SHORT COURSE SERIES

WORLD TRADE PRESS®

Professional Books for International Trade

THE SHORT COURSE IN INTERNATIONAL TRADE SERIES

A Short Course in International Business Culture

A Short Course in International Business Ethics

A Short Course in International Business Plans

A Short Course in International Contracts

A Short Course in International Economics

A Short Course in International Intellectual Property Rights

A Short Course in International Joint Ventures

A Short Course in International Marketing

A Short Course in International Marketing Blunders

A Short Course in International Negotiating

A Short Course in International Payments

A Short Course in International Trade Documentation

A SHORT COURSE IN

International Negotiating

3rd Edition

Planning and conducting international commercial negotiations

Jeffrey Edmund Curry, MBA, Ph.D

Olaf Greifenhagen

"Jim" Chinh T. Nguyen

Yves A. Speeckaert

Published in arrangement with World Trade Press by

ATLANTIC

PUBLISHERS & DISTRIBUTORS (P) LTD

7/22, Ansari Road, Darya Ganj, New Delhi-110 002
Tel: 40775252, 23273880, 23275880, 23280451; Fax: +91-11-23285873
E-mail: orders@atlanticbooks.com; Web: www.atlanticbooks.com

World Trade Press
800 Lindberg Lane, Suite 190
Petaluma, California 94952 USA
Tel: +1 (707) 778-1124
Fax: +1 (707) 778-1329
USA Order Line: +1 (800) 833-8586
E-mail: sales@worldtradepress.com
www.WorldTradePress.com
www.WorldTradeREF.com (international trade and logistics)
www.BestCountryReports.com (business travel, communications and culture)
www.GiantMapArt.com (Giant maps for building lobbies, conference rooms and education)

A Short Course in International Negotiating
By Jeffrey Edmund Curry, MBA, Ph.D.
Short Course Series Concept: Edward G. Hinkelman
Cover Design: Ronald A. Blodgett
Text Design: Seventeenth Street Studios, Oakland, California, USA
Desktop Publishing: Steve Donnet

ISBN 978-81-269-1252-0
First Indian Reprint 2009

This edition is for sale in Indian sub-continent only.

This book is lovingly dedicated to my wife, Charlotte.

Library of Congress Cataloging-in-Publication Data
Curry, Jeffrey E., 1952–
A short course in international negotiating : planning and conducting international commercial negotiations / Jeffrey Edmund Curry; with contributing articles by Olaf Greifenhagen, "Jim" Chinh T. Nguyen, Yves A. Speeckaert.
p. cm. — (The short course in international trade series)
Includes bibliographical references.
1. Negotiation in business. 2. International trade. I. Title. II Series.
HD58.6.C87 2009
658.4—dc21 09-17850
CIP

Printed in India at Chaman Enterprises, 1603, Pataudi House,
Darya Ganj, New Delhi-110 002

INTRODUCTION

THE GROWING DEMAND FOR GLOBAL SPECIALISTS

Many companies, large and small, have made the error of approaching foreign markets in much the same way that they would their domestic markets. The belief that what worked at home will work elsewhere usually stems from lack of experience rather than from arrogance. The most successful international companies and traders have come to rely on "global specialists" to handle their overseas operations. These specialists may be in-house personnel or, if it's the company's first overseas venture, the specialist might be brought in from the outside on a consultancy basis.

Expertise is demanded in international trade and investment for two powerful reasons:

1. Foreign markets are expensive to enter
2. Second chances are few and far between — some say nonexistent

Upper management must rely on these experts not only to plan the strategy for entering the target market but also to execute the tactics in the most efficient manner possible. The specialist, in turn, can be of greatest service by keeping management constantly informed of the opportunities and risks in the expanded marketplace. He (or she) should never make the mistake of letting the "final result" speak for his proficiency. Attaining that result can be a long, arduous affair, and management is unlikely to provide ongoing support to a venture that denies them timely information. The specialist will use his global acumen to inform and train management in the skills necessary to bring about long-term success. As the specialist moves on to the next project, other staff members must build on the foundation laid out in early negotiations.

The services these specialists provide have never been in greater demand. International trade is a huge contributor to the economy of nations. And it is by no means confined to the major economies. Foreign trade represents not only billions in realized profits but also millions of individual deals and contracts. Each deal or contract, in its turn, contains countless details. These details, which come to represent the difference between long-term profit and loss, weren't arrived at casually. Each one was discussed and agreed upon in a conference room or office or during a telephone call or email exchange. Regardless of the medium, they were all negotiated.

WHY NEGOTIATE?

The word negotiate derives from the Latin infinitive negotiari meaning "to trade or do business." This verb itself was derived from another, negare, meaning "to deny" and a noun, otium, meaning "leisure." Thus, the ancient Roman businessperson would "deny leisure" until the deal had been settled. Negotiation is at the heart of every transaction and, for the most part, it comes down to the interaction between two sides with a common goal (profits) but divergent methods. These methods (the details of the contract) must be negotiated to the satisfaction of both parties. As we will see, it can be a very trying process that's rife with confrontation and concession. Whether it's trade or investment, one side will always arrive at the negotiation table in a position of greater power. That power (e.g., the potential for profit) may derive from the extent of the "demand" or from the ability to "supply." The purpose of negotiation is to redistribute that potential. There's no such thing as "take it or leave it" in international business. Everything is negotiable. It all depends on the expertise of the negotiators.

THE ZERO-SUM GAME

International business negotiations are the archetype of the zero-sum game. One side's gains are directly offset by the other side's losses. Your counterpart is attempting to achieve the maximum concessions while leaving you just enough to keep you interested in the deal. Some business gurus may attempt to interpret this as a win-win situation, but experienced global specialists are a hardened lot. Behind all of the smiles, handshakes, and banquets lurks the reality that both sides are trying to "best" each other. It's an accepted, if unspoken, fact.

In recognition of this zero-sum tendency, many of the so-called emerging markets actually legislate a maximum portion of the deal that the foreign partner will receive prior to the start of negotiations. Other economies simply give the local partner veto power on the project, even if they've only made a minimal investment in it. Still others dictate that local partners will always maintain a minimum 51 percent position in the venture, even if the foreign partner injects new capital. While these rules limit negotiations, they don't close them. Those experienced in international commerce see these as parameters within which they can negotiate a wide variety of concessions. As it turns out, many of these "legislated" contract terms are flexible in direct proportion to the scope of the project. It's important to realize that while the size of the playing field may vary from venture to venture, the overriding concept remains the same: Success isn't winning everything, it's winning enough.

Understanding the realities of the zero-sum game and the concept of "enough" will be discussed in detail in the later sections on strategy. Readers may use this book to assist in their own role of negotiator or as a means to select the proper personnel and strategies for international business. The basic format of this text will move through the who?, what?, where?, when? and how? of international negotiations. It's assumed that the reader already understands the importance of why? in today's marketplace.

Jeffrey Edmund Curry
San Francisco, California

TABLE OF CONTENTS

CHAPTER 1

The Role of the Chief Negotiator

SMALL STAGE, BIG PART

THOUGH LARGE TEAMS of global specialists may be assembled for some negotiations, the real interaction takes place between the two chief negotiators. This chapter will describe the role and characteristics of a chief negotiator and examine how that person's activities control the world of international business. Because in many cases the heads of companies must consider themselves for this role, a self-evaluation checklist is provided at the end of the chapter. This checklist is also useful for readers who may be considering careers as consultant negotiators.

Who Qualifies as a Negotiator?

Not everyone is cut out to be a negotiator, and the demands for international work are more stringent than for domestic work. Negotiators must possess a wide variety of technical, social, communication, and ethical skills. The job demands not only mental acuity but also a high degree of sympathy with the party on the other side of the negotiating table.

One of the mistakes many companies make is to assign a member of their upper management as a negotiator without actually considering his or her negotiating skills. In many cases, being the boss almost precludes someone from being a good negotiator. Such a person may be used to getting their way without question and unable to engage in the give and take that's at the heart of true negotiations. Unless their management style is strongly based in consensus, they'll be unwilling to allow for the needs of their counterparts.

The negotiator must always inhabit the middle ground. He (or she) must enter the negotiation process with the understanding that both teams must leave the table with a sense that they've received "enough." The negotiator's job is to maximize the long-term benefits of the venture while securing short-term needs.

The Chief Negotiator

The chief negotiator (CN) is responsible for unifying the strategy, tactics and overall style to be used by a particular company. He must exercise a high degree of self-control and keep the team on track under trying circumstances. Once the strategy and tactics have been determined, team discipline demands that all decisions regarding changes must have the CN as the focal point. While strategic consensus is important, delegation of responsibility is of little value. The stakes in international business are very high, and the CN must be willing to accept total responsibility for the outcome. This will be true even when subordinates have made key decisions.

The CN's greatest skill is the ability to deal with pressure from a variety of directions. Headquarters, clients, team members, family, negotiating counterparts, and government officials will all demand attention. The CN must be a decision maker who can keep everyone satisfied without being distracted from the pre-established priorities. Handling these responsibilities within a foreign environment, and possibly in a foreign language, isn't a job for the faint of heart.

Special problems often arise between a CN who has been brought in on a consultancy basis and personnel who've been made members of the negotiating team primarily for their technical skills. These conflicts must be worked out far in advance of negotiations. This will be discussed in more detail later but the reader is cautioned at this stage that one of the CN's duties is to present a unified and coherent negotiating agenda at all times.

How Much Technical Knowledge is Required?

Government regulations and corporate specifications make technical requirements a key part of negotiations. Besides the actual specifications of the product at hand, the logistical movement of the product across national borders may, in and of itself, require great technical insight. This is often the case in high-tech and telecommunication projects. While it's certainly necessary for CNs to be thoroughly briefed on the technical aspects of the negotiation, it's by no means a requirement that they be experts. Should the subject of the negotiations be highly technical in nature, team members will supply the proper technical backup when required. The CN must devote his attention to the larger picture.

Candidates for CN should be technically astute with regard to both the company's products and modern day information technology. Most international businesspeople now travel with laptop computers (notebook, sub-notebook or palm-top) in order to compactly carry along the vast amount of data necessary for quick decision making. These "electronic team members" can greatly reduce the number of personnel required to make presentations and/or assist in technical decisions. These machines also bring the added ability to make the CN, or team, more productive during travel or downtime. The CN must not be a casual or neophyte user of this technology as his competence may be judged at meetings by his ability to handle the newest hardware and software. In some ways, the laptop has become as useful, and potentially embarrassing (when they don't work), as the slide projector of yore. Laptops can also become a security risk.

Character Traits

SHREWDNESS

The CN, whether staff or consultant, carries the entire responsibility and trust of the company when acting on its behalf. The successful CN must be capable of allowing the other side to see only what serves the strategy best, and this requires an ethical mixture of honesty and cunning. Forthrightness is a trait to avoid when selecting a CN. People who "wear their hearts on their sleeves" or insist on transparency in all dealings will make sorry negotiators in the global marketplace.

While there's no room for duplicity, the CN must know which cards to lay on the table and when. For this reason, shrewdness heads the list for desirable characteristics.

PATIENCE

Patience is an indispensable attribute. Negotiations can be quite taxing—each offer brings a counteroffer and every maneuver a countermaneuver, while delays eat up time and energy. Corrupt officials, petty management, and incompetent staff members all must be handled with care. As will be seen in the sections on bias, some countries make patience a *cultural requirement* for working in their economic sector. Regardless of the locale, a CN who "flies off of the handle" will be of little use in international negotiations.

ADAPTABILITY

Because negotiations are concerned with each side getting the other to change positions, the CN must be highly adaptable. Having an inflexible strategy and limited tactics will almost instantly bring negotiations to an unproductive close. Beyond the preplanned contingencies, the CN must be able to respond quickly and decisively to unforeseen developments. Negotiations seldom go completely according to plan, nor will they always change in preconceived patterns. Being able to "think on your feet" will go a long way toward success at the conference table.

ENDURANCE

While negotiating is primarily a mental activity, it can be physically demanding. The CN must be available for all sessions and eight-hour days will be rare. Add in travel fatigue, climatic changes, jet lag, foreign food, late-night socializing, and work stress and you have the makings of burnout. Many cultures use the tactic of physically and mentally wearing down their counterparts in order to achieve concessions. The CN (and the entire team) must be on guard against fatigue, and there is no better place to start than during the selection process. Physical fitness, endurance, and a reasonably abstemious nature are highly desirable, and bankable, attributes in a CN.

GREGARIOUSNESS

Negotiating is by nature a social process. Many countries have little in the way of commercial contract law, and the success of the deal in such circumstances is based on trust and friendship. Even when the deal is bound by contract, the "relationship" will play a huge role in finalizing it. A competent CN is gregarious by disposition and excels in social settings. Just as many deals are made across the dinner table as are made across the conference table. The ability to hold a good, off-business-topic conversation with a counterpart, even in translation, will only advance the CN's position. Remember, concessions must be *extracted* from adversaries but they're *given* by friends.

CONCENTRATION

International business can make substantial demands on its practitioners. Time zone changes, language problems, and legal wranglings can all be major distractions from the goals set forth in the strategy. The potential for "losing track" is enormous. Many an executive has returned from an overseas negotiating trip with either a diminished sense of accomplishment or a firm belief that *nothing* went according to plan. For this reason, the ability to concentrate on those issues at the heart of the negotiation is an asset the CN cannot afford to be without. Counterparts will often attempt to put as many points as possible "on the table" in an effort to cloud the main issue. The CN must be able to maintain the team's (and his own) focus at all times.

THE ABILITY TO ARTICULATE

People who can't communicate their ideas or understand those put forth by counterparts are of little use around the negotiating table. Good CNs must be practiced listeners as well as articulate speakers. Everything about them—from their demeanor, to their clothes, to their body language, to how they handle subordinates—will be scrutinized. A CN must also have a keen sense of what is motivating his counterparts in order to communicate the proper image. Make no mistake, the negotiating arena is a stage, albeit small, and CNs play the largest roles.

SENSE OF HUMOR

Negotiating can be a very stressful affair, and there will be moments when it hardly seems worth the effort. A CN must be equipped with a highly developed sense of humor in order to weather persistent storms. Some of the negotiating delays, logistical problems, and social settings may seem like exercises in absurdity, and many of the discomforts of travel can be downright demeaning. Viewing such problems with a humorous eye and avoiding the syndrome of taking yourself too seriously can make all the difference in keeping negotiations on track.

Organizational Qualities

When working overseas, the CN embodies the company in image and practice. Consequently, the CN must be highly organized in order to effectively handle the vast number of problems that will inevitably arise. The CN must be able to select, motivate, and control a team operating under high-stress conditions. He also must be able to arrange and rearrange schedules, as well as oversee staff in difficult circumstances. Every and any logistical detail can make the difference between success and failure.

Because administrative support teams will be unavailable to all but the largest corporations, the negotiating team (or perhaps the CN alone) will be left to its own resources. Problems must be foreseen far in advance, and team members assigned to each task. There's little room for error. Every negotiating session should be preceded by a strategy session and followed by a recap. The professional CN leaves no detail unexamined.

The Importance of Team Solidarity

Whenever possible, the CN should have full control over the selection of negotiating team members. This is key, because the team must think as a unit at all times and have total respect for, confidence in, and loyalty to the CN. There can be no "turf wars" or disputes over the CN's authority or assignments. This may seem extreme to believers in less hierarchical management structures. However, high stakes, stresses, and the adversarial nature of international negotiations can't tolerate anything less than a unified effort if success is to be attained.

CAUTION: Dissention within a team will be exploited by counterparts to the fullest extent.

While team members will have varying levels of authority and responsibility, all direction must come from the CN. Any actions that depart from the preordained strategic, tactical, or contingency plans must be discussed with and condoned by the CN. As we will see later, Divide and Conquer is a very common negotiating technique, and the only defense against it is seamless unity. Lastly, because of the need for centralized decision making, it's wise to appoint a second in command (in case illness or calamity should befall the CN).

Self-Evaluation

In smaller companies, it's often the case that a member of upper management is called upon to act as the CN. This can be for overseas negotiations or in the domestic market should a foreign company come calling. Although it may be necessary for top management to sign-off on the contract or attend meetings for appearances sake, it's by no means necessary that they actually negotiate the deal. In some cases, it may be contrary to the company's best interest to have upper management involved, at least until the details have been finalized. The following checklist can be used by managers, owners, or anyone else wishing to consider a career in international negotiations.

SELF-SELECTION QUESTIONNAIRE	YES	NO
1. Do I have the necessary time and attention to devote to these crucial negotiations?	❑	❑
2. Am I the most experienced member of the organization in terms of international business?	❑	❑
3. Do I understand the culture and commercial nuances of my counterparts?	❑	❑
4. Are my language skills suitable for the negotiation?	❑	❑
5. Have I ever worked with a translator before?	❑	❑
6. Have I negotiated major contracts before?	❑	❑
7. Am I physically well enough to engage in extended and stressful negotiations?	❑	❑
8. Do I have the organizational skills to lead a team that's not entirely of my own choosing?	❑	❑
9. Do I have the technical expertise to run the negotiation?	❑	❑

10. Am I capable of working sixteen hours a day? ❑ ❑
11. Am I at ease in unusual social situations? ❑ ❑
12. Am I capable of living in physically demanding circumstances? ❑ ❑
13. Do I find other cultures easy to accept? ❑ ❑
14. Am I considered a patient person by my peers and subordinates? ❑ ❑
15. Am I considered an extrovert? ❑ ❑
16. Am I capable of accepting full responsibility for the outcome of these negotiations? ❑ ❑
17. Are my organizational skills optimal for leading the negotiation team? ❑ ❑
18. Have I traveled overseas for extended periods on business before? ❑ ❑
19. Will my absence from home cause me only slight emotional distress? ❑ ❑
20. Will my absence from home cause my family only slight emotional distress? ❑ ❑

If you found yourself answering "no" to any of these twenty questions, you may wish to re-evaluate your potential role as chief negotiator.

What to Look For in a Potential CN Consultant

Sometimes the right person to fill the role of CN will not be found within your company, or it could be that the best person for the job can't be spared from their domestic duties. In both instances, an outside company or consultant must be found. Keep in mind that, in some cases, the CN is the only representative of your company at the negotiations, while at other times, the CN's role is to advise your team on strategy and tactics. Either way, making a correct choice and a "good fit" will ultimately determine the success of your strategy. Here are some major points to consider.

- MATCH ETHICS Make it clear to candidates that you want the negotiations conducted in a specific manner. Check references thoroughly on this point. It's even advisable to resort to role-playing in order to assess the consultant's ability to act in accordance with your company's ethical standards.
- MATCH CULTURES Negotiating in Japan is not like negotiating in Brazil. Make sure that the consultant has relatable experience in the target market. Language skills are helpful but not absolutely necessary. If the consultant claims fluency in specific languages, put these to the test prior to making the decision to hire. The same goes for dialects. Remember, Cantonese is of limited use in Beijing.
- MATCH TECHNICAL PROWESS Most consultants specialize in specific industries or services. While some will insist that they can negotiate "anything, anywhere, anytime," you'll be best served by someone who has some expertise in your product or service. This is especially true in high-tech, telecom, and financial services.

- MATCH COMMITMENT Because of the intensity of international negotiations, you can't afford to have a detached, dispassionate CN—consultant or not. The successful candidate must perform as if their own company's future is at stake. If the candidate gives you the impression that this is just another overseas assignment, end the interview. He or she must be deeply and noticeably committed to your success. The counterparts across the table should not be able to detect that your consultant CN is anything other than an employee of your company. In many cases, consultants are given company logo business cards with a staff title, such as "Vice President of Overseas Planning," in order to blur the consultant/employee distinction.

NOTE: It's advisable to check your home country's laws on independent contractors prior to issuing the cards or titles.

- MATCH LOYALTY Many consultants complain of being given the responsibility for making the negotiations work and then having their authority undermined at every turn. Conversely, headquarters management often complains of consultants who are determined to follow their own agendas. Neither case is acceptable. Consultant CNs are paid to define strategy and execute prearranged tactics. They must be given 100 percent control of the negotiations and of any staff who may accompany them. In return, the consultant CN must tow the company line to whatever degree management stipulates. All of this must be made clear *contractually* far in advance of the negotiations. If the company can't find a consultant CN they can fully trust, it's best to forgo the hire. If the company recognizes other useful qualities in the candidate, it may wish to use him or her as an assistant to a staff CN.
- MATCH MOTIVATIONS The majority of consultants will charge for both expenses and fees. Expenses should allow the CN to project an image that befits the company. (Don't underestimate the value of appearances.) Fees should be commensurate with the prospective CN's experience and the size of the project. Fees should also include payments for attaining specific portions of the strategy. Financial motivation feeds commitment. Consultants who will not agree to performance-based pay are best avoided.

CHAPTER 2

Choosing Your Team

Big Guns, Little Guns

How Big Should the Team Be?

There are several reasons to keep your negotiation team (NT) as small as possible. The first few deal with the expense and difficulties that arise when your NT must operate overseas. Flights, ground transport, meals, hotels, communication, conference centers, taxes, and cargo can make a trip for even a small team extremely expensive. Arranging for passports, visas, inoculations, and potential medical care for a large group can easily become unmanageable. Problems and additional expenses may also arise when attempting to deal with various family and business schedules. Finally, for NTs operating overseas, keeping track of large groups in a foreign country is nightmarish at best—ask any tour guide.

The rest of the reasons for keeping the NT compact apply to both domestic and overseas assignments. Primarily, communication is a source of strength within any organization and never more so than within the NT. Premeetings, recaps and midmeeting breaks demand that communication be both precise and concise, as major decisions are made in a matter of seconds. The CN must be able to seek the input of the team quickly, and large groups are cumbersome.

Secondly, as mentioned earlier, presenting a unified front is key. The CN must be able to redirect tactics as counterparts bring new issues to the table. Agreement on tactics becomes more difficult in direct proportion to group size, even when there's agreement on strategy. Keeping the NT small enables the CN to make timely adjustments to the negotiating plan and to disseminate that information quickly. Additionally, small teams are more easily able to withstand the "wedges" that counterparts may attempt to drive between members of large teams.

Thirdly, the members of the NT have other job duties unrelated to the negotiations. The fewer you pull away from their regular assignments the better. There's no sense disrupting the company's core business. As exciting as the international arena is, keep in mind that someone must oversee the old business while others look for new opportunities.

Don't Use the Assignment as a Reward

A very common mistake that executives or CNs make is assigning membership to the NT as a reward for other successes unrelated to the task at hand. This is especially true when the team is headed for exotic locales. Many employees see the trip as a minivacation and a way for them to broaden their personal horizons. Even when the NT will be receiving foreign counterparts at the company offices, being a member of the NT is perceived as adding to internal prestige. Some employees even see it as their right by seniority to be a part of the negotiations. Unfortunately, what (and who) succeeds in the domestic market doesn't always play well internationally. Wise CNs must keep in mind that the blustering Vice President of sales and marketing isn't going to impress the reserved Japanese; nor will the brilliant, but reticent, chief engineer be able to withstand the verbal onslaught of the impatient Americans.

There can be a great deal of "fallout" when a staff member fails to be selected for the NT. The best way to avoid it is to make it clear that only talents very specific to the success of the NT are being considered. Technical, cultural, linguistic, social, and travel skills should be compiled in checklist form (not dissimilar to that for the CN) and circulated among potential team members. Inclusion on the NT should be based on this profile alone, and CNs will find they have much better grounds for defending their personnel choices when approached by determined, but unsuitable, staff members. This is especially true when other executives and managers *assume* they're going to be part of the NT. As a way of preserving morale among those left off of the NT roster, some CNs make the deferrees part of the prenegotiation strategy planning process.

A Balance of Skills and Strengths

It's unlikely that any single team member will embody all of the talents necessary to achieve the company's strategy. The CN must choose a cross-section of technical skills and personal attributes that will create a compact and efficient team. One team member's weakness must be offset by another's strength. Technical prowess must be accompanied by the ability to communicate and apply that prowess. Putting a team together is similar to assembling a jigsaw puzzle: there's no success unless all of the pieces fit.

A common practice among experienced travelers when packing for trips is to never put anything in the suitcase that has "only one use"; the same applies to choosing NT members. A *specialist* candidate is eschewed in favor of the *generalist* unless the technical expertise is absolutely crucial to the effort. If the CN must include these "one trick ponies," every attempt should be made to make them a part of the wider strategy and tactics discussions. If that's unsuccessful, these specialist members should be cautioned to advise in private during negotiations and to avoid direct involvement.

Painting the "Big Picture"

Although many technical types will disagree, it's much easier to impart technical knowledge to a good communicator than it is to do the reverse. Members of the NT must be chosen for their ability to effectively execute the company's strategy and to quickly respond to the tactics of counterparts. This is accomplished only through good communications skills. Scientific and financial technical skills will take a back seat, especially during initial negotiations, as the "big picture" is discussed. Details will be left until much later in the process. Many business cultures prefer to have the details tended to *after* the contract is signed. Bringing massive technical data to the negotiating table may only slow down the deal-making process.

NOTE: Much "expertise" can be carried in file or laptop form, in case it should be needed during discussions.

Tasks Both Large and Small

Major decisions are made every day during negotiations, but not all of the work is momentous. Some companies and consultant CNs make the mistake of including only "big guns" on the team. This causes problems, as no one relishes doing the necessary but tedious (and decidedly unglamorous) work that keeps negotiations running smoothly—getting copies, typing policy changes, taking notes, arranging dinners, and so on.

Including a few junior managers or administrators in the ranks of the NT for the sole purpose of controlling logistics is a wise move. This is particularly helpful if these members have experience working or traveling in the target market. Should the finances or domestic needs of the company preclude this option, these administrative duties should be assigned to specific members of the team, and it should be made clear that these duties are as important as any of the more "spotlight" tasks. As is true in other areas of business, what happens behind the scenes determines success on the stage.

Home Team versus Visitors

The respective sizes of the NT is usually determined by the group that's visiting. This is particularly true if the visiting team is in the position of "buying" from the home team or receiving group. The visiting group should forward a list of its members, stipulating the job title and responsibility of each. The receiving group should assemble their NT to correspond to the visiting team.

It's true that the receiving team has the psychological advantage of operating from their home turf, but they should resist the urge to overwhelm their visitors with an imposingly large NT. Since these resources can be called upon at any time, it's best to see if they're needed before arraying them. The ability to successfully exploit the discomfort of counterparts is very much related to one's culture and requirements for a "success." Some visitors may be in awe of your facilities and staff while others may consider it a vulgar display. Either way, small is generally better when making initial contact.

"Observer" Training

Companies that regularly pursue international trade and investment like to use negotiation as an ongoing training tool by purposely including less experienced members on the team. They're given "observer" roles and often do some of the logistical work mentioned above. This allows them to gain experience that can be put to use in future international negotiations. It's best to make it clear to these junior team members exactly why they're being included in the NT, so that they're keen to gain as much experience as possible, get "bloodied" by their own mistakes, and learn from those of other team members. It's also an ideal way for the company to see how their future CNs handle new and difficult situations. Many executives will attest to the fact that the "rising stars" from the home office often become confused and ill-at-ease when put into the crucible of international negotiations and travel. Conversely, the mediocre domestic manager may flourish in the new international environment.

Those Who Can't "Cut It"

A common question in business when determining whether someone will be a success is, "Can they cut the muster?" (Sorry, folks, it isn't *mustard.*) During the Middle Ages, the *muster* in question was the final pattern cut from cloth by journeymen to be used by the master tailor. Cut improperly, the pattern will never work, and valuable cloth will be ruined. International negotiations have a similar one-chance-is-all-you-get sense of finality. The NT acts as the journeymen and the CN is the master tailor preparing to stitch together a successful negotiation. Below are some types of people to avoid because they won't be able "to cut it."

WHINERS

Employees who constantly complain, even under good conditions, are going to find travel and the stress of negotiations intolerable. These types love to bring up problems but never offer solutions. Every company has them, but successful negotiating teams don't.

CONNIVERS

Unity is paramount for negotiations and people who like to work their own agenda or jockey for position will only undermine the team's effort. These types are generally keen strategists and they may be useful in planning. However, under no circumstances should they ever take an active role in negotiations.

HOTHOUSE FLOWERS

More competent than whiners, these "high maintenance" types can only excel under ideal circumstances. They never complain but are easily set back by the slightest deviation from the norm. Unfortunately, negotiations and overseas travel are rarely conducive to ideal *anything*. Sometimes, the NT must operate when materials and equipment are lost, or work in environments in which electricity is something reserved for special occasions. Technically astute or not, these "flowers" won't travel well. If they must be used, do so only when negotiations are on home turf. An overseas team needs those that can adapt to any environment.

BIGOTS

Negotiations are a zero-sum game based on finding common ground amid very real and distinct differences. Adding racial, cultural, sexual, or class bigotry will only obscure an already complex state of affairs. Bigots (of any ilk) tend to communicate their prejudices more than they realize, and it's not the kind of communication that leads to a successful deal.

THE FRAIL

Regardless of where the team originates, the world outside of the domestic market is filled with sights, sounds, smells, and tastes that pummel the visitor. Part of the success of the NT will be in its ability to assimilate as quickly as possible into the environment of their target market. The hygienic and culinary habits of counterparts and their culture may not meet the standards of the NT's domestic scene. Members who can't quickly and adequately adjust to new environments will only be a burden to the whole team, thus disrupting strategies and assignments. Like the CN, the team must be robust.

Overseas? Domestic? One Core Team

Optimally, once a team is assembled, it should be used for both overseas and domestic negotiations related to international business. (Specialists may be added for individual negotiations.) This is especially true for smaller companies with limited resources. But large companies should not make the mistake of having two separate teams—one for overseas and one for domestic discussions—simply because they can afford the expense. Teams that have operated overseas will understand the stresses and strains being exerted on foreign teams when they come for business visits. This information, used sympathetically or otherwise, can be a key part of the overall strategy and daily tactics. Lastly, using the team for all negotiations will add to its ability to operate as a unit as team members become expert at all aspects of negotiating. They must be able to visit as well as host a negotiation and understand the responsibilities of being on either side of the table.

CHAPTER 3

Controlling Negotiations

WHO'S CALLING THE SHOTS?

NEGOTIATING INVOLVES the recognition and assessment of a counterpart's bargaining position. Overestimating can be as disastrous as underestimating. Your counterparts will only reveal that which they believe is necessary and beneficial to their own plans. Trade strategies, and a good deal of tactics, will be dictated by which side is buying and which selling. This also applies to investment, since an investor is technically "buying" into a company (or market) that's "selling" a piece of its equity. The adage "the customer is always right," seems to put the buyer in the position of strength, as does the golden rule of business (The person with the gold makes the rules!). Unfortunately, reality nullifies both axioms.

Buying and Selling Power

THE POWER OF THE NEEDY

The relative "needs" of the buyer and the seller are really what determines who holds the upper hand. Added to this mix are the restrictions that governments establish to protect their domestic markets from "economic colonization." As many large companies have found out when investing in the emerging markets, even when offering to invest billions, they're still expected to transfer technology, train local management, and pay outrageous real estate costs. Here, the seller is driving a hard bargain above and beyond the actual investment strategy—controlling the supply (e.g., cheap labor, natural resources, consumers), and taking advantage of the buyer's need to expand into the new market. Haggling has taken on market-sized proportions. This is in stark contrast to the policies of 19th-century business, wherein "commerce followed the flag" and nations such as Japan and China opened their markets under threat of military force. It should be noted, however, that even today certain commodities, such as petroleum, are subject to "forceful" negotiation.

On a smaller scale, this type of power play takes place in every negotiation. The asking price is only a starting point; discussions and concessions are won or lost based on either side's belief in what is "fair." In order for negotiators to function, whether it be on a small or grand scale, they must be aware of their own strengths and those of their counterparts.

Perceived Economic Power

First and foremost, negotiators must understand where the company they represent stands in terms of international commercial perception. The representative of a Chilean industrial chemical facility will be viewed as part of an agriculture-based market when visiting Japan. Meanwhile, a Japanese grains representative trying to negotiate a deal in Chile will be perceived as being part of a great technological power. The relative power (and perceived need) that each of these negotiators brings to the table will be colored by the level of economic development in their home market without regard to the product their company offers.

It's a natural part of assessing a counterpart to work from generalities to specifics. Even after very specific company research is complete, a counterpart will still tie the perception of need to stereotypes about economics. While this may be a clear case of bias, there are some substantive issues connected to the relative development of a company's national economy.

EMERGING ECONOMIES

Negotiators from emerging economies come to commercial discussions with handicaps that are readily turned into strengths. Their economies are considered to "need" virtually everything—from cash to food to clothes to roads to telephones. They used to be taken as inexperienced and uneducated negotiators with little to offer except a polite "thank you" to their benefactors. A century ago, such countries would have been unceremoniously colonized. Nowadays, they bargain from the standpoint that, while they can use all the development they can get, they also have a lot to offer. Undeveloped resources, hardworking populations, and untapped consumerism all make these emerging economies attractive markets for buyers and sellers.

But often, there's an unforeseen price. Large companies may find that the raw products they seek are not for sale unless they allow local companies to "add value" to the materials first. Investors find that there is a two-tiered pay scale for labor—one price for domestic manufacturers, another higher one for foreign companies. Sellers of consumer products find that distribution is expensive and not open to foreign operators. Contracts that appear simple are difficult to enforce. All of this is foreseeable with proper research and planning. Negotiators must come to the emerging markets with a vast array of bargaining chips and be prepared to relinquish far more control than they would in other markets.

INDUSTRIALIZED ECONOMIES

Industrialized economies have the unenviable position of needing to invest internationally while still vying for foreign investment to advance their own domestic market. Emerging markets view them suspiciously as exploiters that wish to use lesser economies to feed their own growth. Technological economies view industrialized powers as economic "wannabees" that imitate (or steal) technology but refuse to invest in expensive financial and information services or hardware. Many of these industrialized economies are not too far removed from colonial status, and they still harbor fears of becoming retrograde. Their negotiators see emerging markets as opportunities, but they concede as little as possible "at the table" in order to protect limited assets. The technological economies, on the other hand, are treated as future rivals and legislated out of controlling roles. Negotiating with a company from an industrialized economy requires a recognition of their belief that they've fought their way out of one economic status and feel they're being held back from entering another.

TECHNOLOGICAL ECONOMIES

Companies from technological economies are always perceived as being arrogant, even by members of their own fraternity. At times, it's a well-deserved assessment. Much of this perception comes from the exuberance of believing that "anything is possible." Negotiators from these cutting-edge societies can be very frustrated with the pace of activity in less developed nations, and their attempts at patience often seem patronizing. Because they're affluent, any attempt to reduce their own expenses is viewed as cheapness rather than astute frugality. It's very important that these "first worlders" treat their less developed counterparts as equals. This will limit resentment and increase the chances for success. Negotiating across the table from a "technological superpower" often creates a desire to "drive a hard bargain" for fear of seeming too obsequious. This may lead to failure, since it may appear that risk and profit aren't being distributed proportionally.

Breaking Into a Market

Selling a product or investing in a new country will be met with some suspicion by locals even when the target nation has a high demand and everything to gain by the deal. Varying levels of xenophobia will confront the newcomer before, during and after the market is breached. Entrants must not give the appearance of planning to "exploit" their new found market; creating such fear is hardly a motivator for meaningful discussion. This fear of exploitation is inversely proportional to the level of economic development, while the ability to quash potential exploiters is directly related to the affluence of the target market.

NOTE: It's always best to enter a market quietly and then to build on successes over a period of time.

Creating an atmosphere of "equality" is all-important to early negotiations. This is true even when the deal is severely lopsided. The concept of "enough" must be on the table from the beginning of discussions. The outsiders must feel they're gaining enough to make entering the market worthwhile, just as the hosts must feel they're retaining enough to make the deal palatable. Here are some tips for setting up early discussions.

- MAKE INITIAL CONTACT AN INTERGOVERNMENTAL PROCESS Business works within a framework devised by local and national governments. Often, perfectly good deals are scuttled by officials and politicians who feel they've been kept out of the process. Cries of violating "national sovereignty" or "the good of the people" have been the death knell for thousands of potentially lucrative contracts and investments. Even large companies with seemingly unlimited resources can fall prey to the political process. Trade officials (national or local) from a negotiator's home market and those from the target market can advise upon or actually make the initial contacts. This lends a certain amount of credibility to the deal and keeps those in charge of eventual licensing (import or export) apprised of developments. Don't underestimate how much damage a government can do to a deal nor minimize their ability to assist during legal wranglings.

NOTE: Hell hath no fury like a bureaucrat shunned.

- INVESTIGATE A MARKET THOROUGHLY THROUGH RECONNAISSANCE Putting people "on the ground" to research a market is mandatory if success is to be assured. Preferably, these researchers will be eventual members of the NT and they'll be able to bring their firsthand knowledge to bear on the discussions. Their job will be to make contact with a variety of potential partners/targets and make current assessments of the marketplace. Political and market conditions are changing far too quickly these days to rely on last year's assessment or another company's experience. Research is expensive but not as expensive as failure.
- PLAN AHEAD AND FORECAST CONTINGENCIES If the success of your deal demands that you enter a market and set up production or a distribution chain by the end of the next fiscal quarter, be prepared to fail. Establishing international deals, even between technological powers, can take years before the dust settles. At a minimum, a year will be needed from the time the decision is made to enter a new market until actual operations commence. Even the simple trading of goods can be held up by nontariff barriers such as extensive preimport testing. While negotiations are proceeding the market is evolving and conditions are changing, so be prepared to make alterations to the original plan.
- MAKE YOUR MOVE WHEN THE MARKET CONDITIONS ARE MOST FAVORABLE A number of political, economic and social conditions dictate whether your plans for market expansion will succeed. Negotiations will hinge on proper timing. Your team must be prepared to move when events take a sudden turn. The move by international mining companies to negotiate new contracts in Zaire turned on the sudden military advances of (what proved to be victorious) rebel troops. Negotiating mineral rights with a new, cash-strapped and battle-weary government is significantly easier when done quickly. Waiting only changes the balance of power at the table. When the balance tips in your favor, move decisively.

Breaking Out of a Market

Many emerging market companies face significant problems when attempting to expand beyond domestic marketing. Their negotiators are faced with tiny budgets, restricted research, and self-doubt as to whether they can be players on the global stage. Many of these companies labor under government-imposed travel restrictions and limits on the ability to spend hard currency in foreign markets. They have very limited experience in dealing with foreigners and harbor fears of appearing hopelessly behind the times. Much of this is easily remedied by the following.

- FORM TRADE GROUPS AND POOL RESOURCES Deals can be negotiated on an industrywide basis rather than by one company at a time. This is especially true in countries that are still experiencing central planning. Foreign companies are just as happy (and anticipate) buying products from a co-op as they are from a single manufacturer. Financial resources can be pooled along with the best negotiators in order to bargain from a position of strength. Money becomes less of an issue, as a significant sum can be collected in small increments from a large group.

- PETITION THE GOVERNMENT AS AN ECONOMIC OR POLITICAL BLOC Sometimes, the first part of international negotiations begins in the domestic market with governmental departments. Governments are very susceptible to group demands; even the most stringent socialists have come to see the value of international markets. A trade group or citizen's organization arguing for more jobs and increased income will be much better received than a sole company demanding to increase its market share.
- BRING THE RESEARCH TO YOU Political or economic travel restrictions may limit the ability to do market research but don't eliminate it. It's not unusual for foreign companies to visit potential partners upon invitation. A company or trade group can hold expositions or individual meetings where foreign firms are asked to attend and offer proposals. Some countries even require that a foreign firm be "invited" before their personnel are permitted to cross the borders—this is done regardless of who is buying or selling. During these visits, a great deal of information can be communicated that will play a significant role in future deals. Experienced foreign firms recognize this, and they're prepared to exchange a great deal of cultural and economic data.

The Host/Guest Relationship

FAMILIAR TERRITORY

Much has been made of the sports analogy of "home court advantage" as it applies to business. The theory is that the team that's operating on its home turf will hold a psychological advantage over visitors, who must deal with unknown territory. This analogy holds true for the most part during negotiations, although it may be difficult to ascertain just what home turf is.

For while it's true that visitors to a country may be disadvantaged by the rigors of travel and the unfamiliarity of the cultural surroundings, they may in fact be more at home at the negotiating table than their hosts. Savvy teams with years of experience can be dropped into any country, culture, or business and excise concessions for which their hosts were wholly unprepared. Regardless of the locale, these teams are always "at home." This is a powerful reason to keep a team together for as long as possible.

Another area in which experience overwhelms residency is technical detail. Visitors can put their hosts on the defensive early in negotiations simply by being more knowledgeable about the subject matter. This will be particularly true in high-tech, manufacturing, or transportation. Visitors will use their ability to obtain real-time information that may be completely unavailable to host businesses but essential to negotiations. This is why timely research plays such a big role in international business. Never has the phrase "knowledge is power" been more applicable.

SUPPLY AND DEMAND

Buying and selling also affects the host/guest relationship. A host who is in a buying position wields enormous power at the table, even if technically uninformed. Major international telecom and construction companies repeatedly find themselves on the receiving end of a "hard bargain" when dealing with emerging market governments. Some of these countries are moving directly from the 19th to the 21st century in their infrastructure and do so by playing one seller off of another. By relying on the visiting seller's need to maintain (or establish) market share, the host/buyer will usually adopt a "we only want to see your best" stance.

Visiting buyers can maintain a similar attitude as long as the deal isn't based on a scarce resource. Visitors with an eye to long-term investment will also offer very good terms in the hope that future negotiations will be seen in a favorable light when the stakes are higher. This can be very important in countries where the central government has a hand in every business deal. Military and political leaders may refuse to sign off on a major deal (which could mean thousands of jobs and tax revenues) simply because they feel that the results of earlier negotiations were too "exploitive." Once again, the wrath of the bureaucrat has been roused, and *caveat venditor* replaces *caveat emptor.*

CONTROLLING THE PLAYING FIELD

One of the advantages that hosts have, regardless of the buy/sell relationship, is the ability to make the arrangements for visiting teams. This can involve locale, facilities, hotels, food, and transport. Making your "guests" comfortable can be just as disarming as making them uncomfortable. As will be seen later (Chapter 5), some hosts use this particular form of control as a major part of their strategy and tactics. Returning to the sports analogy, in any competition, it's always advantageous to keep the other side off balance.

Using Financing as a Lever

THIRD-PARTY PURSE STRINGS

The control of financing is also a key part of negotiations. Oddly, the team that is in the "buying" position isn't always putting up the money—at least up front. Many emerging market business deals are financed by foundations, development banks, venture capitalists, and even sellers. Many basic infrastructure and education-related projects are funded by such organizations as the International Monetary Fund (IMF) or the Asian Development Bank (ADB) in order to bring these developing markets into the mainstream. Here the visitor/seller finds little resistance from the host/buyer, who is either receiving the goods and service gratis or at extremely low interest rates. The host is almost extraneous to the negotiations, and the visitor need only meet the usually undemanding terms of the funding organization. Although it's a simple process, it's wide open to corruption, as has been the case in many of the tumultuous nations of central Africa.

ADVENTUROUS CAPITAL

The involvement of venture capitalists (VC) is another way for negotiators to maintain control of the deal. These financiers will, in many cases, come from the home country of the visiting side. The use of VC is very popular with American and British companies when working overseas. Japanese and German companies can actually solicit VC-type funding from their own government organizations for global projects. Regardless of whether it's private or public VC financing, the visitors can be much more demanding, since the VC equity stake will (for the most part) be tied to them.

SELLER BUYS ALL

Many projects are done on a build-operate-transfer (BOT) basis, whereby the seller actually pays for the entire project (usually infrastructure) with hopes of recouping costs and profit over an extended period. Many transportation, telecommunications, and energy projects are conducted in this manner in developing countries, where financial resources are scarce. After several years of cost recovery and profit taking, the project is turned over to the buyer at a nominal cost. Plainly, the seller is in a very strong negotiating position in a BOT project, although the wrathful bureaucrat must still be attended to if success is to be had.

What's on the Table?

Everything is open to negotiation when skilled practitioners are involved. Thousands of details are open to discussion and it's essential to learn to differentiate between the important and the trivial. Many important and profit-busting terms are slipped through on "laundry lists" of concession demands while opponents argue fervently for meaningless demands in an attempt to distract. Listen and read carefully before and during discussions, as concentration is a key element in every successful negotiator's style.

DO NON-NEGOTIABLES EXIST?

Demands should always be viewed simply as strong requests and the term *non-negotiable* should be construed as "We're not prepared to negotiate this point at this time." Majority ownership, land usage, and profit repatriation rates are the usual targets of the designation non-negotiable. There's no reason to accept this limitation if the topics in question are of great importance to your deal. Often, the term *non-negotiable* is applied simply because there's no belief that favorable terms could be granted. At other times, political or cultural sensitivity may not make public discussion possible. Willingness to succeed brings success.

Negotiators must decide what the important issues are and whether the opposition's supposed non-negotiable topics are among them. They must also decide if a suitable counteroffer can be proposed to keep the topic on the table. Another consideration is the practice of "back channel" or nonpublic negotiations. Making a concession non-negotiable often backfires on the practitioners, as they're eventually forced to be more generous on other topics, lest they appear unreasonable.

Chart of Negotiables

Below is a list of major negotiation issues that should be considered for international trade and investment contracts.

TRADE

Correspondent banks
Letters of credit
Product lines
Currency rates
Freight forwarders
Ground transport
Arbitration rights
Taxation
Inspection policies
Tariff rates
Distribution rights

PRODUCT LINE

Quality control issues
Technological transfer
Suppliers
Domestic content
Patents, copyrights and trademarks
Licensing

REAL ESTATE

Acquisition
Construction
Contractors
Leasing and ownership
Government liaison

FINANCING

Equity relationships
Debt acquisition
Currency considerations
Exchange rates
Taxation rates
Repatriation of profits
Payment schedules
Working capital
Banking choice
Stock transfers
Loan guarantees
Reinvestment plans
Exit strategies
Accounting practices
Auditing procedures
Stock valuation

MARKETING

Local versus foreign
Advertising
Product development
Distribution channels

OPERATIONS

Equipment procurement
Utility contracts
Service contracts
Hours of operation

MANAGERIAL DUTIES

Accounting procedures
Accounting cycle
Reporting procedure
Organizational chart
Policy development

CONTRACT ENFORCEMENT

Language of enforcement
Jurisdictional rights
Veto process
Government approval process
Antitrust regulations
Articles of incorporation
Dispute settlement process
Arbitration

LABOR SELECTION

Recruiting
Union relationships
Training
Supervisory contact
Wage rates
Benefit packages
Government compliance

CHAPTER 4

Initiating Negotiations

GETTING THE LAY OF THE LAND

SELLERS AND BUYERS have the same motive—profit—but opposing means of achieving it. The same can be said of companies looking for capital and those looking to invest. Each side needs the other, although the degree of need varies from project to project. Traditionally, buyers and investors set the rules and wait to be courted by commercial suitors. Sometimes, however, the seller calls the shots, as is often the case in the petroleum industry. At other times, an emerging market government seeking technology will play one foreign investor off of another, as has often happened in auto industry licensing.

Usually, the party with the greatest sense of need will make the initial contact, which will set the tone for all pursuant negotiations. Appearing too needy can make the deal unattractive even before it's on the table. Conversely, approaching a deal in a take-it-or-leave-it posture may only attract the most desperate partners, or none at all. Some basic contact points and guidelines can be followed to ensure that when contact *is* made, it's seen in the most favorable light.

Project Summary: Setting the Stage

It's essential that the negotiations get off to an auspicious start. Both the initiator and receiver of the inquiry must be excited about the prospects of the deal regardless of who is actually selling or buying. Many potentially lucrative deals have been stillborn because of too strong, too weak, too furtive, or too naive an initial contact.

Truth is always the best approach, but a company must be careful about how much it reveals at the early stages. Revealing too much information will have a deleterious effect on future negotiations, while revealing too little may attract no one to the table. Preparing a project summary (often called a "sell sheet," although it's not confined to companies that are in a sell mode) will allow a company to effectively and consistently initiate, or respond to, potential proposals.

Whether used for trade or investment purposes, the summary is a key part of the negotiation strategy as it will act as the script for either the solicitation of or as a response to an inquiry. It will set the tone of negotiations and pre-position all counterparts for long-term discussions. It should be prepared with the input of the actual negotiators, as they'll be the ones who may have to defend its content at a later date. All data should be couched in terms that clearly suggest that the "results" are forecasted and that details of the project are subject to change. Since the purpose of the summary is to serve as entree to actual negotiations, the project should be described in the most positive terms the truth will allow. Similar to an executive summary of a business plan, the project summary should include the following:

- HISTORY A brief background on the company should be compiled along with a management profile (even if it's a one person operation). If a successful track record is available, it should be mentioned, but don't include the names of past clients unless previously discussed with them. Mission statements may also be included in this section (but not for simple trade projects).
- PROJECT DESCRIPTION Without being overly technical, state the goal of the project and a proposed methodology. Keep the terms general and avoid jargon unless you are sure the reader will understand.
- DEAL DESCRIPTION Make it clear what type(s) of relationship will be acceptable. Whether it's trade, a joint-venture, or strategic alliance, there's little to be gained by "beating around the bush." Ownership percentages (or ranges) should be stated, and any legal restrictions clarified, if applicable.
- FINANCIAL DATA If a partnership or corporate relationship is being sought, there should be a brief three- to five-year projected income statement for the project. (Balance sheets and cash flow statements should be on-hand if requested.) For trade, assemble projections on receiving (i.e., container loads or units per year) or estimate the quantities available for sale, especially if minimums are required.

NOTE: Be aware that the project summary is a form of advertising and that claims made within it are expected to be deliverable. Basic as the claims may be, complex negotiations will depend on them.

Initiating Negotiations

After the target company or market has been selected, the first move must be made. Whether trading or investing, buying or selling, the party that initiates negotiations has the advantage, as they can research potential candidates well in advance of contact. Strengths and weaknesses of a counterpart have already been exposed, for the most part, and can be allowed for or exploited. Planning (if done properly) is also on the side of the initiator, with every contingency reviewed. Assuming that the research and planning phases are complete, negotiations are typically initiated by either a letter of introduction or a request for a proposal.

LETTER OF INTRODUCTION (LOI)

This is a traditional way to approach both trading and investment partners. Such a letter is especially effective if it comes from a third party that has direct influence on the desired receptor. The letter will include a cordial welcome and a brief background of the subject company, followed by a broad description of the potential topic and a request for direct contact. The direct contact should be initiated by telephone, then followed by face-to-face negotiations.

If the letter is to be sent by a referring third party, it will be in the form of a recommendation (see sample below) that should also include a basic description of the project or trade deal. It's best that the company seeking the referral actually offer to compose the letter. It can then be submitted for the referring company's approval and signature on proper letterhead. This saves the referring company time and assures that the letter will cover what is necessary for a successful contact.

SAMPLE LETTER OF INTRODUCTION

Dear________,

On behalf of the Government of ________, allow me to introduce one of our most successful business people, Mr. ________ of the__________ Company. For many years his company has been a major contributor to the economy of our _______ and Mr. __________ has personally been an active benefactor of the community.

He has asked us to write to you as a means of introducing his company to your locality in the hopes that a successful commercial and cultural bond may be formed between our two peoples. His company is of the highest caliber and his personal integrity is exemplary. We offer this recommendation without reserve and foresee a long relationship between your two organizations.

Thank you in advance for all of the consideration you may offer and please contact this office if we can provide additional information or insights.

With highest regards,

A company that's introducing itself should take care not to appear too pushy or boastful about previous deals. State the goals of the project clearly and concisely while maintaining a friendly tone. The LOI is no place for outrageous statements or humorous turns of phrase that may be misunderstood or simply fall flat.

Because of the slowness and unreliability of the globe's postal systems, LOIs are sometimes sent by fax or email. If that's the case, a back-up copy should be mailed as a matter of courtesy. Bear in mind that some totalitarian countries monitor all fax and email activity and often charge the receiver of faxes on a per page basis—thus, possibly making your plans known to interfering parties or burdening your potential partner with fees and inquiries from government officials. Return communication may be even more expensive and subject to inspection. A little research will help determine whether a facsimile transmission is, in fact, appropriate.

WARNING: More than likely, the LOI will require translation. Make sure that the translation is reviewed by a native speaker other than the translator. Many countries are very sensitive about the proper use of their language and will dismiss a soliciting company out of hand for not taking care with translations. Even when mistakes are forgiven, they'll detract from a professional presentation. Also, make sure that the names, genders, and job titles of contacts are correct. More than a few proposals have been ignored when the letter of introduction misspelled the target company's name.

REQUEST FOR PROPOSAL (RFP)

This method (sometimes called request for quote) of initiating contact is rather common in the developed markets of the West where contracts between companies are seen as impersonal. The RFP is a basic description of a project, product requirement, or service system that's sent to a target company with a direct (some might say blunt) request for a response. It can be used when buying or selling, but it's more commonly used as a description of goods or services to be purchased. Most companies have a set format designed to cover any product or service. Translated versions should be thoroughly checked.

The use of an RFP should be limited to those companies that operate in economies that are bound by substantial commercial contract law and trade agreements. Because many international contracts are negotiated and operated at long distance, the RFP can be a very cost-effective way of introducing business partners.

CAUTION: As will be discussed later in the sections on cultural considerations, bluntness may be interpreted as a form of rudeness in some societies, while in others it will be viewed as timely and efficient. Cultural awareness will go a long way toward avoiding potential faux pas.

How to Respond to Any Inquiry

Developing the proper response to an inquiry is as essential to future negotiations as the inquiry itself. While initiators have research and planning on their side, a respondent has time. There's no advantage to firing off a hasty response nor will waiting too long serve the best interest of either party. The following basic procedures are recommended.

PREPARE OPTIONS

All companies, regardless of size, should prepare to operate in the international arena. Since an inquiry could come from virtually anywhere in the world, it would be impossible to prepare a response in advance. However, this doesn't preclude the gathering of technical data and the compilation of options, perhaps in the form of a ready-made company information packet. Being able to assemble a response in a timely fashion will both speed negotiations and set a professional tone. Having considered all the possibilities in advance also allows a respondent company to proceed with confidence. Like the LOI or RFP, the response becomes the basis for the early rounds of negotiations and perhaps eventual contract terms. Accurate data and a well-thought-out proposal will keep negotiations on track. Remember, fortune favors the prepared mind.

TAKE ADVANTAGE OF GOVERNMENT RESOURCES

Sometimes small companies or traders feel outmatched by large companies that demand responses to RFPs. This same sense of dread will be magnified at the negotiating table. It may be wise to gain the assistance of a governmental trade agency prior to formulating a response. They can offer advice on trade or investment terms and lay out the legal limitations. Such agencies may also be able to supply critical trade data otherwise unavailable to the small or first-time operator and even provide assistance at the negotiating table. Being able to respond to an inquiry with some government backup will only add to the negotiating strength of the respondent.

NOTE: The reader should be advised that for some financial services projects, armament sales, and technology transfers, government agencies may insist on being part of the process. Getting them on your side, especially during the early stages, will contribute greatly to successful negotiations.

REQUEST MORE INFORMATION

Often, an LOI will not contain enough information to formulate a cogent response. Confusion may also occur when an RFP doesn't suitably address technical problems, potential tariff restrictions, or ownership issues. Should this be the case, a company should quickly request clarification or additional data before sending a formal response to the request.

This will not be considered at all presumptuous as long as the request doesn't demand too much detail or the revelation of proprietary information. Often times the sender of the LOI or RFP will welcome such a request as an opportunity to further impress potential partners. Keep in mind, however, that a poorly worded request for more information may serve as a guideline for judging technical or commercial acumen. The request should be couched in terms that show expertise and a general understanding of the proposed deal. "Fishing" for information about "givens" will most likely bring the deal to a screeching halt or, at the very least, label the respondent as naive.

SET UP A QUICK TELECONFERENCE

Much negotiating takes place over the telephone and the same is certainly true of preliminaries. Certain inquiries may necessitate a quick response, and teleconferencing is a good way for negotiators to get a quick fix on the style and professionalism of their counterparts. Also, by setting up a teleconference, the respondent is demonstrating a high level of interest while moving the project along in a timely fashion.

This sense of urgency will be appreciated by some and generate fear in others. Appearing to be "too hungry" for a project may detract from a professional image, so negotiators are advised to rein in their eagerness. Some basic research must precede even a telephone response. Regardless of which side is setting up and paying for the teleconference, both sides will be planning to glean as much information as possible prior to the start of face-to-face negotiations.

REQUEST A PRELIMINARY MEETING

If time and budget permit, a meeting to review the original inquiry may be in order. This meeting can involve the principals of the respective companies or their designated agents. In some cases, diplomatic commercial attachés will represent a company at such a meeting. (Their language and cultural skills will be particularly useful.) However, it should be noted that diplomatic personnel will only get directly involved in large projects, technology transfers, or those projects that have potential political sensitivity.

These meetings should be brief, deal directly with topics covered in the inquiry, and be viewed as basic fact-finding sessions. No commitments should be offered or accepted, but much goodwill should be displayed for possible future negotiations. A preliminary meeting, like the teleconference, is a way for each side to take the other's measure prior to intense (and sometimes expensive) negotiations.

SEND AN RFP

When the inquiring company has sent an LOI and is in a selling mode, the proper response may be an RFP. The RFP should be sent only after some basic investigation of the inquiring company. The research should include the history of the company, an ownership/management profile, and an overview of their total business activities (both related and unrelated to the inquiry). Don't rely on the information found in the LOI. Research should *not* be confined to major corporate dealings but should encompass any type of international negotiation.

Although the RFP isn't binding, it's always wise to know whom you're dealing with in today's marketplace. This is especially true when the bargaining between businesses has political or legal ramifications that may result in economic problems. Many companies have been shocked to discover that the Chinese purveyor they were dealing with was actually the People's Liberation Army or that their Russian suppliers were *mafiya*.

DECLINE GRACEFULLY . . . FOR NOW

Sometimes an inquiry simply isn't attractive enough to warrant actual negotiation. When this is the case, the response should be to decline the offer gracefully. Reasons should be stated in the broadest and most diplomatic terms possible. Under no circumstances should a company respond rudely or (even worse) fail to make any response at all. Besides being unprofessional, such undiplomatic behavior limits the possibility for future projects and negotiations. It's not unusual for companies and traders to maintain contact for years before a single deal reaches fruition. Many attempts may occur before "the right fit" happens, and a well-worded rejection leaves the door open for the future.

Another reason to decline in a timely and courteous manner is that each company or trader comes to represent the business culture of their domestic market. Every country has a reputation that's based on past experience with its commercial representatives. Acquiring a reputation for rudeness or unresponsiveness can work against an entire national business community, not just the respondent. This is especially true in developing economies, where there are few players and word-of-mouth is the main source of information. In this situation, arrogance or poor performance in the preliminaries can get a company (sometimes a country) effectively "blackballed" from all future negotiations.

The Value of Multiple Contacts

Even the most informal, short-lived round of negotiations can be expensive when put on an international scale. Whenever possible, arrange to meet with multiple, often competing, contacts during overseas stays. Besides maximizing the travel budget, competing bids may be taken and played off of each other. Multiple business contacts can, at the very least, result in a competitive price structure.

Be aware that governments requiring "business invitations" frown upon multiple contacts unless prearranged through channels. Pursuing them may even serve as a cause to revoke one's visa. Some host companies may even find the practice offensive (especially if they're financing part of the visitor's travel costs).

Others, like U.S. companies, assume visitors will be seeking out a competitor—they will be doing likewise.

Obtaining an Invitation

It is not necessary to passively await an invitation from a potential client even in those countries that require such documents prior to application for business visas. Target companies may be contacted and the prospects for a business relationship explained. This can be followed up with a request to forward a formal invitation. Be aware that delays may occur, as the target company may need to seek government approval in order to forward the invitation.

These invitations are used by governments as a means of monitoring domestic companies and protecting the local market from foreign exploitation. Don't take the process lightly or attempt to circumvent it. Your travel costs will not be reimbursed when you're sent packing by immigration officials. And posing as a tourist in order to gain entry for commercial purposes can also have serious legal consequences. In some countries, contracts signed by visitors with only tourist visas may be invalidated, especially if it serves the purposes of your counterpart.

WARNING: Many immigration agents in the developing world consider the carrying of business materials or laptop computers as evidence of commercial intent. Laptops, palmtops, PDAs and mobile phones may be seized and the information downloaded or eliminated as part of your "punishment" for visa violations.

HOW MUCH WILL IT COST?

International negotiations involving travel can be expensive for both hosts and visitors, with a disproportionate amount being levied on the latter. For most visiting teams, even the opening round of talks will involve at least a week's time. Hotels, flights, meals, ground transport, materials, shipping, meeting room rentals, gifts, laundry, entertainment, and insurance can easily top US$3,000 per person per week. In expensive locations like Tokyo, that amount can double. And these costs don't include payroll and lost productivity.

Hosts also face the cost of providing meeting areas, ground transport, materials, entertainment, gifts, payroll, and lost productivity. Even the most lackadaisical host can spend a large sum in a very brief period with no guarantee that the investment will pay off. Both sides must firmly believe that they have more to gain by pursuing negotiations than can be had by sitting on the sidelines.

Because communication technology has vastly improved in the last decade, a great deal of the preliminary negotiations can be accomplished by telephone, fax, email, or digital teleconferencing. Actual face-to-face meetings may be postponed until contracts are signed. Whenever budgetary concerns demand and wherever logistics permit, technology should be considered as a substitute for travel.

Negotiating by Telephone, Fax or Email

BY OLAF GREIFENHAGEN

Geographical circumstances and time requirements do not always allow face-to-face meetings with potential business partners. It can also be a question of money when the size of the upcoming deal does not warrant expensive business trips in order to bring about a successful conclusion. A simple request for a quote by fax or a telephone call can be the start, and sometimes the ongoing mode, of very lucrative international deals. This case history demonstrates the information flow necessary and the role of service during teleconference negotiations.

CASE HISTORY:

I was called by a representative of a South American construction company asking us to ship heavy street paving machinery. The client explained that he was very concerned about shipping schedules because the construction project was already late and penalty fees were soon to be charged. I explained that his stated desire to move the machinery "as is" and "immediately" simply could not work. The equipment could not be loaded on "flat rack containers" due to height restrictions, and the cost for loading the equipment "on site" was also prohibitive.

I made a number of telephone calls and found out that we would be able to dismantle the machinery into smaller pieces. Though we now had more pieces to move, the new weights and dimensions allowed us now to move the freight on an ordinary "low boy" chassis. It would not be necessary to hire special rigging equipment. In another call we agreed on the new chassis and that the loading of the cargo at the pier would be executed by a stevedoring company. I was able to provide my customer with an estimate for this transport by a quote by fax. The freight charges were to be on a "collect" basis with the shipping line. My part of this transport would be now limited to bringing the cargo to the pier and loading it on board. After receipt of a wire transfer for those charges, we executed the move. But there were more problems.

My customer had requested to use a South-American shipping line, but it was discovered that this line could not provide us with the equipment necessary to load the cargo. This shipping line was using noncontainerized, "break bulk" vessels. Because the shipping line did not allow us to load the cargo on deck, the freight charges were going to skyrocket—unacceptable.

More phone negotiations ensued, and I found a container line that provided us with a guarantee that the cargo would be professionally lashed and secured, thereby eliminating the liability for damages due to nonseaworthy loading. This, and the hiring of a marine surveyor to approve the seaworthiness of the load, further lowered the cost for standard marine insurance. The customer remained happy, and our risks were greatly limited. The entire move was arranged within seven days, and throughout the entire negotiating process I never met face-to-face with my customer or any other people directly related to the deal. The cargo arrived in South America without damage and well within my customer's time parameters. Successful, quick, and telephonic negotiations.

Mr. Greifenhagen is a sales manager for an international freight forwarder.

The Value of Patience

Patience comes in many forms and it is a required quality for any and all people working in international business negotiations. As mentioned at the beginning of this text, the word negotiation derives from the Latin for "deny leisure" but this is not to imply that there are not times when little is happening. In fact, much of the initial stages of negotiations involves waiting. This is called *downtime* and it can be very trying. Negotiations will always move at the pace of the slowest participant and, though prodding may be in order, patience must rule the day.

Oddly enough, speed can often demand patience. The technological economies of the West, especially the United States, like to move at a very quick pace, which they believe is "the only way to go." Business cultures that move at a more measured pace will have to exhibit patience when attempting to meet the production and delivery demands of their counterparts.

Requests for various types of information can also tax patience regardless of the time demands. Some negotiators like to "peel the onion" and only divulge information as needed. Others demand transparency in negotiations and want everything laid on the table at once for review. Some business cultures, generally East Asian, like to only discuss good news in public and reserve the "downside" for back channel discussions. Sometimes this preservation of harmony forces the bad news to be revealed only after the deal has been finalized.

International travel and communications demand patience even when negotiations are going smoothly. Similarly, outside influences such as foreign and domestic politics, governmental agencies, and citizen groups can all have a bearing on negotiations. In all cases, the ready application of patience will go a long way toward countering their effect.

Reconnaissance

Every good battle plan requires reconnaissance. "Recon" allows a strategist to uncover the strengths and weaknesses of an opponent prior to engaging them. The same is true of international negotiations. While it is preferable to do the recon "on the ground" a great deal of information can be gleaned from secondary sources such as texts or the Internet. Regardless of the source, make sure it is as up to date as possible since global commerce has a rapidly changing terrain. Much of the information acquired during the reconnaissance will have a direct bearing on future negotiations. It will also aid in the development of strategy and tactics. Listed below are types of information that proper reconnaissance should cover for both traders and investors.

- POLITICAL SECURITY Determine the stability of the local government, its attitude toward foreign companies, and the expropriation of assets. Focus on the government's participation in commerce and the oversight agencies that will directly affect the project.
- ECONOMIC Determine the state of economic development within the area targeted. Quantify GDP growth rates, status of governmental finances, current

level of foreign investment, and inflation rates; target sector growth rate potential, and company rank in the proper industrial sector.

- EDUCATIONAL Determine the educational requirements of the participants in the targeted sector. Assess the training needs of the targeted company for possible budgeting. Assess the managerial capabilities of the target market and company.
- INFRASTRUCTURE Determine the status of the national and local system of electrical power supply, roads, water, sewage, waterways, seaports, railways and airports. Place special emphasis on those areas that will have an immediate effect on the project (e.g., electricity).
- TECHNOLOGY Establish the level of access to and current use of technological developments related to the project in both the near- and long-term. Investigate government involvement in or restriction of technological access or development. Determine government policy regarding technology transfers and training.
- FINANCE Determine the ability of the local economy to provide or absorb financing for the project, the convertibility of local currency, access to stable banking facilities, and the target company's financial status. Note the number of foreign-operated banks and their ability to act as "correspondent banks" for letters of credit. Also determine any restrictions on currency flows into or out of the target market.
- ACCOUNTING Information should be gathered regarding accounting standards, asset valuation, intangible assets, fiscal periods, loss rollovers, and tax filing periods.
- TRANSPORTATION Focus on the status of the target market's internal and external air transport. Ground transportation, including auto, truck, and rail stock, should be quantified if in direct connection to the project. Governmental projections regarding transport should also be acquired if readily available.
- TELECOMMUNICATIONS Telecom development is a key indicator of future economic development for many of the newer markets. Phones per capita, access to fax machines, optic cable installation, Internet usage, cellular phone contracts, and international satellite access should all be quantified for virtually any investment project. These factors will determine future growth and current profitability in the global market.
- DISTRIBUTION Traders and investors must have entree to adequate distribution lines. Recon should ascertain restrictions on foreign rights to distribute and the guidelines for setting up a distribution chain inside of the target market.
- INVESTMENT AND TRADE RESTRICTIONS Obtain *printed* copies of the target country's investment and foreign trade regulations. Most nations issue an English version of their regulations although companies may have to pay extra. Do not accept anyone's word or opinion on the topic. Current information in this area is vital so it is wise to take note of pending regulations or the tendency of local legislators to pass retroactive laws.

WARNING: Many emerging markets have regulations that are flexible in direct proportion to the size of the deal although it is not openly stated in the law.

- TAX STRUCTURE Some nations place severe tax restrictions on certain forms of foreign trade or investment. Areas to concentrate on are repatriation of profits, import/export tariffs, local content requirements, export processing zones, membership in the World Trade Organization, corporate income tax, expatriate taxes, and trading bloc membership.
- LEGAL ENVIRONMENT Determine the level of protection afforded foreign operators. Similar to investment documents, obtain as much of the information as possible in writing. Focus should be placed upon arbitration requirements, central government and local jurisdictions, copyright/trademark protection, licensing requirements, joint venture/partnership restrictions, property ownership capability, liability laws and limits, WTO oversight, shipping standards, customs regulations, business visas, and internal travel restrictions.
- PERSONNEL POLICIES Few countries permit the wholesale importation of expatriate staff. Focus on foreign-to-local staff ratio quotas, minimum wage requirements, local/expatriate wage differentials, management training stipulations, work visas, benefits allotments for locals, hiring and firing standards, housing prices and restrictions for expats, liability insurance, as well as employment contracts.
- REAL ESTATE AND LEASE PRICES Determine the pricing structure for property ownership (if available) by foreigners. Many of the developing nations have a two-tiered leasing structure that places a heavy burden on foreign companies. Some localities even require foreigners to pay rent a year in advance. Leases and property prices are always open to negotiation and "going rates" should be determined far in advance of formal talks.
- CORRUPTION Bribery of governmental and business officials is a very real if unstated part of international commerce, and all nations suffer from it to varying degrees. As a rule, the poorer the market, the greater the potential for corruption. Determine the extent of the problem in the targeted industry as well as the attitude of the local population and officialdom. Formal negotiations may open with a request for "facilitation money" or "consulting fees," and it is best to have a prepared response. Research may also determine that an industry or economy is far too corrupt to warrant further inquiry.
- ATTITUDES TOWARD FOREIGNERS Get a fix on the host country's view toward foreigners in general (xenophobia is alive and kicking worldwide) as well the attitudes concerning your particular nation. National biases may be racial, geographic, cultural, political, moral, or religious in nature. Determining these stereotypes in advance will allow for proper strategy and tactic development as well as team selection.
- CULTURAL HISTORY Learn everything possible about the culture surrounding the targeted business activity whether it be a simple trade or a multibillion dollar investment. Do not underestimate the role of culture on business negotiations—this holds true for both sides of the table.

Scheduling the First Meetings

The first impression each side makes will most likely have a major effect on the style, progress, and eventual outcome of the negotiations. Scheduling the first round of meetings is an important task for both sides and should be handled in a manner that preserves the professionalism of all the attendees. Bear in mind that some business cultures consider maintaining the "discomfort" of counterparts as a basic negotiating tactic. Both visiting and hosting perspectives will be considered, and the reader may act in accordance with their particular position.

THE SCHEDULE

Whether buying or selling, visitors should never schedule meetings until they have been able to gather their required research. If this means postponing a trip for several weeks, so be it. Unlike the hosting company, additional vital information may be unavailable to visitors during discussions. If budgeting permits, try to arrive in the host country a day or two in advance of meetings in order to get the lay of the land. Unless it is a very short trip with few time zone differences, do not schedule meetings for the same day as arrival. Scheduling meetings to begin on Monday after a Saturday arrival is an optimal pattern. Some hosts may attempt to monopolize this downtime with social events, so visitors may wish to keep their arrival (and departure) schedule vague as a countermove. Intrusions on free time may be unavoidable in countries that require invitations for business visas (countries such as China still like to keep close tabs on business visitors under the guise of constant hospitality). Remember, even if you are a solo negotiator, time away from the table is as important as the time you spend at the table. Schedule both and stick to the schedule.

Visitors that are in a selling mode will be at somewhat of a disadvantage as they will be pressed to adhere to the schedules of the hosts. This is an even greater reason for precontact preparation as the buyer/hosts may wish to meet ASAP. Postponing for a few weeks to prepare may cause the loss of a sale. Sellers must have their bags packed and their materials in order at all times in today's market.

PASSPORTS/VISAS/INVITATIONS

Many countries will not admit foreigners whose passports are within six months of expiration. Getting renewals or new passports overnight is an expensive and unnecessary venture. Some countries (especially those with totalitarian central governments) have severe restrictions on overseas travel and may require lengthy background checks prior to passport issuance. All team members should have current passport status as part of their qualifications. Team members that hold multiple citizenship, and thus passports, can be particularly useful for negotiating teams.

It is vital to secure visas for admission to host countries *prior* to departure. Do not rely on the ability to obtain visas at the port of entry as this will often lead to delays and sometimes shakedowns by immigration personnel who may be well aware that important business is at stake. Some countries require special visas for business personnel (generally more expensive) and issue severe penalties, even expulsion and "blackballing" if business visitors are found to be holding tourist visas. It is advisable not to jeopardize your business over a US$150 visa fee.

Much of the developing world contains governments that like to keep a tight rein on foreign business ventures. Such countries require that foreign companies have a formal, written invitation (email may not suffice) to enter the country on business. Be aware that such an invitation is not carte blanche to conduct whatever business is available. In fact, its secondary function is to restrict visiting companies to solely dealing with those that invited them. Domestic companies in disfavor with the central government will have difficulty inviting foreign firms. Visitors may even find that they will be restricted to doing business with state-owned or favored companies.

NOTE: While your own government may have a somewhat laissez faire attitude toward business, your counterpart may be subject to direct scrutiny or even oversight by government agencies in every aspect of their operation.

ACCOMMODATIONS/MEETING ROOMS

The choice of accommodations will have a direct impact on how a company is perceived. If the host chooses (and pays for) low- or mid-range hotels for their visitors, it will send a message about their standards. When visitors choose the lodging, it should be done in a manner that reflects their economic status without flaunting wealth. The second proviso is especially important when working in developing economies. Showing up the hosting company, whether buying or selling, is not an auspicious way to open negotiations. Also, very rarely are luxury accommodations necessary. As mentioned earlier in the text, it is not wise to include members in your negotiating team who cannot function in anything less than "class A" surroundings. Keep it simple, keep it apropos.

Meeting rooms are an important part of the negotiating process and can be used as part of the overall strategy. Host companies are generally determined to meet on their own turf, but some find their own facilities lacking. Meeting at the visitor's hotel is often amenable to both groups although it does shift the responsibility for the facilities from the host organization. Visitors find this neutral ground to be beneficial as it allows them to control the pace and length of the meetings. More on meeting rooms will be discussed in the later sections.

EQUIPMENT AND AMENITIES

The comfort of the meeting facilities is something that both visitors and hosts must be concerned with during meetings. Chairs, tables, air conditioning, beverage service, catering, lighting, noise control, and toilet facilities can all contribute to or detract from the quality and depth of negotiations. Even the ability to smoke during discussions can have a deleterious effect on meetings. The inclusion of negotiators who have heavy smoking habits or are allergic to tobacco smoke should be reconsidered.

NOTE: The world is increasingly becoming one large "no smoking" area. Plan accordingly.

Specialized equipment needs such as overhead projectors, computer or Internet hookups, telephone systems, voltage conversion, and wheelchair access must be reviewed by both parties well in advanced of meetings. Similarly, fax, photocopy, and secretarial services are other areas that, if required, should be reviewed in advance. Additional cost for this equipment and services should also be budgeted.

NOTE: Do not assume that every facility is as well endowed as your domestic operation or that the host company will supply requested services or equipment for free.

JET LAG, WEATHER AND HEALTH ISSUES

Travel between time zones with as little as a two hour difference can cause problems even for the experienced. Major international travel with fifteen-hour differences can be devastating to thought processes and even physical health. Do not underestimate its effect, and plan for a certain amount of temporal acclimatization. Negotiators need to be operating at 100 percent if success is to be achieved, so don't agree to meetings immediately upon arrival or early the following day. Budgeting an extra day prior to meetings is a good investment.

Acclimating to the local weather is another area that will require some preparation. Journeying from Jakarta to Montreal in December can wreak havoc with travel plans, especially when a high degree of ground travel is required upon arrival. Similarly, arriving in central Vietnam during the rainy season can put severe restrictions on internal travel. Weather and research go hand in hand.

Health issues can derail negotiations as easily as a suspicious balance sheet. Malaria, amoebic dysentery, and diarrhea are very real aspects of international travel and hence exert influences upon negotiations. Preparation in the form of predeparture medical advice, over-the-counter medication, avoiding overindulgence, and the generous application of common sense will keep negotiators at the table and away from the toilet.

NOTE: Many tropical and subtropical nations require immunizations. Carry your immunization record with you when you travel. It can be an expensive and time-consuming process to arrive "in country" without the proper health documents. Also, some governments currently require AIDS testing for lengthy stays.

CLOTHING

Related to weather, health, and negotiating style is the issue of proper clothing. While London financiers may prefer Saville Row suits and silk ties, their counterparts in South Africa may sport open-collared, light-weight shirts to do the same work. Research will supply visitors with the information they need to look the part and feel at ease during negotiations. Dry cleaning and laundry needs should also be reviewed before travel, as being rumpled, dirty, or underdressed can undermine your position during important discussions. Negotiating team members should be properly briefed on the climatic and cultural clothing requirements prior to departure. Once again, keep it simple and appropriate.

MEETING LENGTH AND AGENDAS

Time spent overseas is always expensive but there are diminishing returns when marathon negotiating sessions are scheduled. Visitors, especially those with potential jet lag problems, are cautioned to keep meetings (and recaps) to roughly the length of their normal working day. Exhaustion is the greatest enemy of negotiators and is sometimes plotted as a tactic by host counterparts with greater personnel resources available.

Agendas should be planned *jointly* ahead of arrival and schedules adhered to as strictly as possible. Moving smoothly from point to point in a timely fashion is far preferable to drawn out, disorganized sessions attended by the remains of a haggard team. Chief negotiators, on both sides, must guard the limited resources of their teams if success is to be had.

NEGOTIATING AXIOM: Plan the work, work the plan. Replan the work, rework the plan.

HOLIDAYS AND RELIGIONS

Negotiations should be planned in accordance with events occurring at the host location as well as the needs of visitors. Discussions during Christmas in London or during Carnival in Rio de Janeiro will hardly be productive. Similarly, inviting a Beijing company to Minneapolis during the Lunar New Year period will also be met with some resistance. By monitoring the religious and traditional holidays of *all* attendees, negotiations can proceed without distraction or interruption.

Religious requirements of negotiators must also be considered. Restrictions on work, movement, fasting, and worship periods may have a direct bearing on the progress and outcome of negotiations. Hosts and visitors must know whom they are dealing with and seek to accommodate. Be aware that religious biases can be as destructive to discussions as racial, sexual, or cultural prejudices. Before meetings are scheduled, both sides should be briefed on any special needs.

FLIGHTS, GROUND TRANSPORT AND TRAFFIC

Airlines spend considerable advertising funds to show business travelers that they can provide comfort and relaxation at 35,000 feet. Business class was invented on international flights to appeal to the types of people that take part in negotiations. Even a good intercontinental flight can be exhausting, so it is wise to invest in the most comfortable flight possible. Budgets may preclude first-class travel and even business class can be pricey on transoceanic travel. Sometimes just the choice of the airlines can greatly contribute to comfort and that comfort translates into acuity at the negotiating table.

RULE OF THUMB FOR INTERNATIONAL AIR TRAVEL: Money saved in economy class will eventually be spent several times over at the negotiating table.

Ground transport supplied by hosts or the choice of rental vehicles by visitors will reflect a company's image and standing. Unless a visiting team is familiar with the host terrain, local drivers should be hired in advance (hotels can be a useful source) but be aware that drivers supplied by host companies may be reporting on pre- and postmeeting activity and conversations. Vehicle choice should, like hotels, be in line with both company image and budget.

Traffic is a growing concern throughout the world. Delays and missed meetings do not further the cause of negotiations. Some cities, like Bangkok, are so snarled by vehicles that business guides recommend that hotels be selected at a distance no greater that five blocks from meetings. Schedules will also have to reflect traffic problems when multiple meetings will be required at locations throughout a city. Schedulers should tap the hotel as a resource for information on a city's traffic congestion.

CULINARY

Visitors must be aware that most of the world's cultures take great pride in their culinary ability and are personally offended when the cuisine is rejected by foreigners. Some business cultures are especially keen on linking business meetings with dining but all groups do to some degree. Arrive prepared to have new dining experiences. Business dining or not, overseas travel can become a gastric nightmare if precautions are not taken. As mentioned earlier, fussy eaters or people with delicate constitutions will have a difficult time working in the international business arena, but even seasoned veterans should watch what and how much they eat. Try a little of what is offered and avoid overindulging from cup or plate. Prudence is the name of the game. Don't let the dinner table keep you from making it to the negotiating table.

Hosts should be briefed on any special culinary needs of visitors. These needs may be religious or philosophy based (e.g., alcohol, meats, dairy). Some may be related to medical problems such as salt intake or MSG allergies. It is incumbent upon visitors to inform their hosts well in advance of arrival that special diets may be required.

MEDICAL

Specialized technical meetings or contract signings by corporate officials may require the special inclusion of team members with medical problems. Medical care varies in degree, quality, and style throughout the world. Some of the developing nations are a long way from being able to supply what many travelers would consider basic services. The local pharmacy in such places may be the corner herb store. If modern medical resources will be required, they should be secured in advance of arrival and costs budgeted. Do not assume that all of the world's major metropolitan areas have the same resources—some countries have only a very thin veneer of modernity. For extended stays, emergency medical evacuation insurance can be found for what generally proves to be a steep price.

GIFTS

Gift exchange among business associates is a standard practice in many cultures and is not to be confused with bribery. If negotiations are taking place in such a culture, visitors must prepare accordingly as neglect of this practice shows a lack of understanding (and research). Keep the gifts small, for transport reasons, and preferably company related. Executive model pens, briefcases, binders, cufflinks, neckties, or sweatshirts or jackets with company logos are suggested. Artwork, if produced in the visitor's country of origin, is also acceptable. Do not, under any circumstances, offer gifts produced or purchased in the host company's market.

CHAPTER 5

Face-to-Face

Sizing Up Your Counterparts

FIRST IMPRESSIONS are a big part of society and business as a whole, and they're even more significant in international business. Starting off "on the wrong foot" can seriously damage negotiations before they've even started. It does not take long to create a good impression and even less time to create a bad one. The following tips can spell the difference between a negotiation success and a lengthy, expensive failure.

Impressive Behavior

PUNCTUALITY

No one in the history of commerce has ever erred by being on time. Plan on setting out for meetings with time to spare, particularly when unfamiliar with the location. Even when counterparts have a seeming indifference to time, punctuality will always keep the professional ball in your court.

APPEARANCE

Often, hosting companies will wish to meet their visitors at the airport. Regardless of the visitor's fifteen-hour flight with the four-hour layover, a professional appearance must be maintained. Plan on changing into business attire (or at least a set of fresh clothes) prior to arrival. Wise travelers always carry a change of clothes and their toilet kit with them, just in case their check-in baggage gets lost. Never let your counterparts see you at your worst, especially if it's the first time they see you.

The visitor's accommodations must have facilities that permit the negotiators to maintain hygiene and laundry. This can sometimes be difficult in the developing economies and may even require equipment (e.g., irons, steamers) to be brought along. Negotiating staff must be capable of looking their best under the bleakest of circumstances. This is another reason why high maintenance personnel shouldn't be selected as negotiators.

Hosting negotiators also need to be concerned about their appearance, particularly when they're acting as sellers or attempting to attract investors. Researching their visitor's business standards and acting in accordance with them is recommended. Stubbornly adhering to "the way we do it here" will only make the negotiations an uphill battle.

ENTHUSIASM

Chief negotiators and those working solo must "psyche up" for every round of meetings as if it were the first round. Any feeling of "here we go again" must be banished. Enthusiasm must flow from the top and every member of the team must feel its effect.

Visitors always have the more difficult time maintaining their level of enthusiasm and even more so as their international experience grows. The charm of travel soon becomes a burden and the long stays away from home wear on one's personal life. This isn't just true for negotiators who leave behind families, although the effects are more telling in their cases.

Assigning new duties or allowing subordinates to take key roles (with guidance) during meetings will keep everyone on their toes and force them to focus anew. Another technique for rejuvenation is the inclusion of novices on the team. This can allow the old-hands to hold forth, and giving experienced team members the opportunity to "strut their stuff" can work wonders.

Keeping a good balance between work and play will also serve to maintain a high level of enthusiasm. Make sure enough free time is scheduled and that social events aren't entirely work related. Team members and solo players will need some time to themselves without being made to feel guilty. Burnout is rampant in international business (particularly for staff with high travel rates) and it's usually the result of overscheduling.

TEAMWORK

When meeting counterparts for the first time, it's important that an organized, cohesive team spirit be evident. The first meeting with counterparts will indicate to them just how much work lies ahead. The psychological impact of meeting a monolithic team that is both organized and directed can be devastating. Conversely, disorganized, feuding teams spell success only for the opposition.

It's important that teamwork be demonstrable to some degree at the first meeting (airport or otherwise). Such visual cues as uniformity of dress, prominent company lapel pins, or even matching binders should be linked to a willing deference to the team leader. Counterparts will know that they've just met a team with a single purpose. Maintaining this level of cohesiveness will become essential if Divide and Conquer tactics are to be thwarted.

CONGENIALITY

Like punctuality, congeniality is conspicuous in its absence. Being affable and outgoing at the first meeting will only serve to ingratiate you to counterparts. If the time comes to take a less cooperative stance, so be it. When necessary, it's always easier to move from congeniality to a less agreeable posture than in the reverse direction. Be aware that not every culture expresses its friendliness in the same way. Cultural research will provide negotiators with the verbal and visual cues necessary to pick up on (or display) friendly behavior.

WARNING: Bear hugs may be demanded one week and polite bows the next. Congeniality wears many faces.

RESPECT

The term "respect" is often used but greatly misunderstood. In its literal sense, it means to "look at intently" (though few of us would consider staring a sign of respect). Some equate it with "admiration," while others construe in it a sense of "equality." For the purposes of this book, respect will be viewed as the opposite of contempt.

Treating counterparts with a sense of respect (until they prove otherwise unworthy) is the most positive way to enter negotiations. As with congeniality, moving from respect to contempt is easier than the reverse. Also, if you're willing to fly halfway around the world to deal with contemptible companies just for the sake of profit, what does that say about your own company?

Often, people are unaware that they're expressing contempt or that they're being condescending or patronizing. Visitors who complain about food quality, accommodations, road conditions, local service personnel, or even the weather may cause their hosts to believe that the local culture falls beneath their guest's standards. Hosts who comment unfavorably on the conditions of the visitor's homeland or political situation will be causing similar harm. Feelings—and negotiations—can be hurt in a thousand avoidable ways.

How to Host Introductions

AT THE AIRPORT

When meeting the visitors at the airport, check in advance to make sure flights are on schedule. Arrive early depending on the degree of difficulty and amount of time forecasted for your visitors to get through customs and immigration. Hosts should make every possible effort to ease both of these processes for visitors especially if specialized equipment is being transported for the negotiations. Precontacting customs officials (when possible) to give them a "heads-up" can greatly speed the process when specifications have been forwarded by the visitors. This bit of graciousness will impress the visiting team/negotiator and immediately place them in your debt—a very propitious position for hosts in the selling mode.

If the director, president, or general manager cannot be on hand for the greeting, send the next highest official available. *Never* send just a driver. Host personnel should include a translator if possible (and necessary) as well as a tasteful, professional looking greeting sign to catch the eye of the visitors as they approach. (No marking pen on cardboard signs please.) A computer laser print of the name in extra-large type works well. The sign should also be printed in the visitor's native tongue regardless of their ability to understand the host's language. It is an extra touch that will go a long way. Make sure spellings have been triple checked. If the visitor's company logo can be included, all the better.

If the airport is a mob scene, as most international airports are, an area off to the side or a private room should be set apart for the ceremony (yes, ceremony). A culturally related presentation is wise as it reinforces the idea that the visitors are entering a new culture not just a business venture. Otherwise, a brief group welcome and wishes for a mutually successful outcome are in order. Individual introductions should be done by a predesignated member of the host team. Do not let the introductions proceed in a haphazard manner. A welcoming packet of information should be distributed to all members of the visiting group at this time.

Keep the ceremony brief and make it clear that the visitors will be taken to their hotel ASAP. If it is a morning arrival, it is certainly acceptable to extend a dinner invitation but keep your visitor's fatigue and jet lag in mind. No actual business

SUGGESTED CONTENTS FOR INFORMATION PACKETS

Official governmental welcome • City and country maps

Meeting agendas • List of local restaurants

Cultural activities list • Shopping information

Sight-seeing information • Local events schedule

Transportation guide • Logo T-shirt or hat

should be conducted until the visitors are prepared both physically and mentally. Let the visitors control the first day's agenda. Rushing the process may be interpreted as a tactical maneuver rather than efficiency. Visitors should then be driven to their hotel (at host expense) and their check-in should be facilitated by a member of the host team regardless of who made the reservations. Check back after a short interval to make sure the accommodations and service are adequate.

NOTE: A well-treated guest is an agreeable guest and agreements are what negotiations are all about.

AT THE COMPANY FACILITY

Welcoming visitors to the company's facilities is an exercise in graciousness and intimidation. Hosts must simultaneously make the visitor feel welcome and make it clear that this is not neutral turf. Keeping home court advantage is, after all, the reason negotiations are being conducted at the host facility.

Hosts should present their company in the best possible light but should not seek to put on airs. A small electronics manufacturer on the outskirts of Caracas cannot pretend to be on equal footing with IBM, and it would be counterproductive to attempt to do so. Hosts need only to be comfortable in their surroundings in order to maintain advantage.

A brief formal welcome should be first on the agenda with all pertinent staff members being introduced. (Some cultures move from least important personnel to most important while others do the reverse. Also, some cultures permit a second-in-command to take the lead in these situations.) These introductions should be followed by a short (less than an hour) tour of the facilities. Specialized, detailed tours can be arranged later. Some companies may offer a small welcoming gift at this time, although it is not required. Professionally printed name tags should be offered to visitors and worn by hosts as well. Check the spelling and be capable of making corrections in-house.

How to Make an Entrance

AT THE AIRPORT

Foreign visitors must also be prepared to deal with a certain degree of inconvenience upon arrival at airports or frontiers. Often inefficient, officious customs and immigration personnel will add hours to an already long day. Keep frustration to a minimum as it may only delay the process. Acting indignant or taking a "don't you know who you are dealing with?" attitude simply won't work. If particularly sensitive equipment or personnel are brought along, the host company as well as embassy personnel should be alerted in advance in order to facilitate entry. Keep in mind that in many countries, any altercations at the point of entry may result in the host company being held responsible. This will definitely be the case when a formal invitation is involved. Confiscated equipment, limited visas, a fine, and a government reprimand for the hosts is a less than auspicious way to begin negotiations.

Once the passports have been stamped and customs cleared, allow time for the hosts to offer their welcome. If infirm or elderly members of the visiting team require immediate exit from the airport, let the hosts know well in advance. (The airphone or on-board Internet access are the best way to keep hosts updated if there are in-flight delays or special updates.) Beyond the grooming concerns mentioned earlier, visiting staff should be attentive and enthusiastic upon arrival. Though it may be a lot to ask after twenty-four hours in transit, every member of the team must exude a happy-to-be-here attitude.

AT THE HOST FACILITY

If the hosts have not chosen to meet at the port of entry, or there are multiple contacts, the first meeting may occur on their turf. Visitors should arrive punctually and be prepared for a certain amount of ceremony before work begins. Small gifts such as company logo pens should be brought along but only distributed in return for welcoming gifts presented by the host. Do not upstage the host's generosity or lack thereof.

The host may wish to give a tour of facilities prior to the start of formal discussions. Visitors can only hope that the host has read this book and keeps the tour brief, otherwise endure the process with aplomb. Enthusiasm is required but asking too many questions will only extend the tour. Visiting staff under no circumstances should indicate that they find the facility lacking or comment upon employee working conditions in an uncomplimentary or concerned fashion.

WARNING: Political or social activists should not be part of the negotiating team. Unsavory working conditions and low wages should have been revealed and discussed during the research process well in advance of travel. If unforeseen and unfortunate circumstances do arise, they should not be discussed within earshot of the host until the team has had a chance to formulate a position. If you are a solo negotiator, do not let knee-jerk reactions to events jeopardize the deal. Take time to think through the problem before stating your objections or opinions.

Visitors should always dress for initial meetings with an intention to err in favor of formality. Business suits should be worn (even in hot climates) as a sign of professional respect until the proper tone of the negotiations has been set by the host. Visitors should be prepared thereafter to work in anything from suits to polo shirts. Some companies ask their hosts in advance regarding dress standards so as to facilitate packing. Business related social events that may require special clothing, such as golf or hunting, may receive this same type of inquiry.

The first meeting may turn out to be a completely social event with little "real work" being done. The cocktail receptions, luncheons, cultural tours, and dinners may all appear as innocent forms of welcoming but they are in fact a means to take the opposition's measure. Members of either side may be engaged in idle conversation, but background information will be solicited. Social skills will be assessed and pecking orders delineated. Cultural acumen, marital status, education, strategy, and business sophistication will all be exposed then duly noted. The opposition is looking for chinks in the armor as they pour the champagne. Visitors must keep their guard up, and all team members should be briefed about maintaining their dignity as well as a unified front. Generally, a word to the wise is sufficient, but special care should be taken with younger, inexperienced members of the team. Also keep in mind that turnabout is fair play.

AT THE HOTEL

On occasion, the first meeting is held at the visitor's hotel. Sometimes this is due to a lack of proper space at the host facility or it may be a question of travel time on the first day. Long-term scheduling of meetings at the visitor's hotel is discussed later.

The visitor suddenly finds himself confronted with a duty to be both host and guest for a very important part of the negotiating process. A hotel that reflects the company's status should have been selected in advance with the needs of this meeting in mind. Some companies will rent meeting rooms while others will utilize the living room space of a suite. When these choices are not available or within budget, the lobby or the hotel dining room is an acceptable substitute as long as some degree of privacy can be found.

Visitors will be held responsible to a degree for any shortcomings of the hotel (or its staff) and it should not be selected casually. Appearance, quality, clientele, location, service, and even union representation may all play a part in how the visiting company is viewed by their counterparts.

Guests should be welcomed by a member of the visiting team and escorted to the proper area. If traveling alone, the negotiator should not wait to be called from their room but instead anticipate their guest's arrival in the lobby. Cordiality is appreciated worldwide. If business is to be conducted on the first day, it would ensue after brief introductions and well wishing. Adjournment to the dining room, meeting area, or suite would be in order. Some form of food and beverage should be offered throughout discussions.

Regardless of a buying or selling position, the visiting team will be in charge of running the meeting just as if they were back home. They will be judged on how well the discussions progress and the quality of the physical surroundings. All room amenities (even air conditioning) must be in order and checked in advance. Visitors should not assume that the hotel staff (or the physical plant) will be on par with home market hotels regardless of the classification. When things go wrong, visitors should take full responsibility and never attempt to blame the local staff as this will reflect poorly on the host company. It will also say something about the visitor's willingness to bear accountability.

NOTE: When visiting developing economies, do not be surprised if your counterparts show amazement at the hotel's facilities. Most will have never been inside such a structure as a result of public edict or finances. If this is sensed, a brief tour by the hotel staff may be arranged. Never approach this as "see how much I can afford" but more from the standpoint of how impressed you are with what their country has to offer.

Personality Tips

Negotiators should not assume that the physical and oral cues that are used to assess personality types are universal. Only detailed cultural research will prevent both sets of counterparts from creating or receiving the wrong impression. The following is a list of personality cues that vary from one society to the next.

- A smile in one culture denotes pleasure while in another it signifies discomfort.
- Reticence for one group speaks of shyness but in another it declares wisdom.
- A strong handshake betokens self-assuredness for some but boorishness for others.
- Eye contact indicates honesty to many but is a source of disrespect to an equal number.
- Touching denotes friendship for the outgoing but an invasion of privacy for the introvert.
- A sullen demeanor for one person covers anger for one but sadness for another.
- Slouching signifies weariness and boredom in the West but disharmony in the East.
- Loud speech can mark an authority figure in some cultures but a loss of control in others.

These cultural signals need to be understood in order to be properly utilized. The greatest mistake that negotiators, and travelers in general, make is that they take a great deal of time to learn and interpret what others are doing without assessing their own actions. Personalities can be appraised quickly and accurately when all of the cues are placed in context. It is the context that requires the greatest research and insight.

CHAPTER 6

The Function of Bias

PERCEPTION VERSUS REALITY

CULTURAL BIASES can be both a weapon to avoid and a shield to hide behind. The dividing line between weapon and shield is that between unfavorable and favorable stereotypes. Negotiators must learn to use their counterparts' biases to achieve the most favorable result.

Every culture is perceived by other cultures as having both bad and good features, and these are usually based on some kernels of truth. The Japanese are seen as intelligent but uncreative. The British are snobbish but polite. The Germans are precise but rigid. Americans are self-centered but clever. Sometimes these characteristics are linked to national borders and sometimes to ethnicity (Asian values demand . . .), religion (Muslims always . . .), geography (Westerners consider . . .), or politics (Socialists insist on . . .). However, human nature makes it easy for both whole cultures and individuals to believe the positive about themselves and discount the negative. Any self-respecting Japanese will staunchly defend national intelligence while quietly rationalizing the lack of Nobel Prize winners. Germans will likewise extol their engineering prowess while downplaying the inflexibility of their legal system.

Using Your Counterpart's Bias to Your Advantage

Negotiators rarely have the time to address the problem of biases head-on, and besides, to do so means running the risk of offending a potential business partner. The most efficient technique is to play to the positive stereotypes and defy the negatives. This method will keep the counterpart off balance and in a constant state of trying to figure out the other side. Meanwhile, the negotiator maintains only a positive image in the mind of their counterpart. This requires a good bit of research, coupled with the ability to quickly pick up on the individual biases of counterparts.

WARNING: Don't attempt this technique until you are clearly aware of the counterpart's biases. Otherwise, you may waste a lot of energy dispelling stereotypes that don't exist.

Finding Achilles' Heel

Negotiators must make a resolute effort to clear their own minds of prejudice, if for no other reason than that prejudices stand in the way of efficiency. Assuming that counterparts are intelligent, reasonable, insightful, honest, forthright, precise, clever, punctual, or sophisticated is just as bad as assuming they're not. Skilled negotiators must be able to detect their counterparts' strong points as well as their weak ones and to act accordingly. Rarely can success be found by being oblivious to an opponent, and there's only a slightly better chance in granting the benefit, or drawback, of the doubt.

Perceptions are based on available information. The axiom "All things come to those who wait" doesn't apply to international negotiations. Active, directed cultural research with a great deal of input from expatriates should be accumulated prior to negotiations. Information should be judged by its source and all viewpoints solicited.

WARNING: Don't use cultural materials published by the government of the target country as primary sources. They'll probably be riddled with their own particular biases.

Once introductions have passed and negotiations have begun, each side will be attempting to check the accuracy of their respective research. Negotiators should deal only with the reality facing them across the table. There's no value in attempting to force the facts into a preconceived pigeon hole no matter how well researched. Predictions can depart from outcome. Negotiating, like accounting, must use its poor forecasts as a tool to restructure the process. Missing the mark is a reason to *improve* research—not to drop it.

Economic Prejudice

The developing world and the technological economies continually eye each other with the intention of profit. The former wants to skip a century of nondevelopment to secure cutting-edge products at cut-rate prices. The latter sees millions of unjaded consumers willing to snap up products that have long since run their course in the domestic marketplace. This economic disparity can be piled on top of the standard biases already at work.

Negotiators should be aware that countries that have experienced significant colonization well into the 20th century are very sensitive to this issue. Companies from foreign lands will not always be greeted with hardy welcomes. Instead, they may be met with protests by local citizen groups, as has happened in parts of India recently. The phrase "Investment, not investors" is fast becoming a rallying cry in many developing countries. These economies are demanding access to the world's cash supply without signing on for what many of them see as the "cultural decadence" of their benefactors. Foreign negotiators may find themselves being held responsible for a whole host of problems that they neither had anything to do with nor intended to profit by.

In previous centuries, "commerce follows the flag" was the rule of international business (e.g, the Opium War); today's precept is closer to "culture chases commerce." Negotiators in developing economies must realize that although they've been directed to drive hard bargains, the patience of foreign investors has long since worn out. International companies are no longer willing to take accusations of "cultural imperialism" seriously. For them, 21st-century technology brings 21st-century culture, with all its inherent problems.

Both sides of the table must realize that a take-it-or-leave-it attitude will not produce useful results. The key for each side is the ability to understand their counterpart's position and, to some degree, manipulate it as part of the overall strategy. Such planning will be discussed in detail. For now, suffice it to say that making the other side *believe* it has won is a victory in and of itself.

Playing the "Race Card"

An unfortunate reality of international negotiations is that the race of the participants will have an effect on the discussions. Regardless of the personal feelings of those in charge of the process, racial characteristics need to be taken into account. Understanding one's own racial perceptions, as well as those of counterparts, is an essential part of preparations for face-to-face meetings.

Researching the biases of counterparts and then either playing to them or counteracting them can be an effective tool at the negotiating table. Racial bias is, after all, a weakness and weaknesses are to be exploited. Even where racial diversity is limited or a single negotiator is used, the ability to reinforce or reverse a stereotype at the proper stage of negotiating can completely unbalance the opposition. However, playing the "race card" is a delicate matter that's prone to backfiring, so it's best to have it well planned out in advance.

Cultural Accommodation

Cultural considerations will arise time and again, even when they're not the subject of direct discussion. Each side must come prepared to accommodate the other to a reasonable extent, and such accommodations can be myriad. The days for meetings may be chosen to allow for holidays or religious schedules. Even the time of day can be scheduled based on local activity, as may be the case in hotter climates where the populace traditionally observes some form of *siesta* or *shou shei*. Similarly, negotiations may be interrupted for prayer by orthodox Islamic teams.

Late-night meals, after-hour socializing, marathon sessions, and multiple "time outs" for consensus taking will all require accommodation. Each side should respect the other's need to maintain some of their respective cultural patterns, even when operating on foreign turf.

The Value of Kindness

Kindness may be universally appreciated, but it can also be interpreted as a sign of weakness in some cultures. And the leap from being kind to being obsequious can sometimes be a short one. A kindness withheld can be taken as a slight, while a kindness granted may be viewed as a patronizing act. The phrase "You are too kind" can be taken literally, with the result that the speaker now feels obliged to respond with an even greater benevolence. This is especially true in business cultures with a gift-giving tradition. Research will allow negotiators to recognize when they've gone too far or have been too niggardly.

Kindness is also an effective tactic. Keeping counterparts in sufficient "debt" while negotiations progress may lead to significant concessions. Negotiators must take care not to allow this ploy to become evident and to remain on guard for turnabout. Kindness can produce *social* debts that may require *economic* payment.

Manners That Matter

What constitutes good manners is by no means universal. International operators are always in a position of trying to determine what is proper and when. Translators, expatriates, embassy protocol officers, and host government representatives are all useful sources of information.

Working in the international arena demands a great deal of flexibility. Extroverts may suddenly have to recognize the value of reticence. Negotiators comfortable with dignified bows as a greeting may be thrust into a world of bear hugs or even an exchange of salutatory kisses. Women used to being treated with deference can find themselves excluded from important conversations. While negotiators may not always find these situations pleasant, they should never be surprised by them.

Table manners are another area that can have a direct effect on business. At some point, international negotiations put the players in a dining situation. The desire to "break bread" with trusted associates is strong in all of the world's cultures. It may be at a private home, the company canteen, or an exclusive restaurant. Wherever it is, you can be assured that the table manners of the participants will be observed and assessed. The inability to choose the proper silverware at a Parisian banquet will mark the perpetrator as culturally backward. Similarly, the inabilty to use chopsticks at a Shanghai luncheon will unveil the negotiator as a cultural novice, while asking for chopsticks in a Manila restaurant may be taken as an insult. Eating fried chicken in Atlanta with a knife and fork may evoke a humorous response, while using a left hand to pick up food in Delhi may elicit wide-eyed stares from one's hosts.

Manners in any form—whether it's knowing how to address someone of senior rank or for whom to hold a door, which utensil to use or how *not* to dress for a particular occasion—are small points that speak volumes. They're the nuances that drive successful relationships and promote understanding. Their presence denotes both cultural research and concern, while their absence signifies naiveṭe or boorishness.

For more on business protocols for individual cultures see the World Trade Press Passport to the World Series (25 country-specific titles).

CHAPTER 7

Site Selection

HOW DO YOU GET THERE FROM HERE?

AS IS TRUE OF INTRODUCTIONS, the location and conditions of the negotiation facility can have direct bearing on the outcome of meetings. Consequently, both sides must take great care to maximize their position during site selection. This isn't always solely a question of psychological advantage but also one of cordiality and pride. Very rarely will the host company permit all, or even the majority, of the meetings to take place on neutral turf, since this reflects poorly on their ability to "hold up their end" of the deal. Hosts must host and visitors visit.

Projecting the Proper Image

Visitors will be incurring a fair amount of expense just to travel to the site, and it's a reasonable expectation, even when they are selling, that the host company will provide a comfortable and convenient meeting facility. Visitors may also insist that the meetings take place in a major city that may not contain a host company office. Hosts may then be required to obtain facilities at additional expense. Some companies do "trade outs" with local purveyors or enlist the assistance of government agencies.

Whether an acquired facility or a company facility is used, it must reflect the host's image as much as possible. If specific conference rooms aren't available, the best office on site should be made over to accommodate the meetings. Don't use employee dining rooms or a vacant storeroom as a substitute. There's no point in putting on airs, but make the effort to promote a professional image. Hosts who take the attitude of "why go to such bother for a single meeting?" may find that it's a self-fulfilling prophecy.

Visitors may be called upon to provide the site for at least some of the meetings beyond the introductions. This will often be true when they're in the selling mode and members of the host team don't have local offices. In this case, any advantage the visitors get by using neutral turf is offset by the requirements of selling. Hosts will be assessing the quality of the hotel/meeting room as a means to determine the status and detail-mindedness of their potential business associates. Here again, extravagance isn't necessary, but penny-pinching will send the wrong message.

Convenience, Conditions and Accoutrement

Every effort should be made to assure that the meeting facilities are convenient to all parties. Convenience is, of course, relative; a certain degree of communication should take place before the arrival of visitors in-country. The availability of ground transport, airport location, seasonal weather, road conditions, schedule conflicts, and, in some cases, even curfew restrictions can influence how visitors view the host's selection.

Besides the location, the physical conditions of the facility can make a difference. Uncleanliness, poor lighting, inefficient telecommunications, or excessive noise levels can greatly distract from discussions and even cause hard feelings. Room temperature, while comfortable for hosts, may distract visitors with too much or too little heat. And, as anyone who has visited the growing metropolises of the world can testify, air quality can bring negotiations to a standstill as visitors take ill. While not all of these inconveniences may fall under the host's control, as much care as possible should be taken to correct them.

Accoutrements such as furnishings, copy machines, overhead projectors, computer links, electrical converters, window views, and, most importantly, comfortable chairs will all speak to the status of the host company. (Sumptuously appointed board rooms are as much about marketing as they are about meetings.) There's little doubt that comfortable surroundings allow for concentration and therefore smooth negotiations—although some host teams do occasionally seek to make visitors (sellers mostly) uncomfortable. Luxury isn't required, but err on the side of efficiency and serenity.

Neutral Turf versus Home Team Advantage

Long ago, skilled negotiators recognized the psychological advantage that comes from controlling the surroundings in which counterparts must operate. It's not unlike the planning that the military uses when choosing the "field of battle." Generals who can dictate when and where a battle will take place have already gone beyond the halfway point toward victory.

A visiting seller who must make all presentations at the host facility is at a distinct disadvantage. The host/seller gains no advantage at all when working at the visitor's hotel, although it cannot truly be considered a minus, merely neutral.

While sellers assess their position, buyers will be working to undermine it by controlling or neutralizing the situation. By constantly making a visiting seller dependent on the host for basic needs and comfort (maybe even extending to food and drink), the buyer can seek concessions in return. It may even take the guise of pandering to the visitor's every request. This approach, very much akin to "killing them with kindness," is an effective one.

Visiting buyers are faced with another set of problems. They'll often neutralize the host sellers "turf advantage" by insisting that meetings take place outside of host facilities. While there may be some additional expense incurred in this method (i.e., banquets, hotel meeting rooms), it will be an investment in potential price, delivery, or ownership concessions.

Responding to the Selections of Your Counterparts

MAINTAINING CONTROL

As mentioned above, meetings should take place in a setting that's mutually convenient for all parties concerned. Neither buyer nor seller has 100 percent say, although it should be obvious by this point which of the two has the upper hand. Novice negotiators often make the mistake of allowing themselves to be drawn onto a field of battle slyly selected by their counterparts.

For instance, visiting teams or solo acts who'll be traveling to an unfamiliar locale will often turn over to their hosts all of the arrangements—from hotels to visas to meeting planning. This isn't simply unwise, it's foolish. Although this may release the visitors from the burden of certain preparations, it also leaves them vulnerable to the host's constant influence. Uncomfortable (or over-priced) hotels that are inconvenient to meeting sites will weigh heavily on the attentiveness and time constraints of visitors, thus decreasing their effectiveness. Hotels and meeting sites may be selected far outside of major cities, thus making visitors dependent on hosts for transport and nonbusiness activities. Sometimes (more often in developing countries), visitors may even find themselves lodged at a hotel that's owned by one of their host's subsidiaries or family relations.

CONTINGENCY PLANNING

The best way for visitors to maintain as much control as possible is to treat the host's selections as suggestions. Find out their intentions in advance and check out the contingencies. Verify the need for having meetings at inconvenient times or locales and offer countersites and schedules. Visitors in the selling mode may find it difficult to insist, but claims of time constraints and flight schedules are effective countermeasures to a host's claims of necessity. Regardless of how much planning the host does, visitors should always have up-to-date research on location and facilities, and they should never accept the host's word as fact. A good map and an informed travel agent can often be effective negotiation tools.

Hosts may also run up against insistent, well-informed visitors who'll attempt to control every aspect of the meeting plans. Buying mode visitors with extensive negotiating experience can be extremely demanding. Their choice of a two-hour meeting at an airport hotel may be deemed insufficient for a sales presentation. (This let's-get-down-to-business method is often used against business cultures that rely on extensive socializing.) Hosts may not be able to sidestep this schedule problem, but they can insist on making part of the process a meal that they host. Besides eliminating the "raw" efficiency of the visitor's schedule, the host will regain some control over the actual meeting process.

Whether hosting or visiting, buying or selling, the key to site selection is to remember that, like the contract goal, it's not unilateral. Allowing the other side a concession doesn't require losing everything. Before site selection becomes an issue, have a preset plan and a number of contingencies. If you can't choose the battleground, at least be familiar with the terrain.

The Envelopment Trap

ATTRACTIVE TRAPS

A common technique used to influence negotiations is "envelopment." Though most common in East Asia, it's used by skilled negotiators everywhere and involves the subtle but constant control of the counterpart's every moment, whether social or business related. It can run the gamut from the heavy-handed methods of a Chinese tour of a cultural site, replete with "special guides," to the London financier who miraculously secures tickets to a sold-out show. It can also take the less seemly form of choosing a meeting site in a remote area with limited communications and transport. It may even go so far as the casual hint that visa arrangements are contingent on the successful conclusion of the discussions. The message is clear—it's time to pay for the hospitality.

HOSTILE HOSPITALITY

Negotiators who find themselves being offered free hotels, endless banquets, chauffeured limousines, or excessive gifts are surely the targets of envelopment. As they become more and more comfortable, they become proportionally more susceptible. The best way to combat this is to give every appearance that whatever is offered is also expected. Negotiators should never grant themselves the luxury of assuming that their counterparts are simply being nice. Refusing hospitality may be the mark of an ingrate but falling for its charms is a sure sign of naivete. The strategy of envelopment is to shower the target with good will and then to withdraw it gradually in order to gain concessions. Envelopment is also a sure sign that the perpetrator has little to offer at the negotiating table and is relying on guile, rather than substance.

Visitors and Agendas

When multiple business contacts will be part of a visitor's negotiating plan, it's essential that agendas be carefully coordinated. Particularly in countries where socializing is a big part of business, many hosts may assume that they have free rein with their counterparts' time. Because of this, visitors must make their time constraints (but not the reasons) clear prior to arrival, as well as throughout their stay. This doesn't mean that hosts need to be informed about every aspect of the visitor's schedule, only those related to discussions with the relevant host. (In fact, the less one's host knows, the better for the visitor.) When multiple contacts are used, visitors are advised to allot a minimum of a full day to each company they wish to contact so as to avoid any appearance of slighting.

Hosts must keep in mind that not all visitors view socializing as part of negotiating and that they may offend their guests with excessive hospitality. Visitors may wish to carry on with standard length working days as if they were back home. Hosts should respect this wish as much as possible. Visitors should be wary of agendas that will result in fatigue, but at the same time, they should make every effort to accommodate their host's wishes to be sociable. Communication about agendas, before and during negotiations, is the key.

CHAPTER 8

The Agenda

CARVE IT IN STONE

CONFERRING AND AGREEING upon all aspects of the agenda for the negotiations is the first step in the long process of the relationship building so necessary for a successful deal. Even when both parties are experienced and comfortable with the legal obligation of a contract, there's still an essential human element in play. This is true even when negotiations are conducted via phone, fax or email. In fact, sometimes the quality of the deal becomes secondary to that relationship.

Taking a Proactive Role

One of the surest ways to waste time and money during international negotiations is to proceed without a fixed agenda. Because the greatest expense will be generated by the visiting team, it's essential that they take a proactive role in crafting the meeting agenda. Hosts in many business cultures may resist the efforts to work by a fixed agenda, as it goes against the grain of their society's view of time. Some hosts also like to "run the clock out" as a means of forcing concessions. Clearly, it works in the visiting negotiator's favor to arrive in-country with a clearly delineated agenda.

Experienced negotiators also recognize that it works well for hosts to abide by an agenda as much as possible. Although their expenses may be fewer, hosting companies (buying or selling) are still tying up managerial and staff time. Neither dragging out the negotiating process nor proceeding in a haphazard manner are productive approaches. Many practitioners of the running-out-the-clock ploy find that their efforts have come to naught as savvy visitors leave, never to return. Even vastly promising economies like China have seen investments take a downturn as their negotiators gained a reputation for being "time wasters."

Time Is Money

Keeping discussions on track may require a brief breaking-in period for counterparts unfamiliar with, or disdainful of, the process. While the agenda may have been addressed and detailed well in advance, setting the tone at the first meeting is essential. Visitors wishing to keep to a schedule must arrive promptly and be prepared to get right to work, regardless of their hosts preparation. Selling-mode visitors will appear eager, while those in the buying mode will give the impression of being prepared to make immediate decisions. Hosts who are ill-prepared for the arrival of guests will be put on the defensive, at least temporarily.

Host/buyers who intentionally create a let-them-wait atmosphere may be hard to hold to an agenda. Sellers must recognize this for what it is and decide whether this same attitude is likely to spill over into the payment process. The best way to combat this type of power play is to schedule multiple contacts with competing companies. Often, recalcitrant buyers must be reminded that they're "not the only game in town." Sometimes, however, they *are* the only game in town (at least the only one the government will allow you to play in), and sellers must make repeated efforts to stick to a time line. This unfortunate battle of wills can be frustrating but must be waged, nonetheless. Efficiency is a learned process.

Surprisingly, buyers may find the negotiators from the selling side also incapable of abiding by an agenda, even one that works in their favor. Sometimes this is a cultural phenomenon, at other times it's just an indicator of inexperience or unprofessionalism. Buyers can, of course, be more insistent about the agenda and can decide whether to continue discussions with counterparts who are unwilling or incapable of committing to deadlines.

These battles of will most often take place between representatives of developing economies and those from the technological powers. The latter will regularly have their patience tried by the lackadaisical approach to schedules taken by the former (whose countries are literally pleading for investment or products). Though it may require a serious investment of time, these developing countries will eventually, through insistence and example, embrace the business techniques of the advanced economies, just as they have the technology.

Milestones

Part of assembling an effective agenda is the recognition and listing of achievements that enable progress to move to the next level. These "milestones" should be mutually agreed upon as the agenda is assembled. Some will be deal breakers, others will merely mark the step-by-step progress toward success. Often, the inclusion of certain points will be contentious. Such topics as "shipment guarantor," "accounting standards," "correspondent bank," or "profit repatriation" can give one side or the other reason to pause. Both sides must realize that the listing of milestones is precontractual and that circumstances may change as negotiations progress.

Milestones may also take the form of promised achievements that each side agrees to if negotiations lead to a deal. They are, in effect, forecasts of "deliverables." The content and due dates of this form of milestone need to be discussed and made part of the formal agenda. Regardless of the developmental background of the parties or their relative view of contract bondage, each side must recognize that business in the latter part of the 20th century moves at too quick a pace to function well without an ordering of events. International trade law is too complex and domestic laws are too stringent to leave details hazy. The use of milestones early in the process of negotiations allows no detail to go unscrutinized.

NOTE: Whether you're a buyer or seller, insist on the use of milestones in your negotiations.

Accommodating the Social Aspects

Conducted in certain countries, international business requires a good deal of socializing, though it may have only a facade of relaxation. These dinner parties, cocktail receptions, golf outings, and cultural tours must all be discussed, agreed upon, and scheduled prior to the arrival of the visitors in-country, just as if these were formal negotiating sessions.

Staff, visiting staff in particular, must be informed and prepared for these events. Both sides must recognize that their counterparts will have other schedules and agendas that are unrelated to the discussions at hand. Neither side should seek to monopolize the other's time nor present them with "surprise" events that would put them in the embarrassing position of declining.

Professional negotiators must be prepared to give up varying degrees of their free time to this social aspect of business depending upon which country they're visiting or delegation they're hosting (see Chapter 19, Country Guidelines). Social events are really a continuation of the negotiations themselves and strategies must be observed and maintained. Many a negotiation has been won or lost over a glass of champagne.

Handling the Reactions of Counterparts

One party will always take the lead in formulating an agenda. Very often, it's the seller or the visitor because these two have the most at risk. Whichever side broaches the idea, it must be prepared for the reactions of counterparts. Having a wide variety of contingencies and enough wriggle-room for schedule adjustment allows for quick and decisive responses on the part of the initiator—both very desirable qualities for negotiators. Here are some possible reactions and responses.

TOTAL AGREEMENT

- This should raise a high degree of suspicion and may be a prelude to the "envelopment" mentioned earlier. Test counterparts by adding or detracting from the agenda in such a way as to be obviously contentious. If they agree to the change without comment, prepare for envelopment. The counterparts are merely hoping to get you so committed to the outcome that you will not be able to refuse concessions late in the process.

- Agreement may also be the reaction of a group who are novices to negotiation and are easily impressed with any sign of professionalism in counterparts. They too can be tested with a contentious change, to which they'll most likely raise an objection. (They should also be informed that your schedule is such that it can't tolerate any changes once negotiations have begun.)

- Total agreement to a first draft agenda is sometimes a sign that counterparts in developing economies have no intention of cutting a deal but only wish to test out their negotiating skills on a foreign team. They see this as providing a learning experience for their domestic managers and preparation for bigger prey. Any suspicion of this should bring a response that solicits references or some form of bona fides. The inclusion of serious milestones with early due dates is another way to smoke out these "students."

TOTAL DISAGREEMENT

- Like total agreement, this is very suspicious. Very arrogant host-buyers can respond in this fashion because they wish to (and often do) have total control of the situation. In such a case, the response should be in the form of a request for an agenda prepared by the counterpart. It may turn out to be not significantly different from *your* original proposal. Whatever it is, if you can live with it, let the other side revel in their "victory." You've just discovered, very early on, that ego will be a big part of their strategy. Use it to your advantage. An ego exposed is an ego defeated.
- Total disagreement may also indicate a novice team that is feeling its way. Seek a counterproposal from them and add portions of it to the original in small increments. If they remain intractable, especially if they are visitor-sellers, they may be under government scrutiny—or simply poor negotiators. Being unreasonable at this stage generally indicates fruitless future discussion. It may be time to cancel the negotiations.
- Review the submitted agenda and make sure that your proposal is reasonable. What you *don't* want is to be written off as an arrogant host or a novice visitor.

REQUESTS FOR MEETINGS IMMEDIATELY UPON ARRIVAL IN-COUNTRY

- Hosts faced with this prospect are obviously dealing with counterparts in a hurry. This should give rise to questions regarding the *need* for such speed. Is it the raw efficiency of a successful company or the desperation of a company in decline? (These possibilities should be researched *before* the visitors arrive.)
- Visitors who receive this type of request may ask themselves similar questions to the ones listed above. Additionally, they may be playing into the schemes of a counterpart who wishes to rush fatigued visitors to a foregone conclusion. If the host insists on meeting on the original arrival date, attempt to readjust flight schedules to arrive a day sooner. Otherwise, stay rested and prepare for a tough opening round.

REQUESTS FOR FEWER AND SHORTER MEETINGS

- If you're a seller, this is a very bad sign, and your company will most likely be given short shrift. Review your needs as originally presented and see if they're realistic. If so, reiterate your agenda with a detailed reasoning for the original schedule. If the buyer's reaction is the same, cancellation may be in order.
- If you're buying or investing, a request such as this by the seller side is usually an indication that they're not in dire need of your input. If you're investing, it may also be an indication that the target company has succumbed to another suitor. Contact the target group immediately and demand some straight answers.
- Buying and selling considerations aside, such a request can also be the result of a very busy company that simply doesn't allot much time for discussion. They may even wish to conduct a large part of the negotiation via phone or online prior to face-to-face meetings. U.S. companies, especially, tend to eschew lengthy discussions in favor of "getting down to business." If your company can live with this prospect, so be it.

REQUESTS FOR MORE AND LONGER MEETINGS

- Some business cultures like to discuss every point of a potential contract at length and are very uncomfortable with the prospect of moving quickly. For the most part, these are companies from developing economies and they fear that their negotiating acumen isn't as good as it should be. Sometimes, they're insulted by the fact that their company (and country) could be dealt with in such a short period of time. No one likes to be thought of as "simple." If they're buying, you may have to submit to their wishes. Otherwise, assuage their fears with promises that expansion of the schedule is possible if need becomes evident upon arrival. If they're merely requesting an expansion of the social portion of the agenda, it's best to accommodate them.
- Often companies new to international business (regardless of how developed their native economy is) are unsure of how to proceed, and so they tend to do so slowly. They'll be doubly apprehensive if they're the visiting member of the negotiations. Requesting more meetings is a way of getting themselves heard and buying time to review counteroffers. Some hosts may wish to play on this fear by sticking to the original schedule; others may wish to allay this fear by expanding portions of the agenda. Buying and selling positions should, of course, be taken into consideration.

CHANGE OF DEPARTMENTS FOR PRESENTATIONS

- Host-buyers who decide that your company should meet with the engineers (rather than with the marketing department, as you proposed) may be subtly saying "thanks, but no thanks" to your program. Courtesy interviews don't warrant the expense of international travel. You may counter with a proposal for a meeting with both departments, but don't be surprised if the personnel from the department you originally requested are suddenly called away on the scheduled date. Here are some alternatives: (1) Offer to forward the technical data or a video presentation to the "default" department in the hope of inspiring enough interest to justify a full-fledged trip in the future; (2) Send a small delegation (one person) to do a down-sized presentation to generate interest while saving money; (3) Schedule multiple contacts with competitors and shop your proposal around.
- Visitor-buyers are rarely shunted to courtesy interviews. If it happens cancel the trip or start looking at competitors. Remember, Microsoft became a software giant *after* another company said that they weren't interested in selling operating software to IBM.

EXCESSIVE SOCIALIZING

- Some visiting companies confuse business with vacation and plan to treat negotiations as a form of junket. Requests for cultural tours and other extracurricular activities can be excessive. If they're buyers, offer to assist in making arrangements but keep the involvement (and expense) of local staff to a minimum. If they're sellers, don't let your hospitality or payroll be abused. Provide information but reiterate the business requirements for the trip.

HINT: Visiting delegations that include politicians are usually on glad-handing missions only. Schedule accordingly. Contact business members of the delegation directly and feel out their intentions. While no business may be conducted on this trip, future negotiations may bear fruit.

- Hosts can also be guilty of packing the agenda with social events. Sometimes, it's standard hospitality for that culture, and special events may be organized to impress. It can also be a symptom of envelopment or an attempt to keep visitors fatigued. Succinctly put, sellers must endure what they can't deflect, while buyers can deflect what they choose not to endure.

INCLUSION OF GOVERNMENT RECEPTIONS

- Visitors from developing nations often request government receptions. This is because they're unfamiliar with commerce conducted without direct government intervention. If they're buyers, arrange at least an airport reception, if possible, and more elaborate proceedings if deemed necessary. Sellers should be assured that such receptions are extraneous to the business at hand (if that is indeed the case).
- Hosts must keep in mind that many business cultures see a government imprimatur as a sign that everything is above board. Others may see it as the host company's attempt to bring an outside force to bear. Therefore, don't offer to include government receptions until the counterpart has been thoroughly researched.

THE MULTISITE AGENDA

- Buyers may wish to see and meet at a host's offices, showroom or factory in an effort to determine the size of the operation. Within a relatively small radius this can certainly be accommodated. For the first round of negotiations, only the largest players should be granted the time and expense of anything beyond a day's travel. Keep in mind that some competitive research is conducted under the guise of negotiations. Don't reveal the full extent of a large operation until you're fully aware of a counterpart's intentions.
- Hosts in a selling mode may wish to show off facilities that may be of little interest to their visitors. Counter such agenda requests with statements to the effect that you can't commit to multisite discussions until after the preliminary discussions in-country. Don't let counterparts "run out the clock" on expensive travel plans. If time permits, visitors may find the visitations insightful.

Using Go-Betweens

As in the case of letters of introduction, often a third party can assist in the preparation of the agenda for the first round of negotiations. When trade focuses on sensitive goods or when investment is bound to be the subject of political scrutiny, a go-between can serve as a neutral (or at least dispassionate) party. Trade agency officials (generally, but not necessarily, from the host country) can be very useful in this capacity. Management personnel with successful international track records but with unrelated commercial interests can also serve as prime candidates for the go-between.

Only in the most sensitive scenarios, such as the reopening of trade after an extended embargo, should go-betweens be suggested from the outset. Normally, it's best to wait to see if there are any major "sticking points" in the agenda before resorting to third-party assistance.

NOTE: Readers should be aware that go-betweens called in for agenda setting may be asked by counterparts to join the actual negotiations as a form of referee. Consent to such intervention carefully, as the go-between may become an ally for the opposition.

How to Avoid Being Sidetracked

Once the agenda has been set, care must be taken to assure that it's abided by throughout the negotiations, unless major developments dictate otherwise. Counterparts unused to working under the restrictions of an agenda may neglect its time requirements or seek to sidetrack the proceedings with new topics. Some teams continually arrive late or seek to rearrange topics for discussion in an effort to throw off the timing and attention of counterparts.

Strong leadership by the chief negotiator (or lead negotiator at subsessions) must continually insist that the agenda be observed. Even when selling, a degree of displeasure must be shown at any attempt to rework or "massage" the agenda. Problems can first be addressed by simply calling attention to the transgression. Continual or egregious violations should be addressed directly, with inquiries about the counterpart's intentions. Sellers must use their own discretion as to how much diplomacy is in order; much depends on a counterpart's cultural background. Buyers and investors generally need only to make their displeasure known once before the problem corrects itself.

The Value of "Transparency"

Economies based in contract law repeatedly decry the lack of "transparency" (contractual or legislative clarity) in the developing world. While it's true that the process of compiling "hidden agendas" is somewhat culture based, it can also be the reaction of any group that perceives of itself as weak or disadvantaged. Large companies and those from technological economies must continually be on guard against counterparts refusing to divulge their real motives for negotiating. For instance, discovering two days into negotiations that the visiting team is using your company solely as a foil for discussions with a competitor can be very aggravating. Or worse, your hosts are using negotiations to gain technical acumen before embarking on a joint-venture in a part of their domestic market that excludes foreign investment. Complaining will seldom gain back the time and money already lost.

Part of the research on potential counterparts should be inquiries into the companies they've done business with in the past. Back-channel inquiries, domestic trade agencies, and Internet forums are all good sources for this information. Discretion is the best approach, but very few legitimate companies fear due-diligence-style research.

The Foreigner Who Can Say "No"

During the 1980s, *The Japan That Can Say "No"* was one of that country's most popular books, and in the mid-1990s, a similar book on Chinese negotiators was mandatory reading in Beijing. "No" has always been an effective tool for skilled negotiators, and it is especially useful when fixing an agenda. Visitors often have a difficult time turning down agenda proposals by hosts because they don't wish to appear culturally insensitive. This can even be true when the visitor is the buyer or investor.

Gaining a firm grounding in the host culture (business and social) will provide the negotiator with the insights necessary to propose or respond to a negotiating agenda. Though airport receptions, government soirees, evening sessions, and twelve-course luncheons may not be necessities, they may ensure smooth negotiations. Agenda setting can be a way for each side to test the other's acumen and will. At other times, the research acquired during this phase may reveal that negotiations aren't immediately feasible. The answer "no" will give your counterparts an idea of what to expect at the negotiating table. Use it judiciously.

CHAPTER 9

About Translators

MAKING SURE YOUR MESSAGE GETS THROUGH

THE ABILITY TO MAKE oneself understood is essential if any agreement is to be reached. International negotiations often require the use of translators to attain this goal. The optimal translator will understand both the linguistic and cultural nuances so necessary to communication. Translators must also be adept at comprehending the intricacies of everything from body language to seating arrangements. Rarely will a solo negotiator or team have sufficient language skills to operate anywhere in the world. The quality of the translators involved will greatly influence the negotiation's outcome.

Using the Language Skills of Team Members

On occasion, a member of the negotiating team will have the requisite language skills for the target market. Their ability to translate prenegotiation documents and set up telephone conferences will be highly useful to the group. However, they may not be a wise choice for use as the full-time translator during negotiations. Because their inclusion on the team was most likely for their commercial and analytical skills, the team member would be prevented from giving his or her input if required to act as translator. Only if the team member is in a very junior level staff position should his or her language skills be put to use during regular negotiation sessions. Upper-level management personnel should only be used in extreme cases. Having the vice president of marketing act as a translator isn't an efficient use of personnel.

Looking In-House for Translators

Large companies in cosmopolitan cultures have the advantage of diverse staffing. Language skills abound and should be tapped when possible. Employees who speak Dutch, Vietnamese, or Portuguese may already be on staff and have many advantages over translators brought in from outside of the company. They are already familiar with product lines, company background, and ethics. They'll also be eager to be part of an upper-level company program and thankful for the opportunity to take advantage of company-sponsored travel. Finally, their loyalty to company goals during negotiations should be assured.

Unfortunately, there's a downside to using an inexperienced, in-house translator. Translating during fast-paced negotiations can be very nerve racking. Employees unfamiliar with the effects of stress aren't good candidates. Also, employees new to high-level discussions may find themselves enthralled with the activity and distracted from their translating duties. Asking the opposition to repeat itself isn't professional grade translating.

Check to make sure that an employee's language skills are really sufficient for the task at hand. (Schoolbook French will be of little use in Paris, and Americanized South Vietnamese dialects will play poorly in Hanoi.) Travel and stress skills should be at the same level as the rest of the negotiating team. If they can't handle the negotiating atmosphere, drop them from consideration regardless of language skills. Translators are supposed to be an aid—not a burden—during negotiations.

Translators: What To Look For and Where

Negotiators should hire a translator familiar with both their company's domestic culture and that of their counterparts. When hiring from outside of the company, get the best talent that the budget will allow.

While it may be necessary to advertise, accept only professionals with references. Keep in mind that merely speaking the required language fluently doesn't guarantee a good translation or translator. As in the case of in-house employees, the ability to handle stress and the foreign travel experience, as well as having a working familiarity with the topic of the negotiations at hand, are equally important factors.

Most major metropolitan areas have translator services that can provide professional translators for extended use. Government agencies can also provide translator contacts and services. These services are very practical for hosts wishing to hire for local usage. Visiting negotiators may also wish to utilize these companies. Visitors who are preparing for extensive overseas negotiations are better served by hiring in their domestic market and making the translator part of the team. It may be expensive but it's essential that the translator be directly answerable to, and paid by, the negotiators for whom they're translating.

WARNING: Don't let counterparts provide translation services for you, and be wary of asking one's host to help procure a translator. Disloyal translators can do irreparable damage.

Each side of the negotiating table should have its own translators. As practical as it may appear, using a single translator will result in quick burnout and resultant communication problems. The translation process demands intense concentration, even for the most fluent, and working for both sides is far too exhausting. Additionally, translators need to be part of the pre- and postmeeting sessions that are important to keeping strategy in line. Their comments on tone, body language, and cultural nuance will provide essential information to negotiators. A single translator will not be able to supply this service to both sides.

Proper Care and Handling

It's very important that translators be made to feel that they're part of the negotiating team and process. Keeping them "outside of the loop" until discussions begin and shunting them aside at the end of each day will greatly limit their effectiveness. They should be treated as regular and essential members of the team and included in social events related and unrelated to negotiations. Like other negotiators, translators need to keep their spirits high; being treated with respect, courtesy, and friendship helps. It also inspires loyalty beyond the paycheck.

If they're being paid by the hour, make it clear what's billable and what's not. Staff must also be clear about when (and when not) to utilize the translator. Giving the translator bonuses for work "above and beyond the call of duty" is recommended.

NOTE: If visitors are using a local professional in a developing market, they may wish to make payments incrementally rather than wait until the end of negotiations. Giving the translator a little walking-around money and a few tips will help maintain their loyalty and spirit.

Translators must be well informed. This doesn't mean they need to know all of the company secrets. They should, however, be apprised in advance of the basic technical data and terms to be used during discussions. Some ideas and terms don't translate easily, and it's unwise to expect the translator to come up with interpretations for complex ideas or technical jargon on the spot. It's also a good idea to let the translator become familiar with each team member's speech patterns—another good reason to include them in social events. Brief forays into dialect or slang can derail the translation. Let the translator, and team members, establish a rhythm prior to negotiations.

NOTE: Don't assume that the translator knows basic business or trade jargon. Many a simple trade discussion has gone awry over even common usages such as "free-on-board" or "after market."

Basic Protocol

Not knowing the basic protocol for working with translators will mark the negotiator as a novice and cause translation problems. The following are basic protocols for using translators:

1. When counterparts are speaking, look at them, not at their translator. Continue to look at the counterpart as the translation is given, with occasional glances at the translator. Negotiators must interpret body language as well. You can't see a counterpart smile if you aren't looking.

2. Listen intently. Unlike normal conversation, there's no expectation of an immediate response. Don't formulate one during the translation. Listen, then formulate, and then respond.

3. When each side has a translator, the respective interpreters should only translate when *their* team speaks. They should take notes as their counterpart works and confirm the translation only. Negotiators should verify the translation with their own interpreter while formulating a response. Ask for clarifications if necessary, but don't interrupt.

4. Negotiators should speak in clear short sentences and never for longer than thirty seconds at a time. Pause and allow the translator to interpret. If it's a lengthy speech (as in a welcoming ceremony), make sure that the translator has been given a transcript in advance. This will permit the use of rhetorical phrasing (and lengthier sentences) while still assuring that all points are covered and properly interpreted.
5. Translators are usually seated just to the rear of negotiators, never "at the table." This permits their movement among participants and a certain degree of confidentiality (that is, whispering), when necessary.
6. When translators from opposing sides conflict on a major point of interpretation, ask for clarification. Don't assume that your interpreter is always correct.
7. Never express public displeasure with an interpreter's performance. If the translator was hired by your team or is a staff member, save criticisms for postmeeting discussions. Preserving the translator's dignity will go a long way toward preserving their loyalty. Also, keeping it private gives the opposition one less weakness to exploit. If the translator was hired by counterparts (not a good idea to begin with), express your displeasure to the counterparts. It's their employee, so let them deal with the problem. Seek immediate improvement or replacement.
8. Keep translators close at hand and maintain their confidence. It's not unusual for translators to be approached by the opposition in an effort to solicit information. This is especially true of a visitor's interpreter if they happen to be indigenous to the host country.

Keeping Counterparts Off-Balance with Secrecy

Translators often speak languages beyond those germane to the negotiations. If they share these skills with team members or the chief negotiator, it can be an important tool of communication that will keep counterparts off-balance. Reverting to a third language for intrateam discussions can be both convenient for the team and disconcerting for counterparts—assuming, of course, that the opposition lacks similar language skills.

It's a similar tactic to the one used by hosts that insist upon (or find themselves in the fortunate position of) providing a single translator for both teams. Hosts carry on audible side-conversations in their native tongue while visitors are too restrained to ask the "neutral" translator to fill them in. While considered bad manners in the West, both tactics are common in Asia. Some negotiators eschew such tactics, others have the mettle to ignore such a ploy by counterparts. Still others make clear to the opposition that such "secrecy" is considered a sign of bad faith.

Tips for a Successful Trade Mission

BY "JIM" CHIN T. NGUYEN

1. A delegation leader should be a high ranking and recognized public figure.
2. Identify a couple of dependable and trusted contacts in the host country and work with them on logistics and screening of foreign companies prior to your visit.
3. Take advantage of your country's contacts in the embassy and chambers of commerce in the host country.
4. Organize a premission briefing prior to your departure to inform participants about protocol, itinerary updates, and basic cultural advice.
5. Bring along a qualified interpreter on your trip. If you cannot afford one, then make sure you have one waiting for you overseas.
6. Create a mission profile book that contains pictures, names, and descriptions of participating companies and personnel.
7. Learn how to pronounce names of host contacts correctly and clarify their positions and job titles.
8. Bring small, tasteful gifts for each contact. Gifts are appreciated in every culture.
9. Don't discuss political ideology and religion.
10. A small delegation is more manageable than a large one.

Mr. Nguyen operates a successful international marketing company in San Francisco, California USA

The Importance of Properly Translated Written Materials

The translation of written materials for use in negotiations is essential to efficiency, as well as being a mark of courtesy and professionalism. For those in a selling position it's mandatory. Repeat, mandatory. Whereas a certain amount of grammatical and accentual leeway will be granted translators during the heat of discussions, none can be afforded here. Proposals, letters of introduction, references, and financial reports should all be translated, checked by a native speaker, and submitted along with the originals. Faxes or emails sent to establish meeting dates and times should be composed in the native language of the receiver when possible. If the language is too obscure or a translator is unavailable, the default language for such correspondence is English.

WARNING: When translating financial or numerical data, take care to observe the proper use of commas and periods when denoting currency or thousand unit groupings. These are not universal.

COMPANY MARKETING MATERIALS AND BROCHURES

While preferable, it's not necessary to reproduce four-color company marketing collateral or sales brochures in foreign language editions. This can wait until a long-term position has been established in the foreign market. Prior to that, translations placed as inserts will suffice. Triple check that translations are accurate and have no double entendres before sending them to the printer. When they return, have them checked again. Misprints can have humorous or even insulting results.

CONFESSION: In 1986, the author approved marketing documents that had been translated from English into Japanese in advance of upcoming meetings. The Japanese were less-than-impressed to find that every subheading in these lavishly printed brochures had been printed upside down. There's no such thing as too much checking.

BUSINESS CARDS

Some countries (like Japan and South Korea) place enormous importance on business cards. Regardless of which country negotiators hail from or seek to visit, business cards should be translated into the language of one's counterparts. It's a small task that speaks volumes about a company's intentions and attention to detail. As is true with other documents, take care with the translations.

Well known or trademarked acronyms (e.g., IBM) need not be translated nor do words included in logos (such as Toyota). Company descriptions that are normally included on cards should be carefully scrutinized after translation. (The author's card was once translated from the English *research and analysis* to the Tagalog words for *reading and thinking*.)

Job titles should also be carefully translated as they'll be used during negotiations to match counterparts. Some additional research may be required to determine the distinction between "deputy director" and "vice president" or between "trade assistant" and "sales manager." Don't inflate job titles but, if error is to take place, make it to your benefit. Also, make sure the "vice president of sales" doesn't become the "president of selling vice"—such things happen with embarrassing regularity in international business.

Double-sided cards are the best format, with addresses fully translated and contact numbers clearly stated for international usage. Email addresses should appear in their original format with the Internet service company clearly stated. Some visiting companies go so far as to include their temporary in-country address and contact numbers.

NOTE: In some cases, these cards may be all that remains at the end of negotiations. Make them work for you.

CHAPTER 10

Negotiating Styles, Part 1

MAJOR PERSONAL STYLES

INTERNATIONAL COMMERCIAL negotiation is a zero-sum game that pits every gain against a loss. And when successfully completed, losers believe they've won and winners give every indication of bearing up under defeat. Language and fortitude are used to create a belief that everyone will walk away from the table with "enough," even if one side's portion (hopefully the opponent's side) is far less than forecasted.

Each negotiator and every negotiating team must choose a style that will best serve their goal. The same style will not work in every situation, nor will every situation permit every style. Negotiators and teams must be flexible, able to change style as easily as they change locale. The same research skills that have been focused outward should now be turned inward, as honest and thorough self-assessment will permit the most appropriate choice of both personal and team styles.

Choosing a Style That Fits

Below is a listing of twenty-three different personal negotiating styles. Rarely does a person use one style to the exclusion of all others, and there's a great deal of crossover. It's rare (if not impossible) for someone to adopt a style that runs contrary to their personality. Also, these styles are often countermeasures to each other. (A full listing of countermeasures are suggested in Chapter 15.)

Negotiators strive to be believed, and they must believe in their own discourse if they're to be successful. Even the most talented actors have limits of range. (Robert De Niro can convincingly portray a maniacal gangster, but he probably won't succeed as Oedipus Rex.) Potential negotiators must research their own talents and virtues to determine which style or combination of styles best fits their personality.

Chief negotiators must make similar decisions when assembling a team. One can't have a soccer team comprised entirely of all-star goalies. Diversity is required. Assembly of the right combination of talents, styles, and flexibility will result in a team that can handle virtually any negotiating session. Team leaders must also be on guard against members who endeavor to utilize styles that are incompatible with team goals.

AGGRESSIVE

Many people see themselves as aggressive but few actually fill the bill. Aggressive negotiators run roughshod over opponents with little regard for their counterparts' positions. They take no prisoners and grant no quarter, and the word "concession" isn't found in their lexicon. Aggressive negotiating does have its place if used in small doses, while constant belligerence will rarely result in a penned contract. Skilled negotiators will assume an aggressive posture only when supposedly non-negotiable points are being discussed.

WARNING: As is true in daily life, aggression brings its own additional pricetag. Aggressors throughout history have been outflanked in their mad rush for success by more patient opponents. Aggression is best used as a temporary negotiating tactic, not as an overall strategy.

COMPLIANT

Compliant negotiators are the archenemies of counterpart aggressors. Their style demands that many points are readily conceded early in negotiations in an effort to draw the aggressor farther into the process. Major points are purposely kept off of the agenda until late in the negotiations when the aggressor believes they'll continue to receive concessions. In reality, the compliant side has "run the clock out" and will start demanding "payback" for earlier concessions. The aggressor has been enveloped and placed in the position of possibly scuttling very expensive negotiations and returning home empty-handed. Compliance can be a very effective style but only when used by hosts. It requires strict control of the agenda and the ability to recognize when counterparts have been sufficiently lulled.

NOTE: Compliance is particularly successful when a great deal of PR surrounds the proceedings and visitors have been sending out signals of imminent success.

PASSIVE

Passive negotiators aren't always what they seem. Often utilized by developing economies with little contract law, passive negotiating convinces the opposition to put all of their cards on the table in the belief that everything is mutually acceptable. The passive side presents nothing and simply nods—and counterparts believe they're in agreement. But the nod denotes understanding only. Once all has been revealed, the previously passive negotiators start "cherry picking" the points they find palatable and actively (sometimes aggressively) reworking those they don't. Passive negotiators rarely present their own program; instead, they nitpick the opposition's program in an effort to keep them on the defensive.

Passivity is also used by novice negotiators to learn about the cultural negotiating styles of economies with whom they're unfamiliar. Seeking only an education and not a contract, they pursue their research by letting the opposition reveal data and techniques to be used against "bigger fish" in future negotiations. Many medium-sized technology companies were lured to developing Asia in the late 1980s and early 1990s with promises of market penetration. But unbeknownst to them, they were there to provide practice sessions for negotiators soon to lock horns with Motorola, Seimens, and NEC. Passive "research" negotiators also travel outside of their borders to see how potential counterparts behave on their own turf. Either way, they use up time in fruitless negotiations. This style and strategy is considered deceptive by some cultures and "just business" by others.

One hallmark of both types of passive negotiators is that they don't seek out any input during the agenda-setting process. Research teams can also be recognized by their requests for information unrelated to the negotiations at hand.

WARNING: It's very costly to mistake passivity for agreement.

IMPASSIVE

The impassive negotiator is purposely unreadable. Inscrutability isn't the exclusive domain of the Chinese; it's been successfully used by skilled negotiators around the world for centuries. By creating an image of being indifferent to either winning or losing on any particular point, impassive negotiators cause their counterparts to believe that some secret is being withheld. The impassive buyer also causes the opposition to go to extreme lengths to please. Because they can't see what pleases or displeases, sellers often "shoot the works" in an effort to get a reaction from the sphinx across the table. Skilled, impassive buyers can get a great deal more with silence than they can with vocal manipulations. In this case, money doesn't talk—it stares.

Impassive sellers attack from the opposite direction. Selling and indifference, though seemingly antithetical, aren't always so. Sellers who have many suitors can name their own price as well as pick and choose among the suitors. It's basic supply and demand. A seller who is impassive creates in the buyer's mind a sense of insecurity that the sale may not be "permitted" or that a competitor will get it instead. This attitude of "if you don't meet my price someone else will" puts the buyer in the unenviable position of begging to spend money. Impassivity by sellers is a highly effective style for both trade and investment, but it requires counterparts who are short on research. Buyers truly must believe that their counterparts are "the only game in town" for it to work. First offers, no matter how lucrative, must be met with a dispassionate eye. Practitioners, whether buying or selling, must be masters of the poker face.

INTIMIDATING

Intimidation is the instillment of fear in opponents and fear is a forceful motivator. Unfortunately, it's a short jump from fear to loathing, and loathing is no basis for a relationship. Therefore, fear should be applied judiciously, so that the recipient feels its effect but is unaware of the process. Fear in international business is usually couched in terms of being excluded from a market or a particular money-making endeavor.

It is not easy to be intimidating, and for commerce it's strictly a matter of attitude rather than physical presence. It shouldn't be confused with aggressive behavior, although in some circumstances it can take that guise. Above all else, intimidation at the negotiation table requires the will to back up words with action. Also, intimidation requires the cooperation of counterparts. (They must choose to be intimidated if this style is to be productive.) Skilled negotiators have high fear thresholds but thresholds nonetheless. Learning *what* intimidates counterparts and *when* will determine if this style of negotiating will ultimately work. The following statements indicate that intimidation is at play:

- *"Of course you realize that only a limited number of contracts will be issued this year."*
- *"We understand how important this deal must be for your company."*
- *"Yours is the third company we have spoken to this month regarding this matter."*
- *"We hope you're more successful than the other (insert your nationality or industry) companies we've met with."*

- *"Are you aware of (insert your competitor's name) interest in this project?"*
- *"Our government takes special interest in ventures that involve foreign companies."*
- *"We understand that your company has other interests in our country."*
- *"If agreement isn't reached by the end of today's session, we must understandably consider other offers."*
- *"We would like our legal counsel to review your proposition."*

TECHNICAL

Technical negotiation centers on the data of the product or service under discussion, and it counts on the opposition being worn down by the onslaught of technical details. Many negotiating teams purposely include a member who is highly knowledgeable about technical processes. Besides being able to answer the occasional question, they can also be used to thwart the opposition's attempts to downplay (or overplay) the monetary value of the technology.

This style comes into play in joint ventures where partnership percentages are determined by the agreed-upon value of what each side "brings to the table." Manufacturing economies tend to value physical property (e.g., factories, hardware) over intellectual property (e.g., manufacturing processes, software) while technological economies have reverse values. The technical negotiating style strives to foster a belief in the opposition that their lack of knowledge precludes them from being able to determine market value.

WARNING: The technical style requires that the opposition be made to see the limits of their knowledge only in a particular area. Making the other side feel stupid will be of little value in the long run. Also, translators must be well-versed in the data if this technique is to be effective.

FINANCIAL

Oddly enough, many business negotiations (and negotiators) strive to downplay the role of money making. Many cultures wish to avoid appearing greedy, while others merely wish to keep the opposition focused on other issues until it is time to deliver the unfortunate fiscal news. The financial style of negotiating specifically plays upon the discomfort that counterparts feel when discussing this all-important issue. When used as part of an overall buying/investment strategy, practitioners of this technique talk in terms of money at every juncture of the agenda. All points of discussion must be made compatible with the bottom-line. If a subject can't be shown to contribute to profit, counterparts are asked why they're wasting time talking about it.

NOTE: Americans are famous for their financial focus during negotiations and are sometimes considered boorish for their efforts. Boorish but rich.

As a tactical maneuver, financial negotiators can browbeat the opposition much in the same way that technical negotiators can. Suddenly switching the focus to finance can put bogged down discussions back on track as counterparts strive to back away from issues in which they are not conversant. Besides having the financial knowledge necessary to make this style work, practitioners must also be dispassionate debaters. Remaining unemotional will permit the negotiator to avoid accusations of greed and allow the pursuit of topics on a "just business" basis.

LEGALISTIC

Contrary to popular belief, lawyers are notoriously bad negotiators—the logic being that if they were good at it, judges would be unnecessary. But this isn't to say that a legalistic negotiating style has no place at the table. All business is constrained by law to some degree, and negotiators must be concerned with its effect on the business relationship they're attempting to mold as well as the direct effect upon ownership, taxes, and staffing.

In most of the developed West, legal considerations (and lawyers) are *expected* at the negotiating table. Here the legalistic style is used to remind all participants of their responsibilities and potential benefits under local and international law. Time consuming and petty it may seem, but a team or single negotiator with only minimal legal knowledge will be at a decided disadvantage. When one side adopts this posture, counterparts must be quick to respond in kind.

The developing world is a different matter. Many Asian business cultures prefer to carry on business both above and below the table. The same is true of many South American, Middle Eastern, Eastern European, and African communities. Agreement with the process is not as important as understanding and manipulating your counterpart's reaction to legal wrangling.

Foreign buyers working in such markets will find that adapting a legalistic approach to negotiations at key intervals will result in the granting of major concessions. However, using it as an overall strategy will most likely derail the process completely, as sellers will not be able to envision any profits if kept within the narrow constraints of their domestic legal system. Foreign sellers who attempt to secure legal protection for every negotiated point in these cultures will find the going difficult, if not impossible.

When you are acting as host to sellers from cultures that prefer to work outside of a tight legal structure, the use of the legalistic style will keep the negotiations firmly in your hand. Counterpoints will be disconcerted and obligated throughout discussions. When you are hosting a group of buyers, negotiators should use legalistic tactics only to that degree that will protect payment or investment transfer.

NOTE: Regardless of the legal wrangling at the table, contract execution may not always be ideal if the respective governments don't have similar commercial codes. Additionally, using or responding to a legalistic approach will require added research time—and therefore cost. Foreign negotiators should always have a basic knowledge of the host's legal system and applicable international laws.

SECRETIVE

Many negotiations are conducted wholly or partly in secret. This may be the result of personal privacy issues involving participants, high level diplomatic sensitivity, legal ramifications, or a desire to keep the press at bay. Demanding that the discussions remain secret is also a strategy that can influence the outcome. Secrecy eliminates outside pressure and concentrates the participants on the issues.

And it can be used to keep counterparts from seeking outside assistance or information once negotiations begin.

If you or your company is the subject of such a request, regard it with care. Secrecy isn't always easy or inexpensive to maintain. Make inquiries about the reason for such furtiveness and make sure that it will not restrict your own negotiating style or content. If the conditions for secrecy are accepted, negotiators must prepare accordingly.

NOTE: Secrecy creates a very restrictive atmosphere and it should be requested or acquiesced to only under special circumstances.

Single negotiators from a team are often contacted by their counterpart and solicited for special "side meetings" that are to be kept hush-hush. Team members should be instructed to agree to nothing until they've had time to consider the fallout. Individual negotiators must pledge to inform CNs of any attempts by counterparts to meet with them. Team leaders must be prepared to deal with this prospect and be aware that, oftentimes, the weakest link is singled out by the opposition. If your team initiates such secret side meetings, it should realize that counterparts may be offended and view the remaining sessions as suspect.

DECEPTIVE

Only the most naive of negotiators will deny the value of deception. Use varies by degree from one team to the next, but it's omnipresent. Disputes over its use arise only between groups that commit lies of omission and those that proffer outright deceptive information or promises.

Misleading counterparts and shielding intent are tools that all successful negotiators use. Adapting deception as the main strategy is only productive if the intent of the negotiations is short-term and doesn't focus on contract signing (i.e., gathering of research). Successful long-term relationships can never be based on a wholly deceptive strategy.

Deception as a style is most effective when used in small doses. Because all negotiators are guilty of it, they're also willing to forgive a bit of deception by counterparts. They may even be planning on it. Deception will be discussed in more detail in Chapter 15 on tactics.

NOTE: Negotiators who can't deceive effectively are destined to defeat. Letting opponents know your every move and the depth of your strategy is no more effective at the negotiating table than it is on a battlefield. Deception, like truth, is but a tool.

EXPLOITIVE

All opponents have weaknesses that can be exploited. Negotiators must determine for themselves which weaknesses to exploit and when. The zero-sum nature of the process demands a certain amount of exploitation. When best practiced, the exploitive style involves a careful study of counterparts before and during discussions. As the weaknesses become apparent, the practitioner makes rational (never emotional) decisions to capitalize on the flaw immediately, to let it pass, or to reserve exploitation until later in the negotiations. Therefore, the assessment of a counterpart's failings should be a large part of the negotiation planning process.

Exploitive styles must be conducted with great subtlety as very few counterparts are so desperate as to welcome or tolerate outright exploitation. Weak, undeveloped economies are especially paranoid about any form of what they deem exploitive. (Unfortunately in these same economies, the term is often used to describe any profit made by a foreign company.) Exploitive styles will generally involve the use of deceptive tactics, and therefore they rarely survive long-term scrutiny.

The most common form of this style calls for taking advantage of a counterpart's ignorance of the true value of their resources in the global market or of their inability to access that marketplace directly (e.g., Southeast Asian labor).

NOTE: Like deception, exploitation is used to some degree by all negotiators. Keeping an eye on the longevity of the deal will enable negotiators to determine proper dosages and timing.

STUBBORN

There may be no such thing as a truly non-negotiable topic, but inflexible behavior abounds at some negotiating sessions. Choosing stubbornness as an overall style is risky as it may force the opposition to become equally stubborn on points it feels strongly about. Historically, immovable objects are easy to out maneuver and real long-term stubbornness is the Maginot Line of negotiating styles.

Some negotiators use stubbornness as a way to distract counterparts from true motives. Relenting on a supposedly non-negotiable point will bring concessions—important ones—as a form of payback. Like many other styles it should be used only on occasion, as constant use results in predictability.

AMBIVALENT

Ambivalence is something that negotiators never consciously choose as a style, but it's often there as a character default. Professional negotiators and teams never suffer from it, but may find themselves sitting across the table from counterparts rife with its effects. Ambivalent teams and individuals that are unable to make or hold to decisions can flummox discussions as easily as stubbornness can. By being forced to review subject matter again and again without reaching a conclusion, the opposition may become frustrated to the point of termination.

Many teams that are new to the international market or those under local governmental scrutiny suffer from ambivalence. Their leadership works under the premise that no decision is better than a bad decision. (No decision is a decision.) Even when the proposal works in their favor, they still believe it is too good to be true. Most ambivalence stems from a lack of research concerning the particulars of the deal at hand.

WARNING: As will be seen in Chapter 11 on team styles, the time consuming internal discussions that are associated with ambivalence should not be confused with consensus building.

PRAGMATIC

Pragmatism can be very formidable, both as a strategy and a tactic. Taking to the high ground of efficiency will place counterparts on the defensive and force them to review their proposals purely from a practical standpoint. However, it does require that negotiators have already done the same with their own positions. Recommending practicality when your own positions are idealistic (at best) will not lend credibility to your maneuver.

As a strategic style, pragmatism demands extensive research and a complete, well-thought-out plan that can be laid out in some detail early in the negotiations rather than incrementally. The plan should provide potential courses of action for counterparts as well. If done properly, the opposition will gladly choose from options provided by your plan. Pragmatic strategies require that you think of everything. The numbers are laid out for all to scrutinize. Prenegotiation planning sessions involve a great deal of devil's advocate type role playing. Be aware that some counterparts may resent your planning of *both* sides of the negotiation, even when the proposal plainly overshadows their own concepts and provides them with a substantial piece of the commercial pie. Efficiency isn't loved the world over and it's often seen as a relative term with cultural overtones.

Pragmatism is most often used as a tactical style to get negotiations back on track. Statements like "let's cut to the chase . . ." or "time to cut through the haze . . ." are dropped into the discussion as an indicator that quibbling should cease and real issues get resolved. If diplomatically phrased, no one side will be held culpable. Pointing fingers will merely take up more time and detract from the argument for practicality. All discussions run the risk of tangential debate; a call for pragmatism will refocus everyone on the agenda. However, practitioners should take care that they don't dismiss their counterparts' proposals or arguments out of hand. Good listening skills and an understanding of the milieu in which counterparts must function will greatly assist in establishing when a pragmatic style is most appropriate.

NOTE: Even pragmatists must have fallback positions, in case their original proposal isn't accepted.

BRINKMANSHIP

Brinkmanship as a negotiating style is purely tactical in nature and involves the issuance of ultimatums on specific points. The threat of the ultimatum (or "the brink") is that discussions will be called off unless an issue is resolved immediately or in a specified manner. It's more bullying than negotiating and can only be used effectively by a powerful opponent, most likely in a host-buying position.

This style can't be used very often, although many negotiators have effectively used it early in discussions and then held it as an implied threat throughout the remaining sessions. Counterparts that are evenly matched will rarely deploy it, and novices are warned against even considering its use, no matter how tempting. Negotiation by ultimatum, even when practiced by professionals, always—repeat, always—leads to resentment. Its use in simple trades, and short-term deals will make any continued relationship difficult.

ARROGANT

Similar to ambivalence, arrogance is an unconscious choice as a negotiating style. It's also what inexperienced negotiators often call their well-organized, successful counterparts. Wise negotiators must be on guard against both conditions.

Regardless of your opponents position or attitude, behaving in an arrogant manner will only add an emotional edge to your counterparts' demands. Remember that negotiating is about bending the opposition to your will, not driving them away. There are two main causes of arrogant behavior. One is a feeling of inferiority on your part. The other is not understanding that your counterpart is being made to feel inferior. Reactions and the accompanying behavior are unconscious but not uncontrollable.

In the first case, the practitioner isn't comfortable with his own status, facility, appearance, proposal, or company. The response is to assume a supercilious pose to hide a lack of confidence. If the opposing side is skilled, they'll see through this amateurish guise immediately. If they're not skilled, what was the point of feeling inferior?

In the second case, where negotiators' behavior gives the appearance of arrogance, they have most likely been acting in a manner that disregards the counterparts' viewpoint. Understanding the opposition is a necessary part of the negotiating process. If they feel inferior (and maybe rightfully so), it's in a negotiator's best interest to dispel that notion; keeping the discussions among "equals" makes the granting and receiving of concessions easier. "Inferiors" begrudge every concession they must grant and see every one received as a form of justice. Domineering agenda planning, the throwing of lavish parties that can't be reciprocated, arriving late for meetings, constant cultural comparisons, and implications that you're here to "help" the opposition will only aggravate the situation.

NOTE: Avoid the arrogant style by being vigilant of your own behavior and the opposition's reactions.

SELF-RIGHTEOUS

Many negotiators exude a sense of altruism that can often backfire and is seldom appreciated. Even when successful, companies wishing to put a human rights, religious, environmental, or political equity spin on their commercial negotiations may create more problems for themselves than they solve.

If used at all, the self-righteous style should never be the driving edge of an overall negotiating style, merely a component. The I-know-what's-best-for-you approach will cause resentment in international discussions and gain the practitioner a reputation for arrogance. Political and religious concerns, even if they're company policy, should be addressed during the negotiation research and planning phase to make sure that counterparts share (or have the potential to share) those concerns. Springing those concerns on counterparts or demanding that they be the centerpiece of negotiations will only disrupt the business at hand. Self-righteous negotiators must also be prepared for a grocery list of equally righteous moral demands from counterparts.

WARNING: Some countries (China and Russia, for instance) specifically request that you check your moral baggage on "human rights issues" at customs if you want to do business within their borders. If you have a problem with that, it will only become an even bigger one if these issues aren't resolved prior to the start of negotiations.

OVERWHELMING

There's absolutely nothing wrong with overwhelming your counterparts—as long as you leave them "enough" to maintain their interest in the deal. Buyers are best served by this style and can pursue a "money talks" plan of attack. Sellers can also be overwhelming if they come prepared to counter any misgivings the opposition may have. This requires extensive preparation and solid experience.

Some negotiators are so organized and acute that they can't help but dazzle the opposition. Others consciously maximize their preparation and research to assure success. If this style isn't diplomatically presented and seen as "natural," it will be heavily resisted. When properly done, counterparts may end up using your techniques as a standard against which to judge their own skills.

WARNING: Don't attempt this style until you have at least several years of experience under your belt. It takes time to learn all of the angles of attack and defense. If your company is the target of this form of negotiating, keep your notebooks handy.

FLEETING

Some negotiators have adopted speed as a negotiating style in the belief that it will cover deficiencies in their own position and deflect the strength of counterparts. When dealing with inexperienced opponents, moving negotiations along at a brisk pace may have its advantages. However, the hard-sell, just-sign-right-here attitude can often cause resentment if the deal doesn't provide "enough" for the opposition. If used as an overall style, be prepared to have a fallback plan when counterparts intentionally slow the pace. Additionally, never try to rush an experienced counterpart—it simply will not be tolerated, and it may mark you as a novice.

STERN

Methodical, humorless, and unruffled, the stern negotiator controls sessions with sheer discipline. The histrionics and gimmicks of counterparts pass without notice. Like impassivity, the stern approach requires a poker face but unlike its sister style, motives and technique are made plain from the start. Getting down to business and numbers crunching are hallmarks of the stern. Social activity and smiling are minimal, if present at all.

This style demands a very specific personality type and can be very effective in controlling the content and pace of sessions. Its main practitioners are older, resolute, and highly experienced. (It takes a long time to become grumpy.) If confronted with this style, remember that it's just that—style. Don't let it obscure the substance, or lack of substance, in your counterpart's proposals or arguments.

NOTE: Sternness is a calm form of intimidation. You have to let it work on you if it's to work at all. If you choose it as a style, look for opponents who will readily succumb to its effects.

SOCIAL

Negotiation is certainly a form of social contact, but some participants choose to emphasize its social aspects in an attempt to sway counterparts. Lavish receptions with important (that is, political) guests, private dinners at popular venues, choice seats at sporting events, gambling and shopping junkets, endless cocktail parties, and inclusion at local or family festivities are all designed to make the opposition believe that their best interests are being looked after. The message is, "let's be friends first and business partners second."

This friendly form of envelopment isn't the exclusive purview of hosts. Many visitors already familiar with their host's landscape can use the same social style to demonstrate that they're effective and highly regarded players, both on and off of home turf. The British and the Americans have used their wealth and political connections for decades to let foreign hosts know that they "have been here before" and are already hooked into the local scene. All countries with a major overseas diplomatic presence make ready use of commercial and protocol attachés to line up high-end social events to impress business contacts.

Business cultures that are relatively devoid of commercial contract law use socialization as a way to evaluate and cement relationships. The personal bond between counterparts will, in these cases, supersede the contract. But even in a business culture such as this, socialization can be more of a manipulative technique than a business necessity.

Social functions can be used as a means of tiring out already weary opponents (beware all you jet-lag types) or to distract them from concentrating on commerce in the hope that they'll reveal information or dissention within their own ranks. Less seemly, but not uncommon, is the use of socializing for the purpose of allowing counterparts to compromise themselves or their company. Alcohol and drug problems are exploited, sexual preferences exposed, marital fidelity tested, and company loyalty questioned by personnel in direct (or indirect) employ of the practitioner.

Many visitors to the cutthroat developing markets (and even in some developed ones) have found that late-night carousing with counterparts can devolve into offers of prostitutes (male and female) and the purposeful involvement of local police. Suddenly the visitor needs the counterpart's assistance in clearing the matter up or in keeping it secret. Thus, an evening of social activity has been cleverly engineered by the practitioner into a "debt" that will be repaid many times over at the negotiating table. There is little denying of the effectiveness of both the friendly and less friendly versions of this style of negotiating. Even the most experienced hand can be softened by continual offers of friendship or plagued by a momentary mistake. Avoiding tiring social events and compromising situations can have its problems as well. Very few people wish to appear unsociable (see Stern, above) and turning down after-hours frolicking may convince the profferer that they've committed a faux pas.

Understanding the social restrictions of counterparts (e.g., the Chinese, the Canadians, and the Italians have very different senses of social decorum) will keep you from offending them. Similarly, the avoidance of anything you might be ashamed of will preserve your own position. Always pay attention and never, ever let your guard down.

WARNING: International negotiation is rarely an eight-hour-a-day job, or even a twelve-hour one. It's best to consider yourself in negotiation mode every moment you're awake. Just as peace marks time between wars, rest is something you do between negotiations.

THEFT

Sadly, theft as a negotiating style is growing by leaps and bounds every year. As society becomes more information-based, knowledge isn't only power but also currency. Choosing this as a style is fraught with risk but equally fraught with the potential for profit. Unlike deception, theft isn't universally practiced, and its discovery can bring negotiations to a crashing close. Criminal prosecution and commercial blackballing aren't unusual. Theft is usually practiced by desperate counterparts but many internationally known companies use it on a regular basis to save research expenditures and plan strategy. Any experienced negotiators who claim never to have been victimized by it or to be unfamiliar with "that sort" of counterpart are either self-deluding or not as experienced as they would have you believe.

Theft can take many forms and is used during negotiations to undermine or neutralize a counterpart's position. Phone lines are tapped, faxes, emails or text messages intercepted, conversations eavesdropped on, and files rifled. Laptop computers left in rooms during social events are downloaded or even stolen. Email is intercepted and cellphone conversations transcribed. Baggage handlers, cab drivers, chauffeurs, room attendants, bartenders, airline employees, PBX operators, desk clerks, and local translators can be put on the payroll to deliver even the slightest scrap of information.

Some governments fully condone such operations and assist in the gathering of illicit commercial information. When laptops or software are held overnight at customs, it's a sure sign of government complicity. Totalitarian governments are far less subtle and do nothing to hide their internal control of information. They copy every fax (many nations only have telecom service via government-controlled centers), monitor every long-distance call, and send all email through a central, government-controlled gateway. Any pertinent information recovered is funneled to domestic firms, many of which are government fronts. All of this is conducted under the guise of controlling "political" information or of anti-pornography campaigns.

Discovering that you are a victim of this style doesn't always solve the problem. Unless proof is absolute, counterparts can't be confronted, and skilled practitioners make sure the trail does not lead directly to them. When governments are involved, it's even more sensitive. Some governmental agencies are so bold as to question visiting negotiators about information that was intercepted.

WARNING: Remember, if knowledge is power, then sharing knowledge is sharing power. Negotiators don't share anything until terms have been discussed.

Being a thief hardly guarantees success in negotiations. Though many see theft as part of the "all's fair in love and war" adage, others view it as an equalizer between hapless, David-like enterprises and global Goliaths. Industrial espionage can be surprisingly easy if the prey is unwary, but few successful companies are so oblivious. Many companies respond by leaving information "doors" intentionally unlocked and planting erroneous data, hoping to mislead thieves.

Even without such security measures, detection of theft prior to or during negotiations can turn an otherwise fair-minded counterpart into a ruthless opponent. They may never openly state their concerns but their reaction will be quite visible—they'll take on a so-that's-how-you-want-to-play-the-game attitude and concessions will become few and far between. Negotiations may simply be called off on the spot, with no reason given.

Theft is an extremely slippery slope and its continued employment most often results in detection and punishment in one form or another. It would be naive not to recognize that some companies (and commercial cultures) have successfully employed it over an extended period but mostly while operating under a governmental aegis. For most negotiators, it's a tool with risks that outweigh its benefits.

INDULGENT

Indulging the opposition may seem an odd way to approach negotiations, but both sellers and buyers can use it to good effect. It involves an extremely long-term view. Certain trade and investment negotiations are only the first of numerous rounds of discussion, and buyers and investors are, by nature, likely to approach the talks in terms of "small bites" and incremental involvement. Small successes will build toward larger deals and greater involvement. It's this future that the practitioner of the indulgent style plans around.

Initial deals are negotiated and setup by sellers so that buyers/investors are successful, perhaps beyond their original hopes. Secondary, even tertiary, negotiations have the same result, with the counterpart being brought farther into the net each time. Once they're sufficiently committed, the seller can change style and start making demands. Some sellers even use indulgence as an opportunity to undercut competitors and drive them from the marketplace. Suddenly the buyer finds that his previously indulgent counterparts now control the market and its pricing.

Buyers and investors can also turn indulgence to their advantage by creating "sweetheart" deals that the opposition can't walk away from. Buyers purchase at high prices and investors offer to pump in money with few strings attached. At the next round of discussions, the result is similar. Over time, the practitioner starts demanding price cuts, reduced shipping costs, greater managerial input, or a restructuring of share ownership. Having failed to put safeguards in place during the early "indulgent" sessions (or having overlooked clauses placed by their counterparts), the seller now finds himself outmaneuvered by a patient and clever opponent. Unwilling to lose market share or jeopardize new injections of badly needed equity, they succumb to the new, very nonindulgent demands.

CHAPTER 11

Negotiating Styles, Part 2

MAJOR TEAM STYLES

TEAMS MUST MAKE a conscious effort to maintain a unified front. This can be accomplished through a variety of styles, with specific choices being based on member talent, cultural background, and personality type. A single style can be maintained throughout a single negotiation or turned on and off when required. Though the preservation of unity is the main concern when making a stylistic choice, that unity will flow from member compatibility. When preparing strategy for negotiations, choose the talent first and let those choices dictate the team's eventual style. Also keep in mind that while unity is paramount, the *appearance* of disunity can be used to accomplish the team's goal as well. Much of the effectiveness of any style will be the impression created upon the opposition.

CONSENSUS

Consensus allows the team to disperse authority and responsibility. The group sets policy and makes decisions. The group is consulted on issues both large and small. While a spokesperson may deliver the results of group decisions, no clear leadership role is taken, and the spokesperson may change, depending on the subject matter being discussed. The Chief Negotiator acts solely as a moderator for internal group discussions and may remain hidden at general discussions.

Such group scrutiny is a very time-consuming style, but it has the virtue of being difficult to penetrate. Every decision made by the team requires a form of voting and may result in an inordinate number of session breaks as the team polls itself. Counterparts will find it difficult to pry apart positions that appear seamless. Counterparts may also be worn down by the slowness of the decision-making process and grant concessions simply to keep things moving.

The strengths of consensus-style negotiating are also its weaknesses. No matter how well armored an object is, slow movement invites outmaneuvering, and the same is true for lumbering negotiating teams. Nimble opponents can overload the decision-making process and make consensus building untenable. This is especially true when the agenda hasn't been rigidly set in advance. New issues can be brought to the table until the team requiring consensus gives in to inherent time constraints.

Sometimes the opposition doesn't bother to break the consensus by maneuver but simply calls off negotiations, due to what they see as time wasting by their counterparts. To avoid the problems of the consensus style and maximize its strengths, here are a few tips.

- Only adopt this style when the team is in a buying/investing mode or in a strong selling position where the product, service, or investment opportunity is too attractive or in demand to warrant dismissal.

- Consensus tends to work best when team members are culturally homogeneous and comfortable with subjugation to the group. It can be used with less homogeneous teams but will require extensive briefing and practice.
- Reticence at the negotiating table is required. Discussion must be saved for internal sessions. Counterparts present their positions with the Consensus team requesting only clarifications and reserving rebuttals until later. Any "at table" talk must be couched in terms of "we" not "I."
- Socializing with counterparts needs to be kept to a minimum, as this presents their greatest opportunity for a divide-and-conquer maneuver.
- The Chief Negotiator or team leader must remain as invisible as possible, often allowing other team members to act as spokesperson. Just as the team wishes to disperse authority and responsibility, so too should the counterpart's attention be diffused. Some teams even use false or misleading business titles to distract the opposition from the team's true leadership.
- Internal dissention must be dealt with immediately. Unresolved issues among team members will be very evident to skilled counterparts. Team members who hold grudges or can't separate emotions from business will make poor consensus builders.

COWBOYS

The term "cowboys" generally denotes a highly individualistic approach to business. Its use hardly seems compatible with a team effort. However, cowboys were traditionally self-sufficient people who could work on their own for extended periods while contributing to the group goal: herding cattle for transport. In the case of international negotiations, the goal is to "round up" the opposition and keep them moving in the direction dictated by the "trail boss" (a.k.a. the Chief Negotiator). This may seem a somewhat mawkish analogy, but it's quite apt for certain types of negotiations.

Often negotiations requiring extensive investments do not take place with all members of both teams seated around a single large table. Specialist sessions are scheduled, such as marketing, distribution, technical, or manufacturing. Some team members may be taken to different locations altogether to view branch offices or operation facilities. Decisions and statements made during these extracurricular sessions may dictate the success or failure of the entire negotiating mission. It's no place for the faint of heart. Team members who may flourish in Consensus would find this type of isolation disconcerting. Cowboys revel in it.

Cowboys understand the limits of their authority and the extent of their responsibility. Cowboy teams are composed of individuals who aren't merely specialists but staff who also exhibit generalist management talents. (For example, the head of product development may be a Cowboy, but an engineer is just an engineer.) They're familiar with the company's "big picture" but can discuss it in "little picture" terms. Cowboy teams converge for group strategy and disperse for individual tactical implementation. Team members may utilize any of the individual styles delineated in Chapter 10 when "in the field," as long as these are compatible with company goals.

This is an extremely flexible and adaptive style that is very attractive to up-and-coming negotiators. While it grants a great deal of freedom of action to its practitioners, it also has some stringent provisos and responsibilities. The following tips apply to both sides of the negotiating table.

- Cowboy teams need strong leadership. Not only must the Chief Negotiator be able to provide a clear vision of the team's goals, but he or she must also be able to inspire loyalty and operate effectively without directly supervising the team. Communication lines must be wide open and the ability to delegate on full-throttle. Micromanagers can't tolerate the Cowboy team style and laissez faire managers will similarly fail, as they don't have the requisite ability to bring cohesion to a team that's constantly converging and dispersing. If the CN can't handle the demands of this style, the talents of its individual members will amount to naught.
- Team members must have excellent communication skills and have no qualms about reporting in to the CN. At a minimum, daily contact is required to assure group goals are being met and new information circulated. Although every team member is working on a separate section, it's still a single puzzle.
- The team must be composed of staff who can "work without a net" under adverse conditions. People who need occasional hand-holding simply won't succeed here. Cowboys turn in reports, not requests for advice.
- The loyalty of individual members should never be in question. It's essential that they recognize the difference between self-interest and operating independently.
- The team must be highly organized and well briefed. Because individuals must operate alone for extended periods, they must be armed to the teeth with information. Each team member should prepare for the upcoming negotiations as if they were going solo.
- Agendas that disperse team members must be worked out prior to the start of negotiations. Day one is no time to find out that a Consensus team must suddenly operate as Cowboys.

NOTE: Contrary to what the name might imply, some of the best Cowboys are women. Many female managers are familiar with working toward group goals while being isolated from the normal company structure. Also, in some cultures, the opposition will underestimate their talent simply because of their gender—a mistake that will work in your team's favor.

PLATOON

Platoons operate in a similar fashion to Cowboy teams but with small subteams that have independent team leaders answerable to a single CN. These team leaders must fulfill all of the requirements of Cowboys but also be able to organize and supervise a team of their own. Not all Cowboys make good Platoon leaders, and all Platoon members are not Cowboys.

Platoon style is very useful when large numbers of technical specialists must be brought along for negotiations. Team leaders maintain control of the specialists and run applicable negotiating sessions or side trips. This takes pressure off of the CN and allows him or her to concentrate on wider goals. Team leaders control the work of their subordinates, focusing on the Platoon's independent goals. And while they act as spokespersons for their particular Platoon, they defer to the CN during general discussions.

NOTE: Platoon style negotiating is a good proving ground for future chief negotiators.

DIVIDE AND CONQUER

The easiest way to control negotiations is to control the counterparts' position. Of course, they'll be doing everything possible to prevent that from happening. Turning members of the opposition against each other goes a long way toward succeeding in this particular manipulation. Team negotiating can effectively utilize a divide-and-conquer style, either as the overall strategy or as a simple tactic for specific agenda points. Though it will be discussed here from a practitioner viewpoint, all negotiators must be on the look-out for signs that it's being used against them.

This style works by one of two methods and requires significant skills of observation. Method one calls for the isolation of one or more members of the other team for the purpose of soliciting information—either actual data related to the negotiations or intelligence regarding dissention in a counterpart's ranks. Some practitioners even take this to the extreme of offering remuneration for such information. Intelligence acquired by more subtle means (that is, subterfuge) is often more useful, though it does require a more substantial investment of time.

Once acquired, the information may be used to slyly undermine a proposal or it may be boldly stated at a session and attributed directly to the wayward counterpart ("Your Mr. Chan said last night at dinner that your shipments have a four week lead time not three as you state here. Which is it?") This latter method does two things: it lets the opposition know that you're wise to their game but it also pinpoints the leak. Targeting a *key member* of the opposing team greatly increases the impact of this style, as junior staff members committing such an offense will simply be sent packing. Neutralizing a second-in-command will create general havoc in the opposition. This is a very serious move and should be taken cautiously.

Of course, not attributing the inside information directly ("It has come to our attention that . . .") also has benefits. It creates severe mistrust among the opposition and forces their Chief Negotiator to act alone, since no one on the team can now be trusted. A team effort has just very effectively been turned into a solo act.

These divisive contacts are generally made under the guise of socialization. Much can be learned during a golf game, cocktail reception, or late dinner. Cowboy team members are particularly susceptible, since they may not discover they've been compromised until they return for team sessions. It's also during these dispersed sessions that Cowboys can be approached with the proposal of switching sides altogether (unscrupulous perhaps, but not uncommon).

Keep in mind that experienced teams of all styles will be expecting some form of divisive move by counterparts. It's a technique older than Caesar. In some cases, practitioners are often set up for a fall with information that's more harmful than useful.

LESSON: If you head down a road you weren't supposed to be on, you're hardly justified in complaining about the directions. Know the opposition and "watch your back."

The other method of this divisive style is the constant exploitation of weakpoints and contradictions in a counterpart's statements. Some teams assign a member of their delegation the duty of taking notes and transcribing them for use in postsession recaps. Laptop computers are regularly put to use for this purpose, as word-for-word transcriptions allow for easy searches and comparisons. By using a counterpart's own words to undermine their position ("But at this morning's contract session your Ms. Hernandez stated that, and I quote . . ."), the burden remains squarely on their shoulders. No subterfuge is involved, only attention to detail. Convincing the other side that they are disorganized will greatly reduce their resistance to granting concessions.

WARNING: Only the most experienced, cohesive teams can avoid some form of contradiction or mistake in their proposals. Once the Divide and Conquer style is detected, expect to become the target of revenge.

JEKYLL AND HYDE

This style is also known as "good cop, bad cop." Part of the team takes a very hard-line approach to the negotiations, while another contingent proposes to act on behalf of the opposition. Stern stylists work hand in hand with indulgers to first browbeat the counterparts and then promise to make everything all right. This may seem quite a transparent ploy to the reader when put in these terms, but it can be, and is, a compelling style in the right situations.

Inexperienced teams are very susceptible to victimization by this style and even more so when they're not operating on their own turf. Being confronted with an argumentative counterpart who is a skilled practitioner of Stern or Intimidation tactics can be very disconcerting. Just when the victim believes that negotiations will end in failure, the Indulgers intercede with offers of a whole new (and decidedly more pleasant) proposal. The discrepancy between the attitudes and positions of the opposition is written off by the victim as the idiosyncratic behavior of a culture they don't fully understand. Most of the time they even thank the indulgers for their assistance in salvaging the negotiations. Ignorance is indeed bliss, and the painful truth usually doesn't become apparent for some time. It's an expensive education and one that most negotiators come by the hard way.

The other situation in which this style is effective is when third parties are included in negotiations. Often this will take the form of a governmental agency that has been invited by the host company as an "observer." As talks progress and the visitor's position becomes apparent, this supposedly neutral observer begins to place roadblocks in the way of the deal. Laws and regulations are cited and governmental review prior to contract signing is suggested. The visitor (soon to be victim) confronts the host and demands to know why such problems were not known ahead of time.

The host now offers to use his "connections" and back-channel lines of communication to help remedy the situation. After days of delay, the government has—miraculously—relented on some, but not all, of the alleged problems. The remaining problems, all of which work to the detriment of the visitor, are no longer subject to negotiation. They're now beyond the control of the host, who shrugs in feigned resignation. None of this takes place until *after* the visitors have revealed the full extent of their proposal, but the process was planned long before their arrival.

This type of bargaining usually takes place in countries where it's next to impossible to find the laws actually written down. Even when you do find it codified and contradictory to the recent ruling, the government observer will simply say it has since been updated. In other words, the laws work only for the host country's companies, not yours. Complaining is pointless. Either sign the somewhat less attractive contract or go home.

HIERARCHICAL

Many teams choose to pass all decisions through the chain-of-command for approval. This can occur when a strong CN has a weak team and prefers to agree to all decisions, large and small, as a means of maintaining control of the company position. It's also quite common when everyone on the team is inexperienced and the CN's choice of style reflects the normal company hierarchy.

While this is safe, it's not necessarily cost effective. Having all decisions stem from a single source can make for consistency, but it defeats the purpose of fielding a team for negotiations. Whether host or visitor, it's still expensive to bring a team to the table and it's best to make use of them. The one advantage that hierarchical teams have is that they can act as a training ground for novices. However, it should be noted that hierarchies tend to preserve themselves and continue in their style even when team members have been sufficiently "bloodied" by experience.

The hope that subordinates will act as filters during negotiations quickly evaporates as observant counterparts detect that decision making is centralized. They no longer wish to talk to anyone but the decision maker and will not bother with sessions in which the central authority isn't present. Unlike Consensus (which efficiently disperses authority), hierarchies focus the power, and consequently all the responsibility, on one person. Ego-soothing perhaps, but just as in the case of the Divide and Conquer scenario, a solo act ends up facing a team effort. Unless the Chief Negotiator is very good and the opposition very weak, defeat in some form is inevitable.

WARNING: Hierarchies share the Consensus style's sluggish vulnerability. If such a team must be put into the field, it should be kept compact. Under no circumstances should a hierarchical team be dispersed.

HORIZONTAL

Horizontal teams disperse authority and responsibility much in the same way as Consensus teams, but without the benefit of the CN's oversight. Each small team, set up along the lines of the Platoon style, negotiates its own single feature or features of the contract as a separate entity. This style is used primarily by very large international corporations that plan to farm out parts of a contract to various subsidiaries.

Its effectiveness lies in the ability of each small unit to cut the best deal possible for its own purposes without having to consider the fallout for other parts of the company. Coming face-to-face with this style can be perplexing; in some ways, it's meant to be. Counterparts suddenly find themselves negotiating with several individual companies when they had only planned on dealing with one entity.

Large companies often save this approach for the second or third round of talks, when the details of a general deal are being hammered out. When planned and executed properly, its outcome is very much a success for the practitioners, but it relies on understanding (if not accommodating) their cohorts' positions. This style forces the opposition to disperse negotiating authority without preplanning. ("Sorry, you'll need to discuss that with our accounting division, we only handle transnational shipping.") Large companies can more readily succeed with this "dispersal" when dealing with smaller firms, because it gives the impression that this is how things operate in the "big leagues." The smaller company, even when in a buying position, is too embarrassed by its size to demand that all details be negotiated at the same table.

LESSON: Pride cometh before a fall.

Unfortunately, some companies (both large and small) choose this style unconsciously—through disorganization and poor leadership. Domestic and international companies alike have been plagued for decades by sales departments that make promises and sign deals that their operations department is unable to fulfill. Cutting a deal that can't reach fruition isn't successful negotiating, it's short-term thinking in a long-term marketplace.

The horizontal style demands strong leadership for the individual subsidiary discussions and a firm grasp of the interplay among those affiliates. Creating intramural problems or causing dissention at headquarters will have an adverse effect on overall effectiveness.

REMEMBER: The key to this style is to make counterparts believe they're dealing with separate entities. The reality of the situation is just the opposite.

DEPARTMENTAL

This style is a more self-conscious version of the Hierarchical method but with the dispersal result of Horizontal negotiating. The Departmental is a very common form of corporate negotiating in Asia, and growth in that region is testament to its effectiveness.

Visitors or hosts are faced with an opposing team that has maintained its basic company structure, subdivisions, and central authority. However, rather than negotiating as a single unit, counterparts send only those staff members to each day's sessions whose job description directly relates to the items on the agenda. These specialty-based "departments" can only negotiate within narrow ranges, but they force their counterparts to reveal the entirety of their proposal for later dissection by another department. Team leaders (and perhaps individual and departmental styles) change on a daily basis, and the CN has the option of overseeing the negotiations from a remote location. The opposition must negotiate with several parts of the same company without ever getting to confront the real decision maker. Also, they're forced to adapt to new personnel repeatedly, which prevents them from establishing a pattern to their counterparts' strategy. Not only does this style wear down the opposition, but it also continually drives them off course.

The Departmental style presupposes a tight control of agenda items and clear lines of communications among the various departments and the CN. Some departmental stylists, usually visiting sellers, simply direct their members to make separate, very straightforward presentations and allow the facts to speak for themselves. This idea of "laying all of your cards on the table" (at least the ones you want the other side to see) can be a very effective way of getting key issues decided early. It requires a team composed mostly of Pragmatists.

WARNING: Counterparts being subjected to a Departmental style should recognize that early negotiating sessions can become primarily fact-finding missions for latter discussions. Lower-level departmental negotiators are given a "shopping list" of details needed for the planning of more important aspects of the deal.

The Importance of Stylistic Diversity

Negotiating situations and counterpart styles vary greatly, even within the same country. Teams and individual negotiators must be able to draw upon as many styles as possible if continued success is to be had in an ever expanding international marketplace. Being adept at only one style will limit the team or solo act to a very small number of situations, and attempting to use the same style under all conditions will result in a very small success ratio.

Another reason to become proficient with as many styles or combinations of styles as possible is that it allows negotiators to recognize the more subtle hallmarks displayed by counterparts. Adeptness may come through usage or observation. A negotiator or team may object to a particular style for moral reasons, but they must become familiar with its particulars nonetheless. Having a firm understanding of a counterpart's style and where it leads will allow for effective preplanning as well as adjustment once discussions begin.

NOTE: Negotiations are like chess. Visualizing all possible moves in advance leads to success.

Planning Contingencies

Nothing ever goes completely according to the original design and waiting for problems to arise before considering solutions makes for poor decision making. Well-thought-out contingency planning is the surest sign that a negotiator or team has matured. Such planning must be viewed as a form of intellectual insurance—not mandatory but wise. The following nine areas should be considered as potential troublespots during negotiations.

- FINANCIAL Very often, discussions uncover financial problems that weren't evident during the planning phase. Information may have been purposely withheld or not. Such revelations, if severe enough, can bring negotiations to a halt, but more often they call for some fancy footwork on behalf of all participants. Never enter a negotiation with all of your financial options "tapped out." They should be open, wide open. If either side is on a do-or-die contract signing mission, there'll be more dying than doing. Finances, and the participants' attitudes toward them, must be elastic.

- LEGAL As previously noted, many nations and localities have a legal structure that is flexible, or inflexible, in direct proportion to the size and scope of the deal being considered. The legal ground in developing economies can shift suddenly, dramatically, and without advance notice. More intractable styles may need quick adjustment to make the deal seem significantly more attractive to counterparts and government officials. Visitors should never make the mistake of throwing their mostly inconsiderable legal weight around.

NOTE: Never convince yourself that you have a complete grasp of a foreign legal system until you're in-country.

- POLITICAL Political moves from right to left, globalist to isolationist, or secular to fundamentalist can happen in the midst of negotiations. Some discussions may be put on hold until the political dust settles, as occurred during Russia's 1997 elections. At other times, long-standing contracts must be renegotiated, as happened to Enron in India in 1996 when nationalist politicians won control over an area undergoing a multimillion-dollar infrastructure project. Politics are very fickle and always "local." If the project is of any size, plan on some sort of political interference, which may range in size from the U.S. Department of the Treasury, to the People's Committee of Da Nang, to the mayor of Lima.
- MORAL In recent years, vast numbers of projects have been derailed, severely altered, or had their contracts retracted due to the moral influence of outside groups. Boycotts are threatened by "concerned citizens" claiming moral authority over the project itself or its participants. Negotiations in Myanmar, South Africa, and China all feel the sting of these interlopers, who tend to argue from a very limited perspective. Companies with a great deal of brand equity (i.e., Coke, Heineken, Shell Oil) must be especially attentive.

  Even when no external forces are at play, participants may uncover information about the project or counterparts that is of questionable moral value. This is always a possibility where the cultural backgrounds of the participants are vastly different. Negotiators must use their own moral compass here and determine in advance what can and can't be tolerated. Similarly, teams must have a moral point-of-no-return worked out in advance. Prenegotiation cultural research will assist in setting these limits.

WARNING: Don't wait until a bribe is offered (or demanded) to determine whether or not the proposition will be accepted. All business cultures have their own set of morals: know yours, know theirs.

- STRATEGIC Conditions of all types surrounding negotiations can change at a moment's notice. Backup strategies must be ready for deployment on a timely basis. Original strategies may have failed, been outmaneuvered, or overtaken by outside events. Never, under any circumstances, should the phrase "what do we (I) do now?" be uttered by professional negotiators. Nimbleness is not an option here; a minimum of two backup plans should be waiting in the wings. Don't confuse these contingency plans with "last-ditch" efforts. Secondary strategies must be considered with an eye toward success, not toward limiting failure.

- TACTICAL A failed tactic does not call for a complete revamping of the overall strategy. When attempting to win a specific point on the agenda, it's best to have many approaches planned, all based on the conceivable reactions of counterparts. Furthermore, each point of the agenda may have different tactical requirements. Some contract details may be bullied through, while others will be won by guile, and a third set achieved with finesse. Skilled negotiators must be able to glide from one tactic to the next without detracting from the main strategy. It's not easy, but contingency planning makes it *look* easy. In fact, if done properly, it can't be detected at all.

NOTE: The more tricks (and sometimes they're just that) negotiators have up their sleeves the better. Commercial *leger de main* requires much planning and practice.

- HEALTH When key members of a team are suddenly taken ill, it's no time to start the search for replacements. This contingency should be planned in detail, especially for the visiting team, which will have far fewer sources from which to draw in an emergency. No single team member, even the Chief Negotiator, can be permitted the luxury of being inexpendable. Everyone must have some form of "understudy" and the hoarding of information must be *verboten*. Besides creating a form of insurance against health problems, it's a great way to train novice negotiators for future roles in the spotlight.

NOTE: Solo negotiators must go to extreme measures to maintain their health. No one has ever regretted being "too careful" with their health during overseas travel.

- CLIMATIC Climate can have very telling effects on negotiations. It can disrupt flight schedules, evacuate cities, cause power outages, snap communications, and ruin health. Weather conditions can even have a deleterious effects on the operation of high-tech equipment needed for presentations or financial planning. And such difficulties can increase as negotiations move farther from urban areas to regions where backup systems are in shorter supply. The weather may not be controllable but it *is* predictable and to a much greater degree every year. Even the most seasoned team (pun intended) must plan for adverse weather conditions—and not just from a clothing or medication standpoint. Presentations must be able to be delivered effectively with or without technical gadgets, and backup communications should be readily available.

NOTE: Visiting teams must recognize that arriving in-country unprepared for the climate will mark their efforts as being underresearched.

- PERSONAL Negotiators lead lives apart from business and often those personal lives intervene with pressing needs. Problems that demand a negotiator's immediate attention will arise at some of the most inconvenient moments during discussions. As in the case with health contingencies, the understudy system must be used by teams when members are called away. Solo negotiators planning overseas travel must make sure that all of their personal matters are in order before embarking on important missions.

WARNING: Spouses, parents, children, and significant others must be thoroughly conditioned to recognize a true emergency.

LEARNING TO AVOID OVERKILL

It's always best to have detailed planning, copious information, skilled professionals, and conducive conditions when readying for negotiations. Fortune favors the prepared mind. However, preparation doesn't demand usage and negotiators are to be warned about overkill. On many occasions, counterparts can turn out to be far more pliable than originally thought. What it takes to overwhelm their defenses and counter their maneuvers may be but a small portion of the strategic and tactical array that was meticulously prepared. Don't succumb to the urge to "go over the top" with the remaining, unnecessary portions of your plan.

Beating an opponent at soccer by a score of two to one assures them some dignity, without detracting from the victor's revelry. Running up the score to ten to one by taking advantage of a mismatch leaves the defeated with less than nothing. Moving the analogy to negotiations, the concept of leaving the opposition "enough" makes for a grudgeless long-term relationship and, in the case of simple trades, opportunities for future business. Trouncing counterparts, even when their behavior has been less than cordial, will not bode well in the long run. Highly organized and prepared negotiators must know when to turn off their bargaining juggernaut and move on to the next set of negotiations.

LESSON: Don't let your own style win out over the substance of your position. Overkill wastes time, energy, and opportunity.

Detecting Changes in Your Counterpart's Modus Operandi

Counterparts are under no obligation to be consistent with their style throughout an entire set of discussions. Their changes may be proactive in an attempt to confound the opposition, or the change may be reactions to strategic and tactical failures. Here are some indicators that a counterpart is preparing to make a stylistic change in their negotiation approach.

- Requests for additional breaks or longer breaks
- Requests for postponements
- The addition of new high-level participants, especially if they're visitors who have been flown in "to beef up" the opposition
- The outright replacement of high-level participants for "personal" reasons
- The reduction of support staff (counterparts may be preparing to cancel the talks)
- Increased requests for technical data presumed to be "common knowledge"
- Requests for a location change
- Increases in the number of or length of social contacts
- Requests for side meetings or specialist sessions
- Prolonged use of a third language unfamiliar to translators
- Increased requests for clarifications of standard topics
- Increased interruptions that require "immediate attention"

Distinguishing "Yes" from "I Understand"

The goal of the negotiating process is to achieve agreement among parties with opposing viewpoints. Reaching an understanding isn't the same as reaching an agreement. Sometimes the problem is linguistic, but most often it's stylistic. The smiling affability of the Social stylist doesn't always indicate agreement, any more than the grimaced detachment of the Impassive practitioner denotes discord.

Negotiators around the world are often shocked to find themselves in discussions that proceed rapidly, and cordially, to nowhere. Others have waged hard-pitched and uphill battles that smelled of defeat only to find on the last day that they've won every concession they needed. Many professionals alleviate the suspense of waiting for the final contract signing (or not) by introducing an incremental or provisional signed agreement after each major point of the agenda is resolved. While this commits neither side to the ultimate bond of a bargain, it does give a good indication of the true direction of the negotiations.

No matter how experienced, negotiators can suffer from the basic human frailty of misinterpretation of the facts. The word or words to the effect of "yes" in many languages can mean "I understand," "I agree," "I have no idea what you are talking about but am too embarrassed to ask for an explanation," "I hear you but have no intention of doing what you have requested," or "I'm paying absolutely no attention to what you're saying. Do go on."

LESSON: Understanding is a mental process. Agreement is a contract signing process. Get it in writing.

CHAPTER 12

Planning to Win

Success is a Choice, Not a Result

WINNING IN INTERNATIONAL business must not be left up to chance. Chance is for gamblers and the vast majority of gamblers are losers, much to the delight of casino owners everywhere. Winners control risk and make it work in their favor, much like those same happy casino owners do. The choice of a proper strategy (by a negotiator or team) controls risk to the point where success is readily foreseeable. Failure is the result of poor strategy, not the level of risk.

This chapter explores the process of choosing a strategy, but it doesn't recommend one strategy over another. Negotiators must make that choice for themselves.

Understanding the Zero-Sum Game

In the introduction to this text the concept of the zero-sum game was proffered as the essence of international negotiations. It's a very old concept that has, on occasion, been pushed aside by such theories as "win-win" and "co-opetition." These latter theories are decidedly less confrontational, but therein lies their weakness. International business is a very high stakes, super-competitive and often brutal form of commerce. While time may soften its edges, that softening will not occur for several generations.

RULE: My gains come at the expense of your losses, and vice versa.

Every negotiator and team must enter discussions with a clear idea of how much they'll need (not want) to take away from the negotiations and a detailed strategy for attaining that objective. Considerations about the opposition are based entirely upon how much they can afford to give up and still remain interested in the deal. No one side will get everything it wants, but both sides must get exactly what they need or what they've been convinced they need. The role of a successful negotiator is to allow counterparts to protect their needs by bargaining away their wants.

The "pie" being negotiated can be cut into an infinite number of slices, but the pie never changes size. Some slices are more important than others (needs versus wants), but the fact remains that the more one side gets, the less the other side can have. Acquisition of 30 percent of the pie by team A means the loss of 70 percent. Team B meanwhile has attained a 70 percent gain and sustained a 30 percent loss. Both sides' gains are offset by the total of both sides' losses. The zero-sum game seems simplistic, but it's often misconstrued as creating winners and losers. It may, but it's not inherent in the system. It might just as easily result in two winners or two losers, based entirely on the goals each side initially brings to the table.

Moreover, the concept of winning and losing in international negotiations is strictly self-imposed. In the example stated above, team B may indeed consider itself a loser if its goal was 75 percent and team A may return home pleased at having exceeded its 25 percent goal. At other times, team B counts itself successful at having attained its goal of 75 percent, not realizing that team A came into negotiations looking for a mere 15 percent of the pie. Who is to say who won or lost? Answer: It's an internal matter. Traditionally, the terms "win" and "lose" mean that there's general agreement on what constitutes the prize. Such accord is rare in international commerce.

Win Enough and Lose Enough

Strategies for successful negotiations will focus on acquiring a mandatory group of needs and as many wants as prudence and the opposition allow. The ability to concede points of the agenda that are of little import, while giving every appearance of concern about their loss, is part of every successful negotiator's bag of tricks.

Every solo negotiator or team must enter the bargaining process with a clear idea of the optimal, moderate, and minimal positions they'll accept on any particular issue, as well as on the whole. This process entails planning for a counterpart's position; internal and external research are key. Determining when "enough is enough" on a playing field that may be out of your control will lead to long-term success for all parties concerned, and participants must be concerned with how the opposition is viewing the discussions. You can win too much.

The following list of questions and planning exercises will help you determine what is "enough." It will also help determine when the process has reached a point that's unacceptable, when benefits are too heavily outweighed by burdens.

LESSON: Knowing when to cease negotiations is just as important as knowing when to continue.

A suitable strategy will emerge *only* after the questions are given thorough reflection. Once the answers have been given, rethink the guidelines from the opposition's point of view. Understanding the other side greatly reduces risk and establishes which parts of the agenda are really up for negotiation.

GUIDELINES FOR STRATEGY SELECTION

1. What is the purpose of opening negotiations with this particular group?
2. What is our (my) main goal in the target market? Trade or investment?
3. What level of agenda control can I (we) expect?
4. What level of agenda control will I (we) accept?
5. Is this a buying or selling position?
6. Is this a host or visitor position?
7. What level of experience does our team (do I) have in negotiations of this type?
8. What level of experience does the opposition have in negotiations of this type?
9. What are all of the issues to be negotiated?
10. What issues are considered *needs* for our (my) position?

11. List the range of settlement for each need from optimal to minimal.
12. What issues are considered *wants* for our position?
13. List the range of settlement for each want from optimal to minimal.
14. Re-evaluate the needs and wants lists.
15. What perceptions do we (I) hold regarding counterparts?
16. Summarize the cultural research.
17. Insert personal information (age, gender, marital status, etc.).
18. Summarize the business research.
19. Consider information received about their negotiating history.
20. Is the opposition perceived to be cooperative or belligerent?
21. What outside factors will affect the discussions?
22. Describe the physical setting for discussions.
23. If a team is to be used, will it be dispersed? If so, where?
24. What communication problems can be foreseen?
25. What language will discussions be held in?
26. Will translators be necessary?
27. What language will the legal contract be in?
28. Is there good legal structure in the market where the contract will be executed?
29. What is our (my) perception of fairness?
30. What is the opposition's perception of fairness?
31. Summarize the ethical views of your company.
32. Summarize the perceived ethical views of the opposition.
33. What level of trust do we (I) have in the counterparts?
34. What is the economic disparity between the participant cultures?
35. What is the economic disparity between the participant companies?
36. What issues do we (I) consider non-negotiable?
37. What issues will the opposition likely consider non-negotiable?
38. What topics do I (we) wish to avoid?
39. What topics will the opposition wish to avoid?
40. What is the current political situation between the respective governments?
41. What is the level of authority represented by our negotiators?
42. What is the level of authority represented by the opposition's negotiators?
43. Summarize the talents and personality profiles of your company's negotiators.
44. What personal styles are available to the Chief Negotiator (or team)?
45. If a team is used, list styles likely to fit with the membership's profile.
46. What is the size and composition of the opposing team?

47. Will team members be assigned to specific points of the agenda? If so, justify each.
48. Will these negotiations lead to future talks or long-term relationships?
49. List a minimum of three strategies for accomplishing the company's goals.
50. List possible opposition strategies and their effect on your company's position.
51. At what point will we (I) consider the negotiations untenable?
52. Can I (we) afford to say "no"?
53. What are the alternatives to a completed negotiation?

Avoiding Imperialism

As noted above, all participants will have needs they'll not wish to relinquish. These needs may not be of a purely economic nature. Sometimes these are dictated by the respective legal structure, as in the case of "local content" laws or mandatory local veto power. The needs may be religious or ethical in root, such as Islamic rules regarding the paying of interest. Or they may be a matter of preserving personal "face" or national dignity, as is often the case with natural resource development projects.

In this last case, large companies or those from the developed economies must be careful to adapt a negotiating strategy that doesn't smack of imperialism. Needs and wants may be obtained while keeping the tone of the discussions as if between relative equals. Part of the understanding of "enough" is the ability to avoid driving counterparts past the level of acceptability before all points have been discussed. Don't let poor strategy selection or the surfacing of imperious attitudes derail talks before all points have been made.

Pursuing Company Objectives

Company objectives must always be paramount in the negotiator's mind, and doubly so when consultants are added to the mix. Once objectives have been set and strategies chosen, they should be written down and made available to all of the pertinent players. This document will serve as the mission statement for the upcoming discussions and should be referred to often.

Side issues will bombard the negotiators, sometimes as part of the opposing strategy, and it will be difficult to achieve focus. Because the documentation of objectives will present security problems, it may be best held by the Chief Negotiator for referral at daily pre- and postplanning sessions. Teams, and even solo negotiators, that don't take this extra step to codify the company's objectives will run the risk of completing (what were believed to be) successful negotiations only to find that they've exchanged wants for needs or missed some points altogether.

LESSON: Objectives are just like the contract terms. Get them in writing.

Non-negotiables: Keeping Quid, Giving Quo

Wizened negotiators often remark that they've lost count of the number of non-negotiable points they've managed to bargain away from counterparts. Putting an agenda point under the rubric of non-negotiable will mark the practitioner as a novice or at least a weak bargainer. Old hands will recognize this as an attempt by counterparts to avoid discussing an issue that they can ill defend.

The reader is warned against confusing a need with a non-negotiable. The best analogy is a physical one: we all need food, but *how much* food we need is subject to discussion. To state that an agenda point must be conceded, without the slightest discussion or alteration invites defeat from many quarters. The opposition may find the point negligible but assume a quid pro quo stance in reaction. They'll grant the concession with the assurance that you'll be just as accommodating when they present their non-negotiables. You get a *quid* that may have been conceded anyway in exchange for a *quo* of undetermined importance. The grandstanding associated with presenting a non-negotiable may also cause counterparts to become obstinate on every other point up for discussion, in the belief that it's their only hope of getting "enough." In other cases, especially when counterparts are buying or investing, they simply get up and walk away, straight into the arms of competitors.

WARNING: It can be a short step from non-negotiable to no negotiations.

The best viewpoint to adopt when formulating strategy is that nothing is non-negotiable but that there are limits on concessions. Even the most extreme need has some wriggle-room and that's what you want to emphasize. Contract points are only conceded by the opposition when they feel they've had some hand in altering your original proposal. Fight tooth and nail, if you will, against every alteration, but let counterparts feel they've taken "enough." (Negotiations *are* about give and take.) It's much easier to give a little and demand the remainder than it is to insist on the whole. For this reason, extremely important needs are often overstated to enhance bargaining power.

NOTE: Counterparts should never be able to determine what your true needs and wants are during discussions. Sudden moves toward hard bargaining strategies when needs are on the table make for easy detection. Once a strategy is planned, apply it to all points, big and small.

Checking Your Ego at the Door

The discussions and atmosphere surrounding international business can be very ego-bruising and very ego-inflating. Neither extreme should present a problem for the professional negotiator. Their equity is not tied up in personal objectives or feelings but rather in their strategy. Fawning indulgence may be called for in one situation while weeks later, the grim austerity that's part of impassivity is the requisite persona. Failure of strategy A only calls for the deployment of strategy B and success is just a job done properly. Nothing personal, just good planning.

This attitude must be reflected not only in the execution of strategy but in the selection of its style and scope. Winner-takes-all strategies by practitioners of intimidation are just as doomed as the resigned failure of a take-what's-left strategy executed by a Passive stylist. There's too much or too little ego in the first case and nowhere near sufficient distribution of "enough" in the second.

LESSON: Objectivity is the essential element when strategizing and planning countermeasures. Focus on the goal, not the reward for achieving it.

Formulating a Clear and Workable Strategy

It would be impossible within the scope of this book to lay out a detailed strategy for every type of commercial negotiation. Instead, a schematic of the process is offered so that readers can apply it to their specific situations. In the following example, negotiations are planned over a five-day period with the subject company aspiring to achieve satisfactory concessions on ten points. Planning is taking place thirty days prior to the start of talks and involves two teams of three each, including the Chief Negotiator.

VISITING TEAM PROFILE:

ATTRIBUTE	CHIEF NEGOTIATOR	MEMBER A	MEMBER B
Company title	Vice president of sales and marketing	Vice president of operations	Engineering staffer
Age	45	37	26
Gender	Male	Female	Male
Languages	English, French	English, Japanese	English, Spanish
Travel experience	Medium	High	Minimal
Negotiation experience	High	High	None
Years with company	15	10	3
Technical knowledge	Minimal	Adequate	High
Team position	Visitor-Seller		
Potential personal styles	Social Impassive Indulgent Deceptive	Social Deceptive Legalistic	Technical Compliant

VISITOR'S OBJECTIVES:

GOAL	WANT OR NEED	OPTIMAL	MODERATE	MINIMAL
Introduction of full product line	N	100%	75%	50%
Internal distribution rights	N	Full	Joint Venture	Selection of agents
Control of internal advertising and marketing	N	Full within government limits	Work with internal partner	Advertising only
Exclusive purveyorship	W	10 year contract	5 year contract	3 year contract
Eventual product licensing	W	10 years	5 years	3 years
Trademark ownership in host country	N	Full ownership by seller	Joint venture with buyer	Trademark reverts to buyer in 5 years
Confirmed letter of credit (L/C) for initial shipments	N	10 shipments	5 shipments	2 shipments
Shipping and insurance paid by buyer	W	Full	Split shipping Full insurance	Full insurance
Minimum order size	W	5,000 units	4,000 units	3,000 units
Third party arbitration for disputes	N	Neutral party, neutral country arbitration	Neutral party	Nonbinding arbitration

HOST TEAM PROFILE:

ATTRIBUTE	CHIEF NEGOTIATOR	MEMBER A	MEMBER B
Company title	Director	Deputy director of purchasing	Associate director of finance
Age	65	45	40
Gender	Male	Male	Male
Languages	Japanese	Japanese, Mandarin	Japanese, English
Travel experience	Minimal	High	High
Negotiation experience	High	High	High
Years with company	40	25	15
Technical knowledge	High	High	Adequate
Team position	Host-Buyer		
Perceived potential personal styles	Impassive Deceptive Technical	Technical Deceptive Legalistic	Impassive Financial
Perceived team style	Consensus		

Which Strategy is Right?

The visiting team above will have a difficult time deciding on a strategy, as its members are less technically acute than the opposition. The hosting opposition may be relying on their ability to overwhelm the sellers with technical expertise to drive the price down. The sellers must determine how much of their position they wish to sacrifice in an effort to make the sell. Buyers must be prepared to sacrifice unit pricing to concessions on shipping, minimum orders and insurance.

For the purposes of this example, assume that the hosts are in a position to completely refuse to buy the visitor's product. Of the team strategies previously listed, choose three in descending order of usage and justify their use by the visiting team. Once you've decided on visiting strategy, repeat the exercise from the Home Team's perspective. Bear in mind that there's no universally correct answer due to cultural and corporate differences.

Case History: Infrastructure Related Negotiations

BY YVES A. SPEECKAERT, MA, MBA

The negotiation process leading to the acquisition of a large public utility in a developing country can be a long-winded and often frustrating exercise. This case history involves my participation in a telecommunications project in a member state of ASEAN. My role was lead advisor to the communication ministry during the various rounds of negotiations and consultations leading to the sale of the national telephone operator. Particular emphasis is given to clarifying the transaction process, identifying the conflicting goals of the key players, and pinpointing the critical success factors to a profitable negotiation.

1. THE STAKEHOLDERS

Unlike the board-level negotiations of merger and acquisition (M&A) transactions between two private firms, the privatization process of a highly visible public utility entails consultation with a much larger pool of stakeholders. The challenge of such a transaction to the foreign bidder is compounded by the diverging goals of the following six key stakeholders of the privatization.

The primary goal of the government is usually to maximize the proceeds from the sale and hence to boost the market value of the utility. The operator's current management team and most employees are concerned with maintaining the status quo, keeping their jobs, and ensuring a measure of continuity. The lenders want to see a return on their investments and ways to minimize the risks of disruption in cash flows. The foreign buyer may have various motivations to buy equity in an overseas operator. Usually, this is a long-term investment, banking on the large revenue and flotation value potential of a service. Lastly, the needs of the end users (customers) are usually covered in the various service obligations of the license.

2. THE PROCESS

Whether you are in the business of building a new fiber optics network, a wireless local loop for increasing access, or improving the management of the network, any negotiation related to public service is bound to be complex and have lasting effects. This, along with the large sums required for capital investment, explains why the process of change is politically charged and not taken lightly by local officials. Talks usually last between six months to more than a year.

The real negotiation actually starts with the release of the invitation to tender (similar to an RFP–Request for Proposal), which sets out the conditions and the schedule of bidding as well as a document concerning the license. From the point of view of bidding party negotiators, this period prior to the bidding is crucial in two ways. Firstly, it provides an opportunity to truly understand and clarify the agenda of the selling party, the government. Secondly, your interest and preparedness are a golden opportunity to establish yourself as a strong contender and to demonstrate the seriousness of your intent. It may also provide you a chance to establish a relationship with one or two high level administrators within the ministry or the regulatory agency. Such a bridge may be both useful as an information channel and a conduit of influence.

The bids from all of the various interested parties must be submitted on the same date and time to the ministry. The bidding document has two components. The first describes the business plan for taking the utility forward while the second offers a bidding price for acquiring the company. Upon review of the bids, and sometimes a clarification period, the government awards the license to one of the parties and executes the transfer of existing shares to the new private entity. This privatization stage is often followed by a period of restructuring via an IPO (initial public offering) or a stock flotation to realize the value of the firm and/or enlarge the circle of investors.

3. CRITICAL FACTORS

There are a number of critical success factors (CSFs) that greatly enhance your chances of ending up in the top tier of bidders in a hotly contested privatization.

- Do your homework on the country and the targeted company. Make sure that you spend the appropriate time and resources to fully understand the type of political, economic, labor, and corporate environment in which you will be operating.
- Seek the advice of a locally based advisory firm. Seeking out a local law firm, a bank, or an accountancy firm is critical to gaining local knowledge, connections, and assistance. The advisory firm will guide you through local politics and assist you with business planning.
- Familiarize yourself with the regulatory environment and government objectives. The government or tender issuing party usually has a short list of key objectives for the country and the treasury.
- Develop a strategic partnership. The strategic partner should be part of the corporate establishment of the country but not necessarily from the same utility or industry as the bid target.
- Develop a sound business plan. An independent assessment of market potential, fixed assets, depreciation, liabilities, and the revenue potential of the company should be included. The business plan should also provide the government with a clear vision of what you intend to do once awarded the license to operate.
- Submit the bid on time and with a professional presentation. Clarity and a sound financial proposal prevail over volume and complexity. Government reviewers often prefer a 100- to 150-page cogent document over a 400-page detailed encyclopedia.

4. FORMAL NEGOTIATIONS AND CULTURE

The negotiation of infrastructure projects is a blend of structured, formal transactions and highly political, relationship-based posturing. In the developing world, for instance, the fabric of the society and culture is profoundly different from that of the investor societies. Although some countries have the veneer of being democratic, the underlying power base is centered on seniority and preferential relationships. Moreover the sphere of influence of the business or political elite in the network is determined by wealth, the number of participants, their negotiating skills, and political connections. The trick in negotiating in these societies is to recognize who has that powerbase and then to be ready for quickly shifting alliances. The implication for the foreign bidder is that successfully negotiating in emerging markets in general means also raising your profile and establishing the right connections to exert below the line actions as well as building a formal case.

The following may also be considered when preparing for privatization negotiating:

- Maintain and nurture relationships at all times.
- Do your homework to identify who is the real power holder in the opposite negotiating team.
- Attempt to understand their mindset and priority list. Country and cultural briefings, active listening, local partners, and relationship building are ways to gather such intelligence.
- Often socializing will play a key role in the relationship and people everywhere like to enjoy themselves. Do not miss an opportunity to share a good time with your hosts and demonstrate your interest in making a lasting contribution to the country's infrastructure.

As a concluding note, infrastructure-related negotiation is not a small undertaking. The right to a foreign public service utility is earned, not simply bought. However, with careful preparation, the right local partnership, and a genuine respect and understanding of the local culture and priorities, you can greatly enhance your chances of a successful bid.

Mr. Speeckaert is an international businessman with experience in South America, Europe and Asia.

CHAPTER 13

Countering Personal Strategies

How to Get the Upper Hand

GOOD STRATEGY ALWAYS starts off as a proactive process, but it must also have the ability to become reactive to new information. This information may be technical, political, legal, financial, or even personal in nature. Many times, it takes the form of unforeseen tactical moves or strategic changes by counterparts. Inflexible strategies and static tactics can only be used by the strongest buyer/investors and even then are subject to defeat by nimble opponents.

Planning strategy is subject to the vagaries of guesswork, and we can all only hope to make the most educated guess possible. The only thing worse than having chosen an incorrect strategy is the refusal to admit that it needs correction. Often, the refusal to change is egobased; at other times, when it becomes obvious that the game has changed, it's a lack of backup procedures.

How To Counteract

AGGRESSIVE

Use the opponent's belief in their own strength against them. They can be enveloped during their headlong rush or allowed to dissipate their energy against an immovable object. Aggressive stylists attack frontally and generally, they lack guile.

- COUNTERSTRATEGIES: Compliant, Impassive, Indulgent, Secretive, Deceptive, Theft.

COMPLIANT

The compliant stylist proceeds with the belief that the opposition is unaware of his intentions until the trap is sprung. This style can be derailed by changes to the agenda or the simultaneous discussion of all important issues.

- COUNTERSTRATEGIES: Pragmatic, Secretive, Stern, Brinkmanship, Theft

PASSIVE

This technique requires that the opposition reveal their plan in detail with little revealed by the Passive stylist. Becoming demanding counterparts and insisting on speedy proceedings can expose and dilute this style.

- COUNTERSTRATEGIES: Aggressive, Exploitive, Fleeting, Intimidating

IMPASSIVE

The Impassive, especially buyers, try to convince their opponents that they are hiding something. The inscrutable founder in an atmosphere of openness. Ask questions, demand answers, hold the agenda hostage.

- COUNTERSTRATEGIES: Pragmatic, Brinkmanship, Overwhelming, Technical

INTIMIDATING

Intimidators are just Aggressors with insight. Their reliance on creating fear can and must be stymied early in discussions. Addressing the style directly acknowledges its effect. Stick to business.

- COUNTERSTRATEGIES: Impassive, Technical, Financial, Legalistic, Pragmatic

TECHNICAL

Whereas Aggressors and Intimidators want you to feel weak, Technical negotiators want you to feel stupid by bombarding the negotiations with data. Putting the focus on larger issues and avoiding minutia defangs them.

- COUNTERSTRATEGIES: Legalistic, Exploitive, Self-Righteous, Stern, Social

FINANCIAL

Finance bargainers constantly put the focus on profit, to the exclusion of other issues. If those other issues are important, you must take either the moral high ground or the realistic mid-range. There is more to business than just money.

- COUNTERSTRATEGIES: Self-Righteous, Pragmatic, Legalistic

LEGALISTIC

Countering this strategy depends on which side of the law you wish to remain. If you find your counterpart's insistence on adhering to the letter of the law a bit tedious and potentially unprofitable, then you need to introduce the reality of the situation especially if the host country has little contract law.

- COUNTERSTRATEGIES: Pragmatism, Deception, Stern

If on the other hand counterparts seem unable to "locate the top of the table" or the right side of the law, you must make it clear that the deal will not be concluded under nefarious circumstances.

- COUNTERSTRATEGIES: Legalistic, Intimidating, Self-Righteous, Social

SECRETIVE

Agreement to secret negotiations can often cause regret as it limits outside information and protective scrutiny. If it's at the planning stage, you can demand to know why secrecy is required. If a change in strategy is required, simply state that you find the situation untenable and can't proceed unless the veil of secrecy is lifted. Either way, fortitude is required.

- COUNTERSTRATEGIES: Intimidating, Pragmatic, Stern, Aggressive, Social, Deceptive

DECEPTIVE

Deception is part of everyone's style to some degree and can never be completely eliminated. Excesses can be toned down, however, by injections of—and demands for—the truth. Don't be too insistent, as the tables may suddenly turn against you.

- COUNTERSTRATEGIES: Pragmatic, Self-Righteous, Stern, Impassive, Legalistic, Intimidating

EXPLOITIVE

Exploiting the weakness of others is rarely tolerated and never appreciated when discovered. Countering it requires confrontation and in some cases turnabout. Becoming emotional about the strategy is to succumb to its effect. It can best be countered by limiting weaknesses in your position prior to negotiations.

- COUNTERSTRATEGIES: Impassive, Pragmatic, Technical

STUBBORN

People who refuse to budge on an issue or who state their position in terms of "non-negotiable" are really expressing their lack of justification for their position. Finding the underlying cause for such obdurance is the key to breaking the deadlock.

- COUNTERSTRATEGIES: Social, Deceptive, Indulgent, Compliant

AMBIVALENT

Like stubbornness, searching out the underlying cause of ambivalence goes a long way toward its cure. Often it stems from simply not trusting the opposition. Unlike stubbornness, ambivalence does react well to a heavy hand.

- COUNTERSTRATEGIES: Social, Deceptive, Stern, Intimidating

PRAGMATIC

The only problem in dealing with pragmatic counterparts is that they may only see the "practicality" of a proposal from a single perspective. Blinders aren't rare in international business, even for pragmatists. It's one of the few strategies wherein a "fight fire with fire" countermove works. Whatever the case, the pragmatist must be approached with reason, not sentiment.

- COUNTERSTRATEGIES: Pragmatic, Stern, Social, Legalistic, Technical

BRINKMANSHIP

Rather than being a whole strategy, driving opponents to the brink is more of a keystone tactic in an aggressive or intimidating style. It can be warded off by forcing the counterparts to place their whole plan on the table at once.

- COUNTERSTRATEGIES: Impassive, Stern, Pragmatic, Self-Righteous, Overwhelming

ARROGANT

Arrogant people tend to feel ill at ease about their own standing. This can either be played to or downplayed. Capitalizing on an opponent's feelings of inferiority can add an emotional edge to the discussions that can reduce effectiveness. It's best to find the root cause and alleviate it.

- COUNTERSTRATEGIES: Exploitive, Compliant, Social, Stern

SELF-RIGHTEOUS

Opponents "riding their high horses" make easy targets, but they can also be some of the most difficult people to counter. They want everyone to look at "the big picture," but only from one side. This emotional tie to their issues makes everything appear as a need. They can be maneuvered into a corner by the rapid and repeated use of the quid pro quo. They can rarely be intimidated because they believe right is on their side, so frontal attacks are useless.

- COUNTERSTRATEGIES: Compliant, Indulgent, Secretive, Deceptive

OVERWHELMING

Negotiators will have precious little time to recognize that they're about to be overrun. If you suspect that you're about to confront an Overwhelming buyer ("I'll take everything you've got but I won't pay more than . . .") or a "driver's seat" sales team ("Microsoft has what you need but . . ."), you'll either have to outcharm them or outrun them.

- COUNTERSTRATEGIES: Social, Indulgent, Pragmatic, Fleeting, Aggressive

FLEETING

Speed can be very irritating, and irritable negotiators don't succeed on a regular basis. Counterparts who attempt to run roughshod are either showing their inexperience or questioning your own. Show them your mettle (buying or selling) by refusing to adjust your pace to their style.

- COUNTERSTRATEGIES: Impassive, Stern, Technical, Legalistic

STERN

It is wise to assume that Stern stylists didn't come by their methods casually. The strategy puts a focus on details and can only move in a straight line. It can't be sidetracked so it must be derailed. Don't bother with cajoling. Just disregard the dour looks and hammer away at the weaknesses in the counterpart's arguments.

- COUNTERSTRATEGIES: Exploitive, Pragmatic, Technical

SOCIAL

Social stylists are the most deadly, least obvious, and hardest to resist of all strategists. They offer fun, friendship, and favorable connections as a means to expose and control your position. Hosts practicing this strategy can be exceptionally persuasive for visitors a long way from home. The social niceties must be observed in every culture, but be wary when they cross the line into manipulation. If the effort is egregious, don't hesitate to make a major strategic alteration.

- COUNTERSTRATEGIES: Intimidating, Exploitive, Stern, Impassive, Deceptive

THEFT

Theft of information as a strategy is difficult and costly to repel. Its prevention is tactical. Its discovery can lead to strategic changes by the victims mostly for the purpose of assuring that they're not victimized again. Severe measures are usually called for if discussions are to continue.

- COUNTERSTRATEGIES: Intimidating, Legalistic, Exploitive, Stern

INDULGENT

Being enveloped by an Indulgent stylist can be a very enjoyable experience right up until the strategy closes off your escape. As will be seen in the Country-by-Country listing of strategies and tactics, some cultures are more given to this methodology than others. Many victims bask in its comfort, hoping to wriggle free at the last moment. It's better to resist its charms from the outset.

- COUNTERSTRATEGIES: Impassive, Technical, Pragmatic, Stern

CHAPTER 14

Countering Team Strategies

How To Keep The Upper Hand

TEAM STRATEGIES are often difficult to expose as they are composed of many distracting personal styles. On top of this, your preset strategy has been thoroughly worked out and may already be in place so you may be unwilling to make any dramatic changes. As equally important as choosing your strategy is the ability to recognize and counter the opposition's choice. Just as each team member must master a variety of styles, so should a team be capable of switching strategies. Some strategies are better than others as counteractions and the weaker team will be the one that must adapt first. Stylistic superiority might give you the upper hand initially but strategic choice will maintain it.

Consensus

A Consensus team forms a lumbering beast that attempts to roll over anything and anyone that's directly in front of it. The speed of consensus taking can be increased or decreased depending on how such a team wishes to maneuver its counterparts. Their reaction to every issue is the same, and they're loathe to change tactics, let alone strategy. Consensus teams plan in detail and execute everything they plan, regardless of outcome. Such teams must stick to an agenda and are very disoriented by counterparts who can (and do) handle change easily.

COUNTERMEASURES

- CONSENSUS When both teams use Consensus, as is very common in Asia, negotiations can be long and drawn out as each side vies to control the field. Countering consensus with consensus is only recommended when the amount of time (and therefore money) devoted to the negotiation process isn't a crucial factor. Host-buyers can always wield the upperhand when countering with Consensus. Weakly positioned sellers should never attempt this "fighting fire with fire" approach.
- COWBOYS Cowboy teams that keep their wits and cool about them can do very well against Consensus but not from a selling position, unless they're the only game in town. Because they can work solo as well as in a group setting, Cowboys can outmaneuver the lumbering Consensus by introducing new items (or new angles on old items) to the agenda and overload the Consensus taking process. During dispersal sessions, they can also put their counterparts on the defensive by questioning their decision-making ability and actual authority. This can be very disconcerting for counterparts of supposedly equal rank.

- PLATOON Platoons have the same advantages over Consensus teams as Cowboys do, with the added ability to include lots of support personnel. They can, in effect, form small Consensus teams to scrutinize issues, while retaining the on-the-spot authority to be decisive. This is very effective if teams have been dispersed to several areas.
- DIVIDE AND CONQUER Consensus lives in deathly fear of discord and expends a great deal of time guarding against it. A divisive counterstrategy must be constant and very subtle. Many of the personal styles become tactical maneuvers (Social, Deceptive, Exploitive, Indulgent), and they can have devastating effects if practiced on an inexperienced Consensus team caught unaware. Experienced Consensus practitioners with long-term team members are virtually impervious to Divide and Conquer strategies.
- JEKYLL AND HYDE Inconsistency is a death-knell for those who believe in Consensus. Buyers that counter it with a Jekyll and Hyde style will have varying degrees of success, depending on the experience level of the Consensus team. Sellers, unless demand is very high, will have no success at all countering with Jekyll and Hyde. The use of a third party (preferably governmental) as the Mr. Hyde portion of the strategy may assist in influencing the consensus process, but it may not break their control of the agenda.
- HIERARCHICAL Hierarchies have all of the weaknesses of Consensus and none of its strengths. In the face of an experienced Consensus team, Hierarchies are no match.
- HORIZONTAL These "subsidiary" negotiators force Consensus teams to bargain on many fronts without the benefit of a central contract. This is not recommended for sellers, as they very rarely get to control the agenda so necessary to making this counterstrategy work. Buyers, however, can greatly reduce the power of the Consensus team by adding this extra set of decisions that must be made with every subsidiary.
- DEPARTMENTAL Consensus practitioners have no central authority and much prefer to deal with those that do. Countering with a Departmental style will shield your central leadership while forcing the Consensus team to respond to your practical concerns. They must deal with many departments, while you deal with a monolith. This is very effective when in a selling position and unnecessary when in a buying mode.

Cowboys

These teams are composed of very informed and determined soloists who have the ability to make group efforts. While most effective when used during dispersal meetings, they can also perform well at centralized negotiations that entail many social events. Cowboys can make tactical changes in a split second. They can hit moving targets as well as stationary, but they're most vulnerable to countermeasures before they become too experienced at their trade.

COUNTERMEASURES

- CONSENSUS Only buyer/investor types should attempt to use Consensus strategies as a countermove. Be forewarned that Cowboys can cause Consensus users to doubt their own methods by magnifying the slowness of the process in a rapidly moving environment. Sellers countering with Consensus methods will most likely find themselves alone on the second day of discussions. The Cowboys will have moved on, leaving behind a brief note to the effect of "call us when you're serious."
- COWBOYS When two opposing Cowboys meet, there's the inevitable shoot-out and bloody result. The question is, will it be deadly or just a matter of "flesh wounds?" If your team is in the buying position, it's best to be slightly more aggressive than your counterpart. There's no reason to back down from a position of strength. Sellers, unless in particularly high demand, should tone their position down. When both sides adopt this strategy, negotiations are fast and furious. Your side must have a detailed plan of where it's heading, because it's a short trip. Weak hearts and slow signers should stay out of the fray.
- PLATOON Solo Cowboy players can be readily handled by Platoons, especially during sessions with a great deal of technical reference. Because Platoons are really Cowboys with backup, this can be an effective countermeasure for hosts who find themselves on the losing side of discussions. While it's an admission that your original strategy was failing, it can salvage your position. There's no official rule book for negotiations, only a listing of successful companies. Ganging up on a counterpart is a strategic maneuver, not a moral dilemma.
- DIVIDE AND CONQUER Cowboys are used to working alone so dividing them can only occur if there's a major discrepancy in their proposals. Experienced teams rarely suffer from such incongruities.
- JEKYLL AND HYDE This "good cop, bad cop" strategy can work on individual Cowboys but probably not so well on the team as a whole. Even on an individual basis, Cowboys are fast on their feet and can exploit the difference in the two attitudes.
- HIERARCHICAL Cowboys in a selling mode detest Hierarchies because they're resistant to dispersal meetings. Hierarchies that face buying-mode Cowboys may meet the same fate as the Consensus teams, unless they can process the decisions quickly.
- HORIZONTAL Horizontal teams have the strength of the Cowboy's dispersal and the added strength of being a truly independent subsidiary. Cowboys end up dealing with several separate companies (buying or selling) and this tends to diffuse their potency. This is very effective when the Horizontal practitioner is in a weakened selling position and must maintain control of the agenda.
- DEPARTMENTAL Similar to Horizontal teams, countering Cowboys with a Departmental style prevents them from getting quick decisions (that is, concessions) but without entirely slowing down the process. Though it's best used in a weak buying position, it can also be attempted by attentive sellers.

Platoon

Platoons have the independent muscle of Cowboys but more depth because of the inclusion of support personnel. They are essential for dispersed sessions where technical acumen will be tested. The use of support personnel also allows for a greater number of personal styles to be utilized.

COUNTERMEASURES

- CONSENSUS Platoons dread the lassitude that seems to come with Consensus teams in a buying mode. By further decreasing their nimbleness, Consensus players make an already weak Platoon weaker. Consensus sellers (with reasonable demand present) can also debilitate a Platoon if the usage is discreet. Be forewarned: if the latter process stops moving altogether, it's over.
- COWBOYS Cowboy counterstrategies rely on either a strong buying position or the encountering of weak Platoons. If the Cowboys in question are highly experienced and technically astute, they may be able to withstand a deployed Platoon.
- PLATOON As was true of head-to-head Cowboy matchups, Platoon scrimmages can be bloody. Buying and selling positions will dictate the level of aggression by the respective teams.
- DIVIDE AND CONQUER Since Platoons are actually small teams, they're subject to divisive techniques. It should be noted that they're also specialized in nature and potentially very cohesive. Any new specialist recently taken into the Platoon may be targeted by Divide and Conquer practitioners, but that same specialist is most likely being shepherded by the team leader. Proceed with care.
- JEKYLL AND HYDE Giving one Platoon a hard time and another an easy ride will go some way toward confusing the opposition when they regroup. It may even serve to plant some dissention regarding the relative effectiveness of the individual Platoons. Keep in mind, especially if you're a seller, that if your counterstrategy lacks subtlety it may be viewed as a lack of consistency on your part (hardly a desirable trait in a purveyor). Buyers can play it to the hilt.
- HIERARCHICAL Platoons can become frustrated with buyers who work hierarchically, because the dispersal is only surface level. Decisions are still centrally controlled, and the Platoon gets bogged own. If sellers counter with a Hierarchical style due to company policy or lack of alternatives, they must keep it as streamlined as possible if they wish to maintain the interest of Platoons in a buying mode.
- HORIZONTAL Like Cowboys, Platoons have a bad case of "authority envy" when it comes to Horizontal teams. Though not an option for every company, these subsidiary teams are an effective countermeasure to any Platoon, buying or selling.
- DEPARTMENTAL This should only be used in a buying mode as a counter-strategy. Platoons have all the strengths of departments and none of their weaknesses.

Divide and Conquer

This style relies on either a) the surreptitious gathering of information from counterparts who've been strategically separated from the group or b) the constant exploitation of small mistakes in a counterpart's position. While almost all teams will use this to some degree as a tactic, some teams adopt it as an overall strategy—usually with a high level of success.

COUNTERMEASURES

- CONSENSUS Closing ranks against a divisive counterpart is often the most effective way to ward off their attack. However, it's not easy to form a Consensus style team on a moment's notice. Such a move must be prepositioned in order to succeed. For some groups (such as Cowboys or Platoons), it's a very drastic change of style.
- COWBOYS Cowboys are very enticing to Divide and Conquer practitioners, since the dividing is done and all that is left is the conquering. However, Cowboys are the nimblest of the nimble and can counter divisive techniques with a full array of calculated and sincerely delivered misinformation. Teams that suddenly find themselves dispersed, socially or professionally, can turn to a Cowboy strategy as long as they operate within a few prearranged parameters.
- PLATOON Platoons are far more cohesive than the larger team they may represent. When meetings are dispersed, Platoons are a very effective counter to divisive techniques, with the proviso that their position has been thoroughly reviewed for discrepancies.
- DIVIDE AND CONQUER Strong CNs and team leaders who are aware of a counterpart's divisive strategy may effectively counter with a similar style. It's not unusual for a team that's gone on the offensive with Divide and Conquer techniques to overlook the weaknesses in their own defenses.
- JEKYLL AND HYDE The attitudinal differences exhibited by members of the same team, if well coordinated, can act as a powerful defense against division imposed externally. Jekyll and Hyde teams already work well together, while still exhibiting a divided viewpoint. Conquering a team that thrives on division is extremely difficult for Divide and Conquer practitioners.
- HIERARCHICAL Weakly controlled hierarchies are easy pickings for divisive teams because they're usually rife with dissention. Hierarchies that are well led and highly organized are virtually impregnable because of their high degree of loyalty to the decision makers.
- HORIZONTAL Close-knit subsidiary teams also thrive in a fragmented environment. It's very difficult for divisive teams to deal with Horizontal counterparts who've essentially been given orders to behave independently.
- DEPARTMENTAL Departments can be a useful counter to divisive techniques by sheltering the decision maker. Any discrepancies in the proposal or commitments made by Departmental team members under the duress of isolation can be easily, if humbly, overturned with statements that authority has been overstepped.

Jekyll and Hyde

Practitioners of this style use one set of members to cajole with a congenial Dr. Jekyll attitude while another set hammers at the opposition with all the wrath of a Mr. Hyde. In its simplest form, one part of the team creates a problem for counterparts that another wing of the team offers to solve. Counterparts end up seeking the "aid" of the opposition to make the deal work. Often a collusive third party (such as a government agency) will act out the Mr. Hyde role.

COUNTERMEASURES

- CONSENSUS Group decision making can ward off Jekyll and Hyde practitioners by stressing the lack of consistency in their counterpart's positions, but only if the counterpart is a seller. If the counterparts are the host company using a local government as their collusive "Hyde," Consensus buying teams are advised to make the solution of any problems the responsibility of the host. Consensus sellers may have to tolerate the tantrums of the Jekyll and Hyde team, but awareness of the strategy will allow them to concentrate directly on Hyde and downplay Jekyll.
- COWBOYS Cowboys rarely encounter Jekyll and Hyde teams because the dispersal process limits the use of "good cop, bad cop." When it does occur, Cowboy buyers can demand consistency from counterparts. Sellers must put the counterpart's Jekyll portion of the equation to work for them by using them as a go-between, once they've offered their assistance. They should be very proactive once they detect the strategy and not wait for the Jekyll contingent to make their own proposals.
- PLATOON Platoons should counter Jekyll and Hyde styles in much the same way as Cowboys, but with the added use of their support staff's multiple styles. They may even wish to inject a bit of Jekyll and Hyde into the process themselves.
- DIVIDE AND CONQUER It's hard for the divisive team to exploit the cleavage in the Jekyll and Hyde team, since it's so highly choreographed. It's better for a divisive team to seek out and isolate weaker members of the Jekyll and Hyde team—in order to determine the presence of internal dissention or the financial details of their strategy.
- JEKYLL AND HYDE When both sides take this approach, it can create long and acrimonious days of discussion. It's only recommended if a team has a very limited number of styles to choose from when entering negotiations.
- HIERARCHICAL When in a good buying position, a hierarchy can thwart the Hyde contingent by simply demanding to close the deal. Hierarchical sellers will find that the situation is very much reversed, and they're now faced with demands to see the "head honcho" at every meeting. Honchos can run but they can't elude Hyde.
- HORIZONTAL Countering with this subsidiary format, if available, greatly diffuses and defuses the Jekyll and Hyde effect because it's very difficult to maintain the schism on so many fronts. This is true for either buying or selling. Unfortunately, not all companies lend themselves to Horizontal strategies.
- DEPARTMENTAL Departments are a useful countermeasure when buying because the decision maker can be detached until problems are cleared up. When in a standard selling position, however, the same honcho problems facing Hierarchies will haunt and daunt the Departmental stylist.

Hierarchical

Hierarchies maintain the centralized authority of a standard managerial flow chart and use team members to filter information for the decision maker. It's used by teams new to negotiating or by strong CNs or consultants who have a weak staff. The opposition must not be able to detect that authority is centralized for this approach to work effectively.

COUNTERMEASURES

- CONSENSUS This style works well in either a buying or selling position because Consensus has many people at its decision core. Hierarchies crumble in the face of these highly organized megaliths.
- COWBOYS Hierarchies that allow themselves to become dispersed are easy prey for Cowboys. A Cowboy counterstrategy would demand tight control of the agenda, which is rare in selling positions even when facing a rookie hierarchy.
- PLATOON Like Cowboys, Platoons that find Hierarchies willing to disperse have already won the field, but the carnage will be potentially even greater. There will be no long-term, amicable relationship unless the Platoon controls the urge to take more than "enough."
- DIVIDE AND CONQUER If the slightest dissention or disloyalty to the central decision maker is detected, it can be thoroughly exploited by divisive teams. Hierarchies are pyramidal in form, and loss of the foundation brings down the apex.
- JEKYLL AND HYDE This style should only be used to counter a Hierarchy when working from a strong buying position. Demands can then be made to deal directly with the central decision maker, who may be more susceptible to Jekyll and Hyde techniques when relieved of the filtering effects of staff.
- HIERARCHICAL This is very common when both sides are feeling their way in the international arena. Discussions appear to be between groups, but in reality it's two individuals battling out the futures of their respective companies. Both sides have made their strategic choices, less by design than by default. Everyone has to start somewhere, and this is where newcomers get their first calluses.
- HORIZONTAL The use of multiple fronts implicit in this style makes it a forceful counter to Hierarchies, compelling them to scatter themselves even when working in a single location. It can overload the central decision maker resulting in reliance on untried and less skilled subordinates.
- DEPARTMENTAL Like Horizontal practitioners, Departments can counter a hierarchy by forcing them to deal with what they believe are separate sets of decision making teams that change with every session.

Horizontal

This strategy is used by large companies that have the advantage of numerous subsidiaries that can negotiate their own separate contracts or parts of contracts while still operating under the company's aegis. This will often come into play during large infrastructure projects, technological transfers, or large manufacturing projects.

COUNTERMEASURES

- CONSENSUS A Consensus buyer who controls the agenda can easily stymie a Horizontal team, regardless of its size, either by taking the subsidiaries on individually or by forcing them to work as a unit. Consensus sellers will find, however, that their decision making process will get bogged down by multifront bargaining.
- COWBOYS Cowboys will only successfully counter Horizontal teams when control of the agenda is assured—by being either buyers or highly demanded sellers. Otherwise, Cowboys may be outmaneuvered by the truly independent Horizontalists.
- PLATOON Platoons have the same limits on their independence and needs for agenda control as Cowboys. Their one advantage is support staff, comparable to that of the Horizontal team.
- DIVIDE AND CONQUER Unless specific subsidiaries exhibit some form of internal dissention, divisive techniques aren't advisable as countermeasures. Pitting one subsidiary against another will produce little of use, since their interdependence isn't vital to the outcome of the deal.
- JEKYLL AND HYDE Any effect that Jekyll and Hyde strategies might have will be diffused over many fronts. In the case of small companies, countering with a "good cop, bad cop" routine will only result in an image of disunity or disorganization.
- HIERARCHICAL Hierarchies are easily outclassed by Horizontal teams, unless the former completely controls the agenda. This is the reason why the big fish eat so many little fish in the international business arena.
- HORIZONTAL When two big fish tangle for control (generally in a huge market), one usually gets swallowed whole, although some subsidiaries may get "spun off" from the new behemoth. The stakes are far too high for anything but these "default" positions, and negotiations may drag on for months. The complexity of such discussions is beyond the scope of this text.
- DEPARTMENTAL Departments working from a buying position will be able to blunt the effect of Horizontal strategists, forcing them to broker deals one at a time through separate subteams. This will, of course, elongate the time frame for finalizing a deal. Sellers may find that their departments must move swiftly to maintain the interests of the octopus' many arms.

Departmental

This strategy maintains the company hierarchy but arrays it horizontally, with the decision maker staying behind the scenes. Department teams are sent out to discuss individual points of the agenda, and each team may have a different leader and style. Each department gives a presentation for its portion of the deal, until the entire proposal is laid out.

COUNTERMEASURES

- CONSENSUS Consensus buyers must be wary of Departments as they can drag out the decision-making process to the former's disadvantage. If Consensus is used, verify the real players from the outset and control the agenda. Finding the decision maker "behind the curtain" will greatly speed the process. Consensus sellers must be prepared to break their proposal down to correspond to the counterpart's Departments.
- COWBOYS Cowboys in buying positions will have no difficulty with Departments, as long as they make it clear that time is of the essence and as long as meetings are dispersed. Sellers using Cowboy strategies may find themselves getting ganged-up on by Departments and wasting time giving repetitive presentations.
- PLATOON Platoons have all of a Departmental style's strength, but they're far nimbler. In a buying position they'll dominate easily, assuming that the sessions are dispersed. Match the Platoons to the Department structure for maximum effect.
- DIVIDE AND CONQUER Divisive techniques should only be used when the decision maker can be clearly identified. When buying, insist that the counterpart's CN be present when each presentation is given, and exploit the differences or conflict between Departments. When selling, isolate weak team members for the purpose of securing information regarding overall team goals.
- JEKYLL AND HYDE Buyers can use Mr. Hyde to force the counterparts to reveal their decision maker, who will then be placated by Dr. Jekyll. After that, all attentions will be focused on the opposition's CN. Sellers, even highly demanded ones, should avoid this strategy altogether.
- HIERARCHICAL Buyer/Investors can cut right to the chase and derail the Departmental strategy by pitting one honcho against another. Sellers may find that they have only been dealing with a "straw man" throughout discussions and that real power lies elsewhere. Departments usually turn out to be former Hierarchies with greater negotiating experience and a tight-lipped CN.
- HORIZONTAL Buyers working from a Horizontal strategy can apply time demands that tend to frazzle Departments hoping to give detailed presentations. Sellers countering with this subsidiary method may be slowed by Departmental lumbering, but they can rely on their company's size to awe the opposition.
- DEPARTMENTAL Like head-to-head Hierarchies, Departmental match-ups are quite common, but more so among experienced international negotiating teams. It's a preferred method because it maintains company organizational structure and lines of communication. The dominating team is usually the best informed and the most secretive about the sources of decision making. Many companies use this as their sole strategy and only vary their tactics from negotiation to negotiation.

CHAPTER 15

Selecting Tactics

PLAYING TO WIN

ONCE A STRATEGY has been chosen, tactics must be devised to assure that the goals are attained. While many strategy categories can also be used as tactics, they differ in that the latter is usually a temporary measure devised to achieve a specific result. As an example, a negotiator may choose a Pragmatic strategy to acquire 25 percent of a software joint venture but rely on daily tactics that are Technical, Legalistic and Financial in nature.

Tactical analysis of counterparts is also very important in choosing one's own maneuvers, and it's at the heart of proactive negotiating. Even sellers in the weakest position should avoid having a tactical array that's 100 percent reactive. As is true in almost all commercial endeavors, *how* something is accomplished has a great deal of influence on *how much* is accomplished. In highly publicized negotiations, the means may actually dictate the ends.

This chapter will deal with the various forms of tactics used in international negotiations and their connection to strategy choice. Readers will be able to formulate their own array, as well as learn to recognize tactical patterns developing across the table.

THE FIRST RULE OF TACTICS: Make the opposition believe it's in control.

Matching Tactics to Strategy

What tactics are available to the modern commercial negotiator? When can they be used? When should they be avoided? What are the limits?

In order to answer the first question, a list of tactics and their definitions follow. Those that are derived from strategies will be discussed in lesser detail; the reader is asked to review those categories in prior chapters. The answers for the second and third questions will rely on the choice of strategy, and a brief worksheet is provided at the end of the chapter to allow readers to make those decisions for themselves with some guidance. The answer to the last question is simple: The choice of tactics is limited only by the ability, experience, acumen, and motivation of each negotiator. It can also be a matter of legal and illegal behavior.

Legal Tactics

AGGRESSION

Aggression has violent connotations in daily life, but in commerce it's used to describe the high end of proactive behavior. While we may have very separate reactions to an aggressive salesperson and an aggressive bill collector, we'll all have to admit that it depends primarily on whether they're working *for* us or *against* us. Aggression only bothers us when we're on the receiving end.

Aggressive tactics can run the gamut from arriving early for meetings to calling counterparts at home to discuss business. It literally means "to attack" and demands that you take the initiative when dealing with the opposition. It shouldn't be confused with tactics of intimidation, whose main design is to cause fear. The goal of aggressive behavior during negotiations is to control the time and the place of discussions.

PASSIVITY

Many people respond to aggression or intimidation with docility in the hope that brief appeasement will lead to less demanding behavior. This is very reactive. In proactive negotiations, passivity can be a way to convince opponents that everything is going their way until parts of the topic deemed important reach the table. A sudden change of tactics by the Passive side at this point will leave their counterparts "enveloped." This is a useful tactic against an opponent who has confused confidence with ego. It can never be used for long, and it must be used in tandem with a reasonable tactic (e.g., Pragmatism or Impassivity) so as not to appear irrational. It's also a tactic that requires a great deal of emotional restraint, due to the often overbearing attitude of the type of opponent on whom it is most effective.

IMPASSIVITY

As mentioned earlier, it's never wise to state that a topic is non-negotiable. But this isn't to say that one can't take a hard line on an issue that is particularly important to acquiring "enough." Although it calls for a good deal of nonchalant behavior, even the most Social of strategists can call upon Impassivity as a tactic. It also requires that the tactician be operating from a position of strength (strong buying or high-demand selling), even if it's just for a single point of the agenda. In practice, it involves reticence and indifference until the opposition has stated their position. Once this has been accomplished, an attitude of "is this the best you can do?" is maintained until all possibilities are exhausted. It's not until the end of the process that the tactician will actually state what it is they need or want from this portion of the negotiations. By doing this, they avoid granting concessions the opposition wasn't expecting to receive or gaining more than the opposition had hoped to give.

EXAMPLE: China's Aggressive style during 1984 negotiations with Great Britain used Impassive tactics when discussing terms for the return of Kowloon and the New Territories. Unexpectedly, Great Britain offered to return Hong Kong Island as well (which had never been leased but had been granted in perpetuity). China's Aggressive strategy had implied that Hong Kong Island would be taken by force, but their refusal to state it outright led to the concession via Impassivity.

INTIMIDATION

Using Intimidation as a tactic usually occurs when one side feels they've been backed into a corner on an issue that's very important to their strategy. Unable to win the concession by means of discussion, they attempt to do so by threat. This has worked in commercial negotiations of all types for centuries. It does have two requirements for effective use. First, the threat must be believable even if you have no intention of following through on it. Strength, or the illusion of strength, must be readily apparent to the opposition. If you have to explain your threat, it's no threat. Second, you must be capable of defending yourself if and when the opposition decides to respond in kind. If you can't take a punch, don't throw a punch.

Intimidation can be a messy business, even when it's a brief tactical move. Because it can change the tone of negotiations so drastically ("the gloves are off"), it's best reserved until late in the proceedings, when all other means have been exhausted. It should never be used as an emotional reaction to nimbler, more experienced (perhaps more intimidating) opponents. Most likely they've purposely driven you to the point where you'll make threats—in the full knowledge that you'll have to back down. Being humble is one thing, being humbled another. Never, ever make idle threats. They can be as binding as a contract.

FORTHRIGHTNESS

Many consider this a virtue but just as many use it as a tactic. Anytime someone starts of a sentence with "to be frank with you . . ." or "in all honesty . . ." they've just switched to Forthrightness as a tactic. What they're about to say may or may not be completely true but it's the portion of the truth that they find most useful. By declaring their own honesty they hope to provoke a similar response in you, thereby getting you to divulge something important.

Forthrightness is most often used during a Pragmatic strategy to keep the discussions moving. It can be very potent when dealing with opponents who've adopted a basically Deceptive strategy. By making a tactical call for honesty, you can force counterparts to alter their plans to some degree, though rarely completely. At the very least, you've made them aware of the fact that you consider their scheme dishonest. Don't assume they'll be ashamed. Forthrightness often brings about nothing more than a recognition by the other side that they have to learn how to better deceive you.

For some negotiators, Forthrightness is merely a pose that covers the overall strategy. It may even be used as part of a grander deception. Forthrightness only requires the *appearance* of telling the truth. The "whole" truth can be held in reserve. *No* successful negotiator *anywhere*, at *anytime* has *ever* spoken the *complete* truth. If negotiators convince you they're being candid with you then they're successful practitioners of the tactic. Belief does not demand truth.

DELAY

One of the numerous oxymoronic terms used by militaries around the world is "delaying action." With this tactic, an advancing enemy is held at bay by a small force using hit-and-run guerilla attacks meant to impede progress until reinforcements can be brought forward. These "little war" tactics are practiced quite frequently in international negotiations as well (mostly when a David meets a Goliath) and they have the desired effect when used judiciously.

Delays may take the form of outright postponements, shifts of venue, calls for internal conferences, loss of paperwork, minuscule contract disputes, feigned illnesses, filibustering, transportation breakdowns, strikes, and even prearranged government intervention. If talks take a turn for the worse and the side that is outclassed lacks the "at table" skills to retake the field, then delaying tactics are called to the fore. The hoped for "reinforcements" can take the form of additional personnel, changes in the economic environment, updated information, the courting of another suitor, or intervention by government officials.

The most powerful reinforcement available to the Delay practitioner is time, or more precisely, lack of time. Delays are usually last-ditch efforts by an opponent who is hoping to "run the clock out" in order to get either what they need or to trigger the call for another round of negotiations. The tactic is best used by host companies wishing to take advantage of their visitor's flight schedule, but it can also be deployed against any opponent that is attempting to work to a rigid time frame. Infrastructure projects, Build-Operate-Transfer schemes, highly publicized construction projects, and government contract work are just a few of the types of projects subject to the pressures that can be brought to bear by delaying tactics.

It's not a tactic that should be trotted out often, particularly when in a weak selling position. Delay is a sign of weakness for sellers, and to display it early in negotiations will only let your opposition "smell the blood in the water." Some buyers like to use Delay as a way of testing how hungry a seller is for their business. This "let them wait" attitude is a very old practice in business and it's not commensurate with the pace of modern commerce (where time is measured in nanoseconds). Unnecessary delays may mark even the strongest buyer/investor as being part of the Old School. It also makes sellers have second thoughts about the payment process. For both buyers and sellers, delays don't create a favorable impression in the minds of the opposition. If you can afford that sort of image or have played every other card in your deck, proceed with delaying tactics. Otherwise, get down to business.

DISTRACTION

When negotiators have decided what's important to them (needs) as opposed to agenda items that are merely desirable (wants), they must make every effort to keep the opposition from finding out which is which. Distraction is a common tactic for this purpose. Negotiators will argue vigorously for points that have little meaning to them, knowing full well that they'll concede them in the end. Important issues are then taken as concessions in a quid pro quo for these early "defeats," or else they are quietly slipped into the standard contract language.

Socialization strategies use a great deal of distraction to elicit information, isolate counterparts, and undermine an opposing CN's position. Late-night parties, cultural side trips, and exhausting multisite meeting schedules all give the opposing negotiator something else to think about—notably discomfort.

Besides the discomfort, the distraction that occurs when one feels they're among friends will be the moment when practitioners uncover dissention or inconsistencies in counterparts. Unguarded moments are highly sought after by the practitioner.

EXAMPLES: Uncomfortable seating, lack of air conditioning in meeting rooms, and frequent interruptions by staff on "urgent" business also serve as distractions. They're often prearranged to do just that by practitioners of this tactic. The greater the discomfort, the greater the level of distraction. Some have been known to go as far as to place late-night anonymous phone calls and arrange for noisy "guests" to stay in hotel rooms adjoining those of the opposition. A fatigued opposition simply can't concentrate. Extreme but effective when dealing with jet-lagged travelers.

LINGUISTIC

One of the challenges of international business is overcoming the barrier of language. Even when all parties involved are using the unofficial language of commerce, English, discrepancies arise—just ask the British and the Americans. Added into this mix are the argots of specific industries, shipping, contract law, and technology. Rather than seeing this as a continual barrier, some negotiators take on linguistic differences as a useful tactic. It can take several forms, all of which contain the "plausible deniabilty" that is often necessary to make the tactic work.

The first involves the supplying of translators to the opposition. It was discussed earlier in the text how these local hires can relay private conversations to their "real" employer, but they also serve other purposes. Host countries usually insist that, for legal use, the contract language be crafted in the local tongue, not the translation. Unattractive items such as veto rights, tax rates, and rules regarding the repatriation of profits are easily hidden or eliminated from the translated version and will not be discovered until well after the deal has been closed. The translated version will rarely be accepted as having any validity. Such a tactic can definitely make negotiations "smoother," but only in the short-term.

Language can also be used as an all-purpose excuse when Deceptive strategies are uncovered, nefarious tactics go awry, or one side has simply been backed up against a wall on a point they "need." Most negotiators who've traveled to the developing markets can relate at least one tale of how, when discussions were just about to derail, the opposition discovered that the dispute was really the result of "poor translation." Even when the opposition has brought their own translator, it will all be written off as a dialect problem. ("So very sorry, we must all be very careful in the future. Now, where were we?") Much pride, as well as the bargaining session, have been saved. Like many other ploys, this one wears with age. Use it sparingly.

The introduction of jargon is also used as a way to assess an opponent's acumen or expose their ignorance on any particular topic. It can also be used to subordinate opponents who wish to position themselves as equals. Especially in the worlds of high technology, finance, shipping, and international law, there are standard levels of knowledge that mark a negotiator as being a true "player" or not. To find out who knows what, the practitioner will purposely use acronyms, contractions, and technical terms in an effort to elicit requests for explanation on what they consider to be basic points of discussion. They'll keep turning it up a notch until they reach a level beyond the understanding of counterparts. If the opposition takes the bait at a fairly low level, the tactic can be used repeatedly to manipulate them into positions that are unfavorable. It's most often used by investors looking for a big share in a joint venture and sellers planning to make a *single*, sizeable transaction. (If you need confirmation of how effective this tactic is on a local level, visit any computer store and tell them you're looking to buy. You'll leave with enough equipment to run NASA and equally enormous "buyer's remorse.")

LOCATION

Location, or the sudden change of location, can be used to disconcert an opponent—even more so when they're "high maintenance" types who require ideal circumstances for optimal performance. Targeted visitors may find that the meeting facility that was touted as being "just outside of the city" is in reality a two-hour drive through backroads. Unfamiliar territory and distance from their psychological link to getting home (the airport) make the victim of this tactic dependent on their opposition. No longer merely counterparts, they have become caregivers. Add into this the accompanying language problems, transport restrictions, and general separation anxiety (homesickness), and the picture is complete. Negotiations will proceed but under the control of the practitioner. It's a tactic that's best used against inexperienced negotiators, as it relies on the target being unused to the rigors of travel. Experienced teams will be only mildly inconvenienced and yawn at the ham-handedness of the ploy.

Another location tactic is commonly used by large companies to awe counterparts. Rather than inconveniencing opponents, they lavish them with every possible thing they could want. Meeting facilities and hotels are top-of-the-line with furnishings designed to impress. Tours are arranged for cutting-edge manufacturing plants and high-tech compounds. No expense is spared. The message being sent out by the practitioner is "we're already at the top. We don't *need* your (product, business, expertise), but we are more than happy to discuss it." If you're on the receiving end of this tactic, be aware that the underlying message is "We really *want* what you have but we're going to try and convince you that it's not worth very much." This tactic never works on Impassive or Stern strategists but the rest of us are highly susceptible to it. Remember, though the lap of luxury is nice, you're still sitting on someone's lap.

INDEBTEDNESS

This gambit entails making counterparts feel as if they're in your debt on several possible levels. The first involves financial debt and is actually best used by a negotiator who doesn't appear to be flush with cash. Unlike the rich Location practitioner above, whose main goal is to make you feel as if their expenditures on negotiations are everyday costs, the Indebtedness tactician subtly lets it be known that every *cent*, *rupiah*, or *ruble* they spend on counterparts is a major exception. Food, lodging, drivers, translators, sometimes even airfares are paid for by the practitioner as an investment in the ultimate outcome of the negotiations.

This ploy is transparent to even the most novice negotiator, yet it still takes its toll. Inwardly, the victims always feel that they have to give their hosts "something for all their trouble." If the tactic works, the victims can be assured that the practitioner has a very clear idea of which "something" will be taken as payment on the debt. If you're targeted with this financial tactic, offer to pay your own way (if you choose). If the practitioner insists on picking up the tab—some will claim it's a cultural norm for dealing with visitors—let them. Enjoy the free ride but constantly remind yourself that they're trying to manipulate you. The sense of Indebtedness fades once the motivation is exposed.

Big companies and governments create a different form of Indebtedness. The tactic is to make the opposition believe that they've been granted a "favor" just by being allowed to come to the negotiating table. The target may even be hosting and paying for the negotiations. It's very commonly used by Impassive strategists and Cowboy teams to foster a sense that all of the concessions will flow in one direction and that they'll be on the receiving end. The tactic works best from a strong selling position ("we've got it, can you afford it?") or a single suitor buying/investing position ("we can afford it, do you have it?").

Debt can also take an emotional form and this tactic is widely practiced by Social strategists who strive to befriend counterparts. The victim will be introduced to the practitioner's family and friends and may even be invited home for dinner. Weekend rounds of golf, dinner parties, and theater trips can all be used to further the friendly atmosphere. By engendering a nonbusiness relationship, the practitioner hopes to ask their new "friend" for a favor during the course of negotiations. This favor will *supposedly* be paid back later, and this wonderful friendship will make doing business all that much better. Like financial Indebtedness, this friendliness often works under the cover of a cultural norm, which it may well be—and a manipulative one, at that. It's hard to resist the charms of this tactic, especially when traveling far from home. Unfortunately, a warm-and-fuzzy feeling doesn't make for a clear head when negotiating. If you're targeted by this tactic, accept whatever level of friendship you feel comfortable with and, like your ego, check it at the door once negotiations start. ("Nothing personal, just business.")

CULTURAL

Cultural differences are often "played" to influence a negotiator's judgment. This can take the form of a host practitioner reminding the opposition of its lengthy cultural history and contributions to civilization. The underlying message here is "we have little experience in international business personally, but we hail from an ancient and esteemed background. Don't try to push us around." It's a tactic that rarely works against an opponent coming from a business culture that relies on a "so-what-have-you-done-lately?" premise. It serves mostly as a confidence builder for the practitioner and, in that respect, it does have some function at the negotiating table. This type of tactician will usually insist on numerous cultural events as part of the agenda in order to hammer home their point. A plethora of such events in the agenda should be a cue to expect this tactic.

Coming from the opposite direction is the practitioner of cultural imperialism. These tacticians care little about their own ancestors, let alone those of the opposition. They present themselves as the manufacturing, technological, or financial saviors of their counterparts. ("We can get your people out of the fields and into the factory in no time.") The tactic is deployed early to check the reaction. If the opposition is suitably (at least partially) impressed, it will be maintained throughout discussions. If the reaction is negative (as it often is, except under the most desperate circumstances), the tactic should be dropped in favor of somewhat less offensive measures.

When the two types of tacticians mentioned above meet, the potential for fireworks is enormous. The use of these tactics is often at the root of the conflicts between technological economies and those of the developing world. The former should not give short shrift to the value of the past and the latter should not rely on it. As mentioned earlier in the text, researching a counterpart's culture is as important as reviewing their balance sheets.

GENDER

Gender roles vary from society-to-society and from company-to-company. In some it's quite common for both genders to participate in business, while in others, business is the exclusive domain of men. That dominion may even be codified into local law. Because it can be a controversial issue, it can be exploited tactically for negotiating purposes. Gender tactics can also lead to the consideration of sexual preferences and influences.

The presence of women at negotiations can successfully unnerve an opponent who isn't used to dealing with women in business. This can be a very potent tactic when sellers from a male-dominated business society are forced to "sell" themselves to a female counterpart. The weakness of their position will be made doubly clear. Female negotiators can also be used to mollify an aggressive male counterpart who is foolish enough *not* to perceive a female as a threat. There's no rule against blindsiding an opponent with their own bias.

Of course, the reverse is true when female sellers face buyers from male-dominated societies. Selling is always an uphill battle and in this situation it may be a 90-degree incline. In extreme cases, the buyer may refuse to even speak to the female negotiator. If the sale is important enough, the wise tactic may be to bow to the cultural biases of the counterpart when selecting negotiators.

Social strategists have another spin on gender; they like to pander to the sexual preferences of their opposition when playing host. Discovering that a counterpart considers himself a capable, if aging, Lothario may result in the sudden appearance of a beautiful (and available) female among the practitioner's negotiating ranks. Similarly, a middle-aged female executive may find herself the object of the attentions of a dashing male counterpart a few years her junior. Both scenarios happen with a none-too-surprising frequency, and the tactic has been a staple in international business, diplomacy, and intrigue for centuries. Add adultery into the mix and the ability to manipulate is even greater. While the young may be targeted for this tactic, practitioners have found repeatedly that "there's no fool like an old fool."

Homosexuality can be tactically exploited in much the same way but with the added ingredient that in many societies it is illegal. Being set up in an unfamiliar environment is not a difficult task. Negotiators of every stripe must keep their wits about them at all times to ward off this tactic. Gender and sexuality are very visceral topics and should not be dallied with lightly. Use of any of the tactics mentioned in this section requires full commitment to the outcome. Once put in motion these tactics are difficult to control.

RACIAL

Racial tactics can be just as explosive as Gender ploys. The most common form of this tactic involves the attempt to make counterparts personally responsible for racial prejudices of the past. Like Cultural Imperialist tactics, this ploy is put on stage early to detect any level of "guilt," deserved or not, in opponents. High levels of culpability or overplayed denials of responsibility will be exploited again and again throughout the proceedings. Buyers will use it to drive the price down, sellers will use it to drive the price up. Concessions will be viewed not as bargaining chips but as reparations. Most of this is directed against Caucasian counterparts even when their cultural background precludes them from any previous sins. The Japanese and the Koreans are also occasional targets of this tactic.

Whereas the above practitioners wish to dwell on how they've been held back, the other variant that plays the "race card" likes to focus on their own advances. These tacticians present themselves as not just racially different but superior. It's their belief that if negative stereotypes (e.g., whites are arrogant, Asians do not value life) can be held as truths by the downtrodden, then positive ones must also be true (whites are technologically advanced, Asians are superior organizers). Similar to cultural imperialism, these "saviors" come to the table already in a strong position hoping to make it even stronger by lording their status over counterparts. The dangers here should be self-evident, but it hasn't prevented this tactic from being deployed often and worldwide. It's rarely productive, never in the long-term. If you plan to use either version of this tactic, you'd better have a damn good reason and a flexible flight schedule.

TECHNICAL

Simply put, this tactic calls for the withholding of technical solutions or problems until counterparts have fully exposed their position. The practitioner must never give any indication that the solution was available or the problem visible until the very last moment. Tipping your hand too soon will dilute the impact and limit opportunities. If done with the proper degree of subtlety, this tactic can be used as often as circumstances permit.

FINANCIAL

This area of tactics is probably the most familiar to the reader, but it bears some explanation. Sellers clearly overstate their asking price expecting to be bargained down to an acceptable level. Buyers state low-ball prices knowing they can afford higher. It's the most basic form of "dickering" known to humankind. (The word *dickering* comes from the term for a set of ten animal hides used as a unit of trade.) Some cultures love to dicker prices and look upon it as a natural form of business. Others, like many Western societies, will only let the seller quote prices without any feedback from the buyer beyond "yes" or "no" statements.

Other financial tactics come into play in international business. Prices may be stated in one currency, then payment demanded in another. Simple trades between the same two companies made only weeks apart may be paid in several different currencies. Negotiators use this system of "arbitrage" to play harder, stronger currencies off against softer, weaker ones. Sometimes, investment is locked into a specific currency as a way to insure equity levels throughout the venture's operation.

Another tactic used during investment-related negotiations is the taxing of repatriated profits. Sometimes the tax is plainly stated and could have been discovered during the research phase. In other instances, it takes the form of a "special exchange rate" that kicks in when the foreign company attempts to convert their profits from the local currency. This isn't proffered until late in the negotiations if at all and it's used to keep the investment perpetually situated in-country. In some cases, the rate can be just 50 percent of the standard rate—a common practice among countries with particularly weak or inconvertible currencies. Foreign companies should be forewarned to take up this issue early in the proceedings. Also be aware that the "special" rate is usually subject to change without notice. If you can't gain a waiver or lock in a reasonable rate, be prepared to spend your profits in the local market.

STATUTORY

Trade and investment law can remain in a state of flux for decades in a target market, with changes every thirty days not uncommon. Developing markets are constantly reworking their laws in an attempt to maximize their domestic economy. Local laws can change even faster than central government statutes and some companies use their local connections to have commercial statutes changed as negotiations proceed. Zoning laws and taxes are extremely vulnerable to this type of manipulation. In most markets, this tactic can be subverted by research that's no more than six months old. In developing markets, thirty-day-old information is the oldest that should be used, and care should be taken to keep an eye on the local authorities. If the project is large and vulnerable, direct contact should be made with government officials prior to the start of discussions.

Another legal tactic used against foreign visitors is the sudden interference by immigration officials regarding visa/passport paperwork. Key members of the negotiations, including the CN, may be detained or sent packing in an effort to dilute the counterpart's position. This ploy is fairly widespread and not just in developing markets. Embassy personnel who've been alerted in advance of your arrival can go a long way toward warding off this type of interference. If such a problem is forecasted, make an effort to have a home country commercial attaché greet you or your team at the port of entry.

Customs officials can also get in on the act by holding presentation materials for inspection. Some may even hold or confiscate luggage for the inconvenience and embarrassment it causes visitors. Don't assume that the other side plays fairly.

STUBBORNNESS

Discussing a point and conceding it are two different things. Even the most unctuous of Social strategists can become tactically stubborn on any particular point of the agenda. The intractability may be real if the point is considered an absolute need, or it may be feigned as a way of gaining a subsequent issue, once the subject under discussion is ultimately yielded (after much hoopla).

Stubbornness can be an effective tactic because it creates a sense of belief in the opposition that they now know "what makes you tick." Of course, it's the practitioner's decision as to whether that belief is factual or not. The obstinate behavior can take the form of a tantrum or the stonefaced repetition of an unvaried viewpoint. Many practitioners prefer to state, with a smile, the same ideas in a hundred different ways. Whatever the presentation, intransigence is the goal. If the position is a feint, care must be taken not to give in too soon and expose the ruse. When it's real, don't belabor the issue to a point where the opposition loses interest in further discussions. Protesting too much can be as bad as protesting too little.

When faced with a stubborn opponent, don't take their behavior at face value. Review what you believe to be their entire strategy and determine if the issue at hand is a potential need, a want, or a feint. If you can't make a clear determination, pose questions that go directly to the counterpart's motivation. Even question the authenticity of their stance ("It would seem to me that this is a minor issue for your ends. Why is this so important?"). If the issue is of little value to your position, concede as soon as possible—don't argue for the sake of it. However, it should be noted that those feigning stubbornness will most likely choose an issue they know is key to your strategy. If it's an important issue for you, state so and offer compromises that only gradually chip away at your own position. If the opposition accepts the early compromises readily, they were most likely feigning their intractability. If not, continue to subdivide the pie until "enough" has been had by both sides. If counterparts concede the entire issue, you can be assured they'll be looking for a payback in the near future.

PRAGMATISM

Practicality is something that any negotiator can suddenly claim as their own. Of course, what's pragmatic for one side may be onerous for another. Stating that something is just common sense assumes commonality of viewpoint. Pragmatism as a tactic can have great impact when discussions become argumentative, confrontational and emotionally charged. Multilateral negotiations, as opposed to the more common bilateral ones, are particularly conducive to the sudden introduction of pragmatic proposals by negotiators who sat on the sidelines and listened to a wide variety of viewpoints. When these "voices of reason" finally pipe up, they can distill all of the workable viewpoints into a single, rational statement.

Moderators are supposed to perform this function but are often remiss. Negotiators who take on this function informally may be called on again and again to take that role. Most who do make sure that their own needs are highly represented in the pragmatic distillation. Wisdom, real or imagined, does have its advantages. Practitioners of this tactic should be warned not to take on a patronizing tone when offering their insights. If anything, make it clear that your tactic is the result of "cherry-picking" ideas from the entire assembly. It's the practical thing to do.

Illegal Tactics

Even the most reputable companies can harbor unsavory elements. Many legitimate businesses have illicit components or beginnings. While the developing markets are very prone to illegal tactics (Russia and China are riddled with corruption), they must be considered when operating *anywhere* in the world. This section isn't an endorsement of these tactics, just an exposition. *Semper vigilans* (ever vigilant).

SURVEILLANCE

Depending on what country you're operating in, surveillance may or may not be illegal. It can take the form of having a person "assigned" to you by counterparts for both business and social events. At the next level it may involve teams of government operatives who "tail" you wherever you go. (The author has a terrible habit of being mistaken for a clandestine government agent in virtually every developing economy he has visited. The surveillance in some locales has sometimes extended through several visits over a period of years—all this while negotiating the most mundane of business. What starts as being intimidating can quickly become irritating, but the paranoia of counterparts and their governments never ceases to amaze.)

The tapping of phones is quite common, while the planting of listening devices and cameras in hotels and offices is well on its way to becoming a standard. (There are stories of a hotel in a major Asian city that is frequented by foreign business travelers in which the in-room phones never actually deactivate when you hang up the receiver. The handset continues to act as a microphone for all conversations.) Some companies even plant listening devices over counterpart's positions at the negotiating table to pick up whispered conversations during sessions.

This isn't just an information-gathering tactic. Sometimes the opposition makes little effort to conceal their surveillance, in the hope that it will apply pressure to counterparts. That pressure may result in added concessions, or it may simply remind everyone of who's in control of the playing field. Avoiding or ameliorating the effects of surveillance isn't difficult or expensive, nor is it always necessary. If you have nothing to hide, don't waste energy trying—let the other side expend their resources chasing shadows. If you do wish to maintain a level of security, or just plain privacy, hold important conversations at random locations and use public phones. Devices to detect "bugs" are relatively inexpensive but users should be warned that not all customs officials are forgiving when they find them in your luggage or on your person.

EXTORTION

The number of businesspeople who've been set up to commit an illegal or immoral act while traveling on business is legion. The objective of the set up was to blackmail the victim into influencing the outcome of negotiations. The tactic can be used against the opposing CN, but it is more likely to be deployed against a more junior member of the delegation. The influence being sought may involve the passing of inside information or the request for outright concession granting.

Practitioners may use prostitutes, planted drugs, "mickey" cocktails, staged fights, planted cash, or information obtained in the aforementioned surveillance to bring their victim to heel. The only ways to avoid these tactics are to pay attention, "keep your nose clean," and don't do anything you would be ashamed of if discovered. All three antidotes are easier said than done. Be forewarned that if you give into the demands of the extortionist there will be no end to their squeezing. They may even continue to contact you after you return to your home country.

DETAINMENT

Detainment is always possible when negotiating with a government or a company with strong political connections. Like surveillance, the legality of this tactic is a matter of perspective. When a negotiation doesn't go as planned, or the visiting group decides unilaterally to call off discussions, detainment may be used as a means to bringing about "resolution." Totalitarian governments are not afraid to use it, or its threat, since detention is the way they treat their own citizens when disputes arise. Even more democratic governments aren't beyond seizing passports and imposing house arrest until business is completed. In some cases, when deals don't reach fruition, foreign negotiators are seized during *return* visits for other business and detained until the first deal gets resolved. (There are many documented incidences of this in China where businesspeople have been seized in Macao and the then-British colony of Hong Kong to be trundled across the border on trumped up charges. The underlying charge however is that a Chinese company didn't think its "enough" was enough.)

The best way to avoid victimization by this tactic is to know whom you're dealing with and to stay on their good side—or at least the middle. Trying to hoodwink a governmental agency or their front companies in a totalitarian country is an unjustified gamble.

FRAUD

Do all negotiators resort to some form of lying? Yes. Is all lying illegal? No. Lies of omission are quite common in negotiating, otherwise there would be little need for strategy and tactics. Everyone would lay all of the information on the table, and their meeting would be over in an hour or two. But not telling absolutely everything that you know isn't the same as prevaricating. The deliberate misrepresentation of fact is generally considered to be immoral and if used to influence the outcome of negotiations, it's most often illegal. But that's not to say that it does not occur on a regular basis.

Some multibillion-dollar business deals, such as the Indonesian gold fields scam or numerous stock schemes, are based entirely on a lie. Happily, fabrications of this magnitude aren't that common. For the most part, lying as a tactic takes the form of overstated income statements, lightly "cooked" balance sheets, overly optimistic marketing surveys, cleverly worded research, bogus lines of credit, doctored statistics, and falsified letters of recommendation. There's the "little white lie" for which forgiveness can be sought and is almost immediately granted. At the other end, there's the "big lie," in which large groups of people must knowingly participate in order for it to work. Everything in between those two extremes can land the practitioner among the wealthy or among the incarcerated.

Some economies have stringent due diligence processes and active fraud squads to police business activities, both domestic and international. Others assume fraud is just a part of the normal business landscape and only seek prosecution when exposure causes public embarrassment. Penitentiaries are well populated with "information jugglers" who underestimated their counterpart's intelligence and reaction to being defrauded. While there is no 100 percent protection against this, and far less when working with translations, major problems can be avoided by trusting no one. Everything that *can* be checked out, *should* be checked out. Make it clear from the start of negotiations that the due diligence process is a standard practice and not a personal attack. Agree to nothing and sign nothing until the important facts of the issue have been verified. Be nice but be skeptical.

STEALING

George Bernard Shaw is credited with saying that "fools imitate, a genius steals." If this is true, then genius runs rampant in some economies. Industrial espionage has become not just a major problem but almost a standard operating procedure in some of the world's greatest and potentially great markets. It can take many forms and isn't always a tactic of last resort by a desperate negotiator. Often, it's their opening gambit.

Professional thieves abound in the world's airports, targeting distracted travelers and their luggage. Much of this is simple larceny, but some of the travelers are the subject of a specific negotiation tactic. Proprietary information kept in presentation materials, briefcases, and laptop computers will be stolen during an "unfortunate incident." This information will be taken directly to the victim's negotiating counterpart or competitor. Any such information uncovered during the surveillance mentioned above will be similarly distributed. Whole networks have sprung up in Europe, Asia, and North America for the sole purpose of stealing commercial information. (Many of Eastern Europe's post-communist states have turned their defunct "secret police" forces to the task of industrial espionage.)

Materials and laptops left in hotel rooms and meeting facilities will be rifled through and downloaded during social events or breaks. Negotiators may even be "mugged" on the streets in what appears to be a common street robbery. Victims can be assured that the thieves were after much more than their wallets.

Total protection from this tactic is only possible when security teams accompany negotiators (as is quite common now for foreign firms visiting the oil fields and mines of war-torn Africa). However, reasonable precautions should be taken by anyone who travels on business with important, saleable information. Those carrying laptops should keep them close at hand and stored in cases that don't readily identify them as computers. The same goes for PDAs and palmtops. Another precaution is to keep proprietary information on separate disks or thumbdrives, encrypted if possible. These disks should be carried on your person and safeguarded much in the same way as a passport or visa.

Hardcopies of information and other important presentation materials should be kept as portable as possible and never mixed in with expendable collateral, like brochures. Keep these with you at all times during meetings and stored in hotel safes when not. (In very chaotic or lawless locales, even hotel safety deposit boxes should be avoided, as the staff may be in the employ of counterparts or their operatives.) The best protection against the theft tactic is to treat information as having "priority one" importance. Sadly, most of this tactic's victims take better care of their traveler's checks than they do their company's secrets.

PHYSICAL FORCE

Businesspeople get threatened, beaten, and murdered everyday around the globe. Sometimes it's the same random violence that we're all subject to, but sadly, the perpetrators are often on the payroll of commercial competitors and venture partners. Physical force may be used to scare someone away from the negotiating table or to keep them at it. It may take the form of a threat or an actual attack. The threat may be stated openly or hinted at with varying degrees of subtlety. The attack can range from a mild roughing up to a savage beating, stabbing, or shooting. Death may be accidental or intentional. The perpetrators may be amateurish thugs or professional enforcers. Those responsible may be private businesspeople or government officials.

Most large companies discourage victimization by this tactic by supplying their traveling personnel with security teams. Those with fewer resources must look out for themselves. This tactic isn't deployed casually, even by government officials, and rarely during early stages of negotiations. While it's most often deployed against visiting negotiators, it may also victimize hosts. Its purpose is to obtain something (money, concession, ownership) that can't be obtained readily by other means. Thorough prenegotiation research should reveal whether counterparts are ready and willing to pursue their ends through violence or other illegal means. Knowing that a counterpart will react violently when backed into a corner is part and parcel of avoiding the tactic. Skilled negotiators should never be surprised that it *could* happen to them. Only the timing and the motive should be matters of conjecture.

Reacting to threats is a continuance of the war of nerves that high-pressure negotiations creates. Threats shouldn't be ignored or mocked. Assume they're real and pursue governmental protection if that is an option. If the host government itself poses the threat, visiting negotiators should seek out diplomatic personnel from their home country immediately. Talking your way out of the problem is an option (you are a negotiator after all), but having a backup plan will make your speaking voice a little less jittery. If the issue in question does turn out to be truly non-negotiable in the strictest sense, concede it and then "get out of town" on the next flight. There may be many things worth dying or taking a beating for, but an agenda isn't one of them.

BRIBERY

Bribery is the grease that lubricates the axles of much of the world's business. Whereas it may be a felony in the United States, in China it's simply considered one of the costs of doing business, like an informal tax system. This isn't to say that business in the United States is completely bribe-free or that every company in China works under the table. What can be stated without fear of contradiction is that all professional negotiators at some time in their career will be offered or solicited for a bribe. A sizeable number of them will participate willingly.

Even the very stringent Foreign Corrupt Practices Act (mandatory reading for U.S. negotiators) passed by the United States in the mid-1970s recognizes that the tactic of bribery is almost unavoidable. Though the act outlaws the bribing of officials for the sake of enhancing one's position during negotiations, it does allow for "facilitation payments" when the practitioner is only trying to get the official to do the prescribed job in a more timely or professional manner. Bribery of government officials is extremely common in the developing economies, where low pay for civil servants encourages the seeking of extra income. The payments can take the form of cash, automobiles, company shares, or lavish parties. Some governments even set up phony companies or country clubs and allow foreigners to become "shareholders" and "members" as a way to cover the trail of payments. While the ruse may protect you in the foreign market, your domestic government may have a different attitude.

Of course, not all bribery involves government officials. Counterparts may offer "sweetheart" deals, with side payments to cooperative management. They may boldly bribe the opposing negotiators in an effort to get them to sell out their company's position or just to obtain inside information. Proffering bribes during simple trades in the world's marketplaces has become almost pedestrian. Accepting a bribe is both a legal and moral choice, but there's other fallout. Once even the smallest bribe has been accepted, it marks the receiver as corruptible, and he or she can only become indignant about the amount of subsequent offers, as the moral high ground has been lost. The bribe tactic may also lead to extortion being used against you—a far cheaper method. Counterparts may threaten to inform the police or your own company unless you start to "play ball" during negotiations.

Being solicited for a bribe brings a rash of other concerns. Some tacticians will solicit for a bribe as a matter of course when they're in any form of buying position. They may even have budgeted for it when planning their negotiation strategy. Turning them down may be taken as a hostile action or as a clear demonstration that you don't understand their business culture. The same could certainly be said of their level of understanding where your culture is concerned, but they're dealing from a position of strength. If you do decide to turn down the request, you'll have the risk of canceling any chances for a deal—unless you're prepared to make other, more legal, concessions to counterparts as compensation. Tacticians have been known to solicit bribes from opponents knowing full well that they can't comply due to legal restrictions. They use this as leverage to coax other concessions from a counterpart when trying to compensate. This clever and effective maneuver can only be counteracted by moral indignation at having even been asked for a payoff and then only if you're in a relatively strong selling position. Otherwise, your choices are limited to two: comply or concede.

Complying with a request for a bribe has the same drawback that any form of appeasement does: one request always leads to another. Counterparts who solicit bribes (as opposed to those who just accept them when offered) are well aware of the manipulative value that bribery has. As in the case of extortion, anyone who can be convinced to pay once can be convinced again, and again, and again. If you're prepared—even budgeted—for it, then repetition presents no problem. Bribery certainly does have a value, as it makes the system run a little faster and a little better. There are places on the planet where you can't even get a phone installed without bribing someone. Some wags have even commented that bribery in the emerging markets generally works out to be roughly the same rate as licensing and lawyer's fees in the supposedly less bribery-prone developed societies. Right or wrong, bribery must be seen for its underlying tactical effectiveness and not merely as a means of lining someone's pockets.

Use Only What's Necessary to Attain Goals

Being well supplied with tactics doesn't mean that they should all be put into practice at once. Letting the opposition know your full capability can greatly limit future discussions. Negotiations can fluctuate in length and extend well beyond the original prediction. Playing all of your options early only allows counterparts to be prepared when the same tactic is trotted out a second time.

Strength at the negotiating table derives from being able to maintain a balance between the means and the ends. Learning to use just enough to get "enough" will come with experience and the recognition that not all heat creates light. Histrionics, power plays, grandstanding, and tantrums have very limited uses during professional negotiations. Negotiators must be great expositors while, at the same time, clever concealers of their own options and maneuvers. Subtlety is the norm for the professional, and finesse usually wins the day.

Daily Recaps

Negotiators should continuously review the successes and failures of their tactical plan, even when it's a simple one. Daily recap session should be held as soon after the close of daily discussions as possible. They must be held in private and well out of the earshot of counterparts. Local translators, drivers, and hotel personnel should be excluded, as they may be providing information to the opposition. Recaps should focus on whether the desired results for that day's session were met and whether overall talks are moving in the right direction at the forecasted pace. Mistakes must be acknowledged and remedies put in place. Teams must keep in mind that blame is not as important as solutions. If the original plan is showing success, stick to it and make sure all members are clear on future implementations. Even a solo negotiator should take time at the end of each session for review and reflection.

One mistake that novice teams make is changing their tactics because the opposition has changed theirs. It should be kept in mind that the reason counterparts have changed is because they're facing a well-thought-out strategy with suitably efficient tactics. There's no reason to believe that their revamped tactics will be more successful. They may even be less so. Having backup plans in the wings will permit speedy changes, in the event that the counterparts' new plan proves more effective than their first.

Assessment Techniques During Breaks

Recap sessions can vary in length depending on the agenda and the strategy of the opposition. Regardless of length, the recap must efficiently provide answers for the negotiator or team. The same questions that were asked in Chapter 12 when formulating the strategy must be reasked for two important reasons: To assure that the areas that are currently under discussion are being resolved in a manner that fulfills the original plan. To assure that all areas that were strategized are being considered with the level of emphasis forecasted. This second reason warrants special scrutiny, because it's easy to lose sight of agenda items during the activity and pressure of bargaining. Many negotiators have returned home with issues that aren't just unresolved but never discussed. And it's not always minor points that slip through the cracks.

WORKSHEET

The worksheet on the next page is provided so that the reader can match possible tactics (column 2) to a given strategy (column 1). The reader is also asked to choose a countertactic (column 3) as if predicting a counterpart's reaction. There's no one correct choice or response for any given strategy, and the reader should consider all of the potential combinations based on the position variants (e.g., host, buyer, visiting investor, third-party visiting trader). Choices must also take into account a true assessment of the reader's experience, technical skill, personality, and company size. Team tactics must reflect the same variables.

STRATEGY — TACTIC — COUNTERTACTIC WORKSHEET		
STRATEGY	TACTIC	COUNTERTACTIC
Aggressive		
Compliant		
Passive		
Impassive		
Intimidating		
Technical		
Financial		
Legalistic		
Secretive		
Deceptive		
Exploitive		
Stubborn		
Ambivalent		
Pragmatic		
Brinkmanship		
Arrogant		
Self-righteous		
Overwhelming		
Fleeting		
Stern		
Social		
Theft		
Indulgent		
Consensus		
Cowboy		
Platoon		
Divide & Conquer		
Jekyll and Hyde		
Hierarchical		
Horizontal		
Departmental		

CHAPTER 16

Closing the Deal

WHO MAKES THE DECISION?

THE DIFFERENCE BETWEEN a successful negotiator and a failure is the ability to close a deal when it has reached its maximum level of distributing "enough" among all participants. It's not that unusual for one side to achieve all of its goals relatively early in the discussions. In other cases, experienced negotiators will "front load" the agenda with their main needs so that they don't waste time on lengthy discussions that end in deadlock. Visitors with travel budget concerns do this quite often. In either case, closing the deal at this early stage leaves counterparts with many unresolved issues and may reveal the closer's true motives. Because of this, the deal is best closed when the agenda has been exhausted.

Don't succumb to the urge to rush the agenda or rely on the ability to "hammer out the details later." If your strategy was well thought out, it should be followed to its conclusion. Consider the fact that counterparts may be depending on your desire to wrap things up quickly as a means to get a contract signed before all of the bad news hits the table. Impatient visitors can be very susceptible to this and will find they have little legal recourse in the foreign courts once the contract is signed.

Buyers usually have the say as to when a deal will be closed, but they can be encouraged to do so by savvy sellers. This is why every salesforce in the world has its "closing specialist" whose job it is to convince the buyer that "enough" has been had and it's time to transact the deal. International negotiations differ only in the fact that the buyer/investor is usually much better informed than a standard customer. Both sides have an equal chance to close the deal, and the more proactive the decision maker is, the greater the chance of controlling the process.

When Is It Time To Close?

Here are the ten questions that must be asked directly or indirectly of all participants to determine if it's time for closure.

1. Have all points of the agenda been discussed?
2. Have the financial ramifications of all points been thoroughly delineated?
3. Have the technical aspects of the deal been reviewed?
4. Have the local and international laws applicable to the deal been researched?
5. Are all active parties to the deal logistically capable of performing their functions?
6. Is the time line set for the deal realistic?

7. Do all parties recognize the short- and long-term consequences of the deal?
8. Are all parties in agreement as to the language and terms of the deal?
9. Do all the parties to the deal trust each other?
10. Do all potential signatories have the requisite authority to act on their company's behalf?

Knowing When to Say "No"

Sometimes the appropriate response to an offer laid on the negotiating table is "no." Declining a deal, and doing so in the proper manner, is sometimes the Silver Medal of international business—not ideal, but respectable. There are many reasons to decline, and doing so doesn't necessarily mean that *no* deal can be cut. Declining may just initiate the call for future talks once the deal-breaking aspects have been resolved. In other cases it may expose the need for the participation of additional parties. Because this potential for future dealings is so important, declining the deal must be done with the greatest diplomacy, even when the counterpart is suspected of the most egregious subterfuge. Although you may have no intentions of ever dealing with these particular counterparts in the future, maintaining your reputation within the international business community for levelheaded dealings is important.

REASONS TO DECLINE OR POSTPONE

Here are some valid reasons for declining or postponing a deal.

1. Cannot resolve financial issues
2. Unable to obtain proper contract assurances
3. Unfavorable legal environment or criminal intent by counterparts
4. The deal is too exposed to political instability
5. Counterparts are noncommittal
6. Counterparts become intransigent
7. Counterparts lack the wherewithal to fulfill contract requirements
8. Counterparts lack the organizational skills to make the deal function
9. Corruption reduces profit to unacceptable levels
10. Economic environment becomes unfavorable
11. Counterparts prove untrustworthy or unprofessional

True failure only occurs during negotiations when a bad deal is cut. Such a deal may even turn out to be bad for all parties concerned. On the other extreme, a perfect deal is rare, because it demands that all parties maintain both their needs and wants. Negotiations are like any other form of business in that they involve risk. Risk management demands that skilled players know when they've won "enough" *and* when they should stay out of the game.

Avoiding Being Victimized by "Practice Negotiations"

The desire to enter the exciting and profitable world of international business can often lead to becoming a victim of someone else's learning curve. Some companies like to use what appear to be formal negotiation sessions as a way of practicing for upcoming discussions with another company. This subterfuge is most often practiced by host companies new to the international marketplace, and they will most likely cast their net from developing economies. They're hobbled either by a lack of research materials in their home country or by budgetary restrictions that prevent them from the foreign travel necessary to securing "on the ground" information about potential counterparts.

Discussions may be conducted in a conventional, even friendly, manner with no indication that they're heading nowhere. Victims may be given every indication that their proposals are sound and acceptable, or they may be fought on every point, regardless of importance. In either scenario, the side with the information deficit is simply testing its strategies and tactics against an opponent similar to its future opposition. The victims of this simulation may have been chosen for their national, cultural, racial, technological, industrial, or economic characteristics.

Negotiators must use their own discretion when they suspect that counterparts or potential counterparts are none too serious about the outcome of discussions. Here are some basic ways to determine the seriousness of counterparts before entering into expensive and time-consuming negotiations.

- Ask counterparts during the early contact phase why they've chosen your company specifically for these talks. If their answers are vague, pursue the next topic.
- If this is their first foray into a technological or industrial sector and you're *not* a leader in that sector, ask what other competitor companies they've contacted. If they say "none," ask why and proceed with caution. If they refuse to say specifically what companies were contacted don't bother with follow up. If they do indicate contact with competitors, ask if actual negotiations took place and the reasons for their results.
- Ask counterparts to give a clear indication of their time line for the project. If they are sellers, ask what quantities can be shipped and when. If they're seeking investment, ask how much of the control of the company they're willing to relinquish. If they're buyers, ask if they've already secured their lines of credit and what quantities will be required for shipment. If they're investors and their inquiries were unsolicited, ask for reference letters.

Some of these questions may appear to be somewhat blunt; the exact wording is left to the discretion of the negotiator. However, getting answers to these questions early on can save a lot of time and expense that would otherwise be wasted on research, travel, and negotiations.

CHAPTER 17

Reporting Results

Is 99 Percent Enough?

INTERNATIONAL NEGOTIATING isn't only a business process, it's a learning opportunity as well. Each session—large or small, productive or unproductive, heated or boring—can offer the participants the occasion to add to their own store of knowledge and skill. After strategies have been formulated, tactics deployed, decisions made, and contracts either signed or declined, detailed reports should be compiled and reviewed. This can aid greatly in several company processes and should be considered part of a company's information database.

The Value of Record Keeping

1. It keeps other members of management informed of important dealings that are taking place far from their view or direct control. It bears repeating that negotiations are very expensive for host or visitor and that cost must be justified. This will be even more important when no contract is forthcoming from the negotiations. The introduction to this book remarked on the need for informed management, and the reader is reminded that such information flow is paramount.
2. Negotiators can review their own actions as well as those of counterparts once they're distanced from the heat of discussions. It can be very surprising how transparent a tactic can be when viewed in retrospect. Just the process of organizing the reports and putting them on paper can lend insight in to what really happened. Negotiators may sometimes have to face up to what appears to be glaring mistakes on their own part. Painful as they may be, the lessons of twenty/twenty hindsight tend to stick.
3. Consultant negotiators must make detailed reports if they plan to continue in that line of work. Simply returning from negotiations waving a contract, or worse nothing at all, isn't going to win the favor of the client. While consultants may not wish to give their negotiating secrets away or expose every blunder, a reasonably straightforward report will, at the very least, let the client know what their money was spent on besides airline tickets and hotel rooms.
4. Perhaps the greatest value of a detailed report is its use as a teaching tool. Every negotiation opens new opportunities for a company to expand into the world's markets. A small company may start with a solo negotiator, then proceed to using a small team and then several teams operating simultaneously. It will need records so that each negotiator or team can build upon the successes and avoid the mistakes of their predecessors. If these reports become lost in the myriad of company documents or they're hoarded by upper management, a valuable companywide resource has been lost.

Guidelines for Post-Negotiation Reports

The following guidelines for writing post-negotiation reports will allow for their long-term use.

1. Compose the report as if the reader knows nothing of the companies or participants involved. The reports may still be in use long after the compiler has left the company or ceased to be employed as a negotiator. The report will have little use as a learning tool if major points have been treated as givens.
2. Treat the negotiations as a whole, from planning through completion. Personnel selection processes, planning sessions, travel arrangements, facility selection, and contract follow up should be included. Negotiations don't take place in a vacuum, so there's no reason to report them as such.
3. Be specific. Reports are filed so that both participants and nonparticipants will have a clear understanding of what went on during discussions. Details about anything and everything that affected negotiations should be included. Generalizations such as "morning sessions went well . . ." or "our offer was not well received . . ." don't address root causes. These types of reports are often referred to as "postmortems" and should have a detailed factual base to match the scientific, though unfortunate, nickname.
4. Give the bad news as well as the good. Few people like to admit their own mistakes, let alone commit them to paper. However, it must be understood that learning comes from mistakes as well as success. If the negotiations were ultimately successful, then the emphasis will be on the positive. If they were less than hoped for or a complete failure, attempts to whitewash them will be readily transparent. State the facts and let them speak for themselves.
5. Summaries should be prepared *daily* while negotiations are in process. Don't wait for discussions to finish in order to try and remember what happened on day one. Teams should have discreet notetakers at every session, and solo negotiators should commit their memories to paper (or pocket recorder) as soon after each session as possible. Talks may drag on for days, and the whirl of travel may turn a whole week into a blur. Accuracy counts.
6. Each daily summary should be followed by a brief analysis of the proceedings to that point. Tactical changes should be noted and their effect on strategy weighed.
7. Since the overall document is retrospective reporting, each daily summary and analysis should also be followed by recommendations for future discussions and advice on how to avoid pitfalls. These recommendations often turn out to be the most valuable part of the report-filing process.
8. Prepare an executive summary. If negotiations are lengthy and the reports contain the requisite detail, the account can run to hundreds of pages. The summary will allow those members of management interested in "the big picture" to get a handle on the process. The summary should contain a recapitulation of the entire negotiation, an analysis and an overall recommendation. Consultant negotiators should gain a clear level of understanding about how detail oriented their client company is prior to embarking on negotiations. Consultants should keep detailed records for themselves.

CHAPTER 18

Commitment

THE STRAIN OF IMPLEMENTATION

THE BURDENS OF TRAVEL are over, tense negotiations have come to a close, the sixteen-hour work days have reverted to normal length, and the detailed reports have been written. Now the real work begins. A common problem among negotiators is that they return to their companies, contract in hand, with the belief that the job is complete. Unfortunately "the deal" is only a piece of paper at this point. Proper follow through by all participants will really be the test of whether negotiations were a success or a failure. Follow through can even save negotiations that were a "wash."

Exploiting the Investment

Investors rarely move into a market unless the timing is right. Those seeking investment generally have strenuous time constraints. Both groups also understand that the window of opportunity can close quickly. Political upheaval, exchange rates, and market movements can turn twenty-four hours into an eternity. And yet, after spending a great deal of time and money on negotiating a venture, either side or both may start to drag their respective feet during execution of the contract. This can happen because investors suddenly become wary of their new partners or because the recipients of the investment feel that, in retrospect, they got a poor deal.

In the first case, the company receiving the investment must do everything they can to assure the investor that the whole process will go as planned. A sudden change in the legal or political environment may even require a return to the negotiating table. Both sides must be committed to making the deal work to overcome these hurdles, but the greater part of the burden is on the investment's recipient. In the second case, the burden of commitment is reversed. Investors must convince their new partner that the deal as contracted will be to the benefit of both parties. While the counterpart's lack of commitment should have been discovered during the original negotiations, new information (or suitors) may be at the root. Here again, a return to the table may be required to save the venture.

Of course, many times there's no real problem, only different senses of urgency. When investment is at the center of the deal, the pace will be set by whichever party has the *lesser* need. Companies hungry for investment will move at the whim of the investor. Investors hoping to gain marketshare in advance of competitors will find that the commencement of the venture will be very much controlled by their new partner. While a certain amount of gamesmanship is to be expected, all parties contracted are recommended to operate in compliance with the stated terms. In today's marketplace, positions of power change rapidly, and the puppeteer can swiftly become the puppet.

Buyers and Sellers

The commitment between buyers and sellers in a simple trade may be significantly shorter in duration than that of investment venture, but it should be no less strong. Sellers that ship late, ship partial orders, or ship inferior or no product at all can put the quietus on the best of negotiations. Buyers that return specified goods, refuse delivery, renege on letters of credit, or pay late or never at all can have an equally devastating effect. Barring extreme circumstances, such behavior by either party shows a lack of commitment to the deal. If the offending party is a long-time player in international business, their procedures should have been uncovered during proper prenegotiation research, and the victims can only blame themselves. A degree of patience and recognition that failure may be an option will be required. Commitment requires that the victims salvage what they can.

If these deal busters are novices, the opportunity exists to save the deal and educate the offenders as to the value of commitment. Often times new players in the arena aren't fully aware of their responsibilities or the ramifications of poor performance in trade. Those on the receiving end of the poor service or products need to make these novices aware that reputations make the difference between long-term and short-term players. They must be assured that they'll be unable to solicit other business unless the contract is fulfilled as written. This posture may ring hollow with the truly devious who make up a small portion of traders. Commitment to completion here will not guarantee full success but will secure enough to make continued contact worthwhile.

Following Up on Failure

Even when negotiations have been a true failure and a bad deal has been cut, follow through can lead to success. A contract is a contract, and novices as well as experienced negotiators will, on occasion, sign "bad" ones. It doesn't change the fact that the contract must be fulfilled if there's to be any expectation of long-term operations in the marketplace. Besides avoiding the legal fallout, following through on a less-than-ideal contract will secure a reputation for commitment and honesty that can be exploited in other deals. It may also lead to a chance to renegotiate the original "sour" deal once counterparts recognize your integrity—not always, but sometimes.

Negotiations that have resulted in one side declining the proposed venture also demand follow through from *professionals*. Rarely are the differences irreconcilable and they may only hinge on changes in the marketplace uncontrolled by the negotiation's participants. If your's is the side that declined the deal, assuming you did so gracefully, maintain contact with the counterparts and express your continued interest in future dealings with their company. Maintaining some form of relationship, even if it's as simple as a company newsletter or seasonal greetings, will keep your company in the "mix" if a potential deal does arise. It may even lead to a referral to a company that can provide the goods, services, or investment opportunity desired.

If your company was on the receiving end of the refusal, take heart and don't take it personally. Find out the cause of the rejection and make every effort to seek a correction. Proposals may be rewritten, budgets reconsidered, product lines reworked, and policies reinterpreted. Maintain contact with the counterpart, thanking them for their considerations while expressing your continued desire to work with them. Resubmit your reworked proposal and offer to reopen negotiations. In the words of experienced salespeople everywhere, "'No' just means 'not now.'" The worst that could happen is that you get a reputation for persistence.

Rules of Follow Through

ONE: BE PROFESSIONAL

The term *professional* is used for those who've attained a high level of expertise in business. They have gotten that far because they've learned to separate personal feelings from their business life. This isn't to say that they aren't passionate about business. Professionals are the most committed of any participants in a deal. For them, "a deal is a deal" and whatever was agreed to must be acted upon by all concerned parties. Personal differences, emotions, wounded pride, or inflated egos aside, a professional will follow through on a contract. Anything less is unthinkable.

TWO: BE OBSERVANT

Following through isn't the same as plunging ahead blindly. Circumstances that surrounded negotiations may have changed significantly. Politics, finance, and even geography may have all taken a turn for the worse since the deal was signed—or maybe for the better. Few contracts have zero wriggle-room and negotiators must build as much of it into a deal as they can to allow for unforeseen circumstances. Those following through must be observant in order to catch those circumstances when they arise. Being able to observe what new found partners are doing is also part of follow through. Whenever possible, members of the negotiating team should be left "on the ground" until the contract is in full force and running smoothly. It's okay to trust the other party, but that trust must be verified.

THREE: BE NICE

Even when the sternest of strategies has been used to close a deal, there is always room for cordiality. Avoid quibbling over meaningless details and proceed with the execution of the contract. Patience will be required to some degree in all business dealings and in the early stages of follow through, especially with novice counterparts, who may put you to the test. Keep in mind that the relationship may last for decades and there's little to be gained by enmity among the participants. It's also best to remember that in the future, *your* mistakes may require the cordial patience of your new partner.

FOUR: BE RIGHT

No one is right all of the time. Successful people learn to keep quiet unless they're sure of their position. Follow through is the period in which all of the problems that weren't worked out at negotiations rear their ugly little heads and the chances to offer solutions are myriad. Your way of doing something may be *a* right way, but don't assume it's *the* right way. New deals in foreign lands or involving foreign companies can bring a whole new set of "tools" to the table for fixing these problem areas. International business has a hundred times more commercial, political, legal, cultural, racial, and geographical variables than the already complex world of your domestic economy. Experts are few and far between in international business circles and their areas of true expertise are limited. Don't pretend to be one on every issue. Study the options, all the options, and choose the best.

FIVE: BE ON TIME

Much of the follow-through process revolves around the setting of standards to be utilized for the duration of the commercial relationship. Each side is demonstrating their interpretation of professional behavior and testing the limits of the counterparts methods. Fair enough. Your goal should be to do all things required of you in a punctual manner. Attendance at meetings, filing of reports, submittal of financial information, shipment of goods, payment of bills, injections of capital, and distribution of profits should *always* be done on schedule—with no exceptions. This will be particularly important in the early stages of follow through, when reputations are won or lost. Setting high performance standards allows you to make similar demands of counterparts. Start early, maintain standards, garner profits.

The Lessons

Be clear on these points when approaching international negotiations.

- Negotiating is a complex process that requires extensive research.
- Paying attention to details isn't optional. It's mandatory.
- Success is a well-planned choice.
- Every moment is crucial.

CHAPTER 19

Strategic and Tactical Guidelines by Country

ARGENTINA

COMMERCIAL ENVIRONMENT

Argentina is one of the more affluent countries in South America, and on the continent it's second only to Brazil in GDP per person. Food processing, with an emphasis on beef and grain exports, is a major industry and there are also considerable manufacturing and tourism sectors. It's the most heavily European influenced of the Latin American countries, and these influences carry over into the negotiation styles. Although Argentina has a past history of inflation and excessive state intervention, its new government is committed to a stable currency and foreign investment. The government has also put a new emphasis on attracting technology firms to this formerly agricultural country. Spanish is the primary language (for business and contracts), although English, Italian, and German are widely spoken.

COMMON STRATEGIES

- FOR TRADE: Impassive, Aggressive, Stubborn
- FOR INVESTMENT: Social, Hierarchical, Departmental

NOTES FOR NEGOTIATORS

The Argentinians see few rivals for themselves in the realm of sophistication. This is conceivable from a cultural if not commercial viewpoint. They're hard bargainers, willing to dig in their heels if they feel they're not being treated as equals.

Concessions are granted in small increments, even when the Argentinians are bargaining from a weak position. Every point of the agenda will be hard fought. Come prepared for the long haul.

Although there has been a great deal of privatization in recent years there are still pockets of entrenched bureaucrats. Proceeding with discretion and keeping a low profile will do much to limit interference.

Argentina is a land of connections and a wide range of "inside tracks"—ranging from family to the industrial sector to politics. The overlap between one's social and business life is substantial, and a recommendation (or condemnation) carries a lot of weight here.

Make contact as far up the organizational chain as possible. Hierarchies are the predominant management structure, with very little decision-making power filtering down the chain of command. Starting in the middle will only prolong the process and extend your negotiating budget.

While written contracts will be detailed, Argentinians prefer to do business with friends. Visitors who exhibit a cultured interest in Argentina and its people will have an advantage at the negotiating table. Meetings will be very formal and pecking orders are observed for seating and introductions. While meals may be part of the protocol, business is rarely discussed during mealtimes.

Be punctual, but don't become upset if your Argentinian counterpart exhibits a more casual approach to time. Visitors, whether buying or selling, are held to a higher standard.

When discussing your own company or business culture, take care to not make unfavorable comparisons with Argentina. And under no circumstances should Argentina be lumped in with the rest of South America.

Politics is a very sensitive issue, and the country's militaristic past is a topic to be avoided at all costs. Even mentioning that you saw the film or the play *Evita* may set off a torrent of comment. British companies, and perhaps even their American allies, may find some residual resentment from the Falklands conflict. In all cases, the fewer political references the better.

AUSTRALIA

COMMERCIAL ENVIRONMENT

Australia is a Western-style democracy. Over the years, its various governmental administrations have, in their turn, embraced Asia and shunned it. Because it's 95 percent Caucasian, it's often seen by its Asian neighbors as a Western outpost. A well-educated nation, it has one of the highest per capita GDPs on the Asian Pacific Rim. Labor unions are quite strong; mining and manufacturing are key industries, although agriculture is a mainstay. Australians are very active as investors throughout Asia, and they export a great deal of food to neighboring ASEAN countries and China. Foreign investment is welcome. Australia is a technological leader in the Pacific, especially in telecommunications.

COMMON STRATEGIES

- FOR TRADE: Aggressive, Pragmatic, Indulgent
- FOR INVESTMENT: Social, Cowboy, Platoon

NOTES FOR NEGOTIATORS:

Australians shun formality and are recognized as some of the friendliest businesspeople on the planet. This belies a tough bargaining ability. They're masters of the Social strategy.

Be direct while negotiating, as the Australians are keen to spot deception and they have no qualms about walking away from the table if they feel you're holding back information. Since formalities are minimal, negotiations move at a quick pace. Show up on time and come prepared. Australian managers tend to be more "hands on" than most, so technical details will be welcomed and understood.

Even when bargaining from a very strong position, avoid the appearance of taking control. Attempting to "lay down the law" will only create resistance. The Australians will already understand the secondary nature of their own position, and reminders of it could foul the deal.

The Australians don't mind putting on a little pressure when they're buying or investing. The limitations of your proposal and the availability of competitors will be cited on a regular basis. Waiting for the price to drop is an Australian pastime.

Keep your offers realistic but leave yourself some wriggle-room. The Australians will haggle, but only to a small degree. Making a hyperbolic offer at the start will not be perceived as the opening of bargaining but as an indication of your lack of realistic goals.

Contracts will be written, detailed, and enforceable. All parties are expected to adhere to the letter of the contract, as the Australians have well-developed commercial law. Handshakes are an amenity; signatures mean business.

Because of their relatively small population and remote locale, the Australians have become experienced travelers and negotiators. They do detailed research on target economies and companies, with an eye toward limiting surprises at the table. Be assured that they'll know all about your company and culture before the first meeting.

The Australians are a tough breed and they enjoy competition. They never shy away from confrontation and will go toe-to-toe with anyone. While their outlook on success and failure is somewhat fatalistic, they encourage long-term relationships and prefer to work with people they count as friends.

BELGIUM

COMMERCIAL ENVIRONMENT

The city of Brussels is considered by Belgians, as well as by many other continentals, to be the "capital" of Europe. All major economic and political decisions regarding the European Union flow from there. Antwerp is the third-largest seaport in the world, and it guarantees Belgium's leadership in international trade and transport. The country has a strong engineering component and a robust steel industry, and it's a top player in the world's diamond market. Because of its role in European shipping, transportation equipment also accounts for a great deal of its exports. The country is a hybrid of Dutch (Flemish) and French (Walloon) cultures, though the twain seldom meet in this country of ten million. This conflict seems inexplicable to outsiders but can have an enduring effect on business negotiations and social gatherings.

COMMON STRATEGIES:

- FOR TRADE: Pragmatic, Stern, Technical
- FOR INVESTMENT: Pragmatic, Hierarchical, Departmental

NOTES FOR NEGOTIATORS

Though socially the Belgians tend toward the casual, business meetings are somewhat formal. First names are rarely used, except among friends; Mr., Mrs., and so on are customary. French or Dutch equivalents can be used as well.

The Belgians are technically astute and prefer presentations with a great deal of factual information. Get right to the point and avoid trying to "sell" the concept. The facts will have to speak for themselves.

This is the land of commercial pragmatists; outlandish schemes will receive scant consideration. Proven technologies and recognized services tend to do the best.

Do detailed research into the background of the company you're contacting. Written materials should be translated into the appropriate Flemish or Walloon. Don't under any circumstances confuse the two cultures when negotiating, as it will cause considerable conflict.

Belgians are generally recognized as tough but likable negotiators. They've established themselves in Europe by being able to understand and absorb other cultures. Belgians have little fear of economic colonization and always bargain as equals.

Don't attempt to "throw your weight around" or otherwise remind the Belgians that they're a tiny country in a very large world. They've heard it all before and can afford to say "no" to just about any deal.

Because of this nation's limited resources and land area, thrift is highly prized. Proposals that squander assets, whether financial or personnel, will be highly criticized. Keep it conservative and watch those pennies. Set up meetings far in advance and confirm them upon arriving in-country. Be punctual, you can assume your Belgian counterparts will be.

Though the Belgians pride themselves on their polyglot tendencies, contracts are enforceable only in the local dialects of French or Flemish. English is widely spoken, as is German and a multitude of other European languages.

Beer production is a national treasure, and business visitors can be expected to enjoy the social aspects of its consumption. The Belgians drink for taste rather than quantity, and they appreciate a fine palate. Visitors who can hold forth on brewing varietals and production methods will find themselves in good stead at the negotiating table. (The same holds true for those with an appreciation for Belgian art.)

BRAZIL

COMMERCIAL ENVIRONMENT

Brazil is the largest country in South America, with a GDP per capita that is almost twice the size of China's. Primarily an agricultural society, Brazil exports a great deal of beef, leather, and textiles, but it also supports flourishing chemical and consumer goods industries. Plagued by recurrent debt and inflationary problems, the government has instituted numerous "austerity" measures to keep the country on track. The communications infrastructure and high-tech industries are target areas for investors and government-backed schemes alike, and they'll remain so for the next decade.

COMMON STRATEGIES

- FOR TRADE: Compliant, Deceptive, Social
- FOR INVESTMENT: Divide and Conquer, Departmental, Social

NOTES FOR NEGOTIATORS

Titles are very important in Brazil and business conversation remains formal. Calling a counterpart by their first name may be reserved for social occasions or for business after a long-term relationship has been established.

Brazilians are very proud of their language (Portuguese) and resent being confused with their Spanish-speaking neighbors. Never refer to them as South Americans and never attempt to speak Spanish in place of Portuguese—although most businesspeople will understand both. Translate business cards and presentation materials into Portuguese, but avoid speaking it unless you're fluent.

Brazil is a lively place and its people emotional. Presentations should have a bit of panache, and the presenters should exhibit a good deal of excitement about the proposal. Sticking to the facts and figures will not impress counterparts, whether buying or selling. Conversely, don't be surprised when your Brazilian counterparts erupt into emotional exchanges among themselves. Such passion is not to be seen as outright dissent but as part of the histrionics that accompany much of life in Brazil.

Brazilians aren't shy about bargaining, and they tend to grant concessions only toward the end of negotiations. While the pace here may be quicker than in other South American cultures, don't expect lightning fast results. If your schedule becomes known, time constraints will be used against you. If you're unfamiliar with the commercial landscape, use an intermediary to guide you to the proper contacts. There's a very large social component to doing business, and meeting the right people will not only lead to fruitful negotiations but will also ensure long-term viability of the project.

For all of their formality and relationship building, Brazilians have a reputation for loading a lot of dubious factual information into the early negotiations. It's their way of keeping you interested while supplying the requisite wriggle-room if things go sour. They're expecting the same from counterparts, participation is up to the individual negotiators.

Regardless of what your hosts may say, get everything in writing, with as many specifics as possible. Never assume that you'll be able to work out those irksome details later or that business can be conducted on a handshake alone. While legal protection for foreigners is good by developing market standards, there's little advantage in putting it to the test.

CHINA

COMMERCIAL ENVIRONMENT

China is a fast rising world economic power, but it still suffers from substandard GDP per capita and infrastructure. Commercial law is nascent and highly favors domestic companies. However, since little commercial law exists, a system of *quanxi* (connections) functions in lieu of contract enforcement. Foreign companies invest in China primarily for its cheap labor rates and in the hope of accessing future consumers as per capita wealth increases. The government is slowly privatizing but it still has a very shaky banking sector. Foreign firms have done well in China, although exporting profits back home is considered problematic due to China's inconvertible currency. Corruption, both public and private, is rampant and virtually unavoidable.

COMMON STRATEGIES

- FOR TRADE: Deceptive, Indulgent, Social, Exploitative
- FOR INVESTMENT: Deceptive, Impassive, Departmental, Hierarchical

NOTES FOR NEGOTIATORS:

The Chinese have little compunction about deceiving foreigners. Don't rely on the other side's sense of fair play. The Chinese recognize how interested foreigners are in accessing this developing market. Investors may be led into agreements that are difficult to either execute profitably or to dissolve quickly.

Profit repatriation is difficult at best and should be an early part of the agenda. Don't wait until the end to find how much you can take back home.

When buying, write explicit quality requirements into trade deals, as quality tends to taper off after the first delivery. When selling, extend no credit whatsoever. If all of the people who are still owed money by Chinese importers got together, they could apply for nationhood.

Friendship, or the appearance thereof, is a common ploy to secure concessions. There may be ulterior motives behind lavish dinners and invitations to meet family members. Accept these events as gestures only.

Competitors are regularly pitted against each other, sometimes at the negotiating table. Letting foreigners fight over them is a long-standing tradition here, but now the Chinese set the terms. Some form of graft will be built into the agreement.

Don't assume that the person who appears to be in charge is actually in charge. Verify, in writing, important issues before moving on to other parts of the agenda. Referring to a two-day old spoken statement will have no weight—unless, of course, you said it.

Never use a translator supplied by your Chinese counterparts. If you're a non-Asian and speak Mandarin fluently, don't be surprised if the Chinese pretend they can't understand you. The difficulty of their language has been a tactical tool for centuries, and they resent having the code broken. Whenever their statements appear contradictory, it will be blamed on an interpreter.

Take notes and be prepared to exploit inconsistencies across the table. They'll be doing the same.

Patience is greatly appreciated, while anger and impatience are considered signs of instability.

Never reveal proprietary information until a deal is completed. The Chinese don't recognize "nondisclosure agreements." In all negotiations, make it clear early on that you're ready, willing, and able to say "no" to their proposals.

The Chinese make much of the "harmonious relationship," and the leader never delivers "bad news." The downside is always delivered late in the negotiations by a second-in-command—often at the banquet that follows a contract signing. Damage can be limited (not eliminated) by early statements to the effect that the contract will be subject to renegotiation if "unforeseen" circumstances change the deal's outcome.

EGYPT

COMMERCIAL ENVIRONMENT

Compared to the other Arabic oil-producing nations, Egypt has a surprisingly low GDP per capita, US$5,500. Its other big industries, textiles and food processing, are keeping the country afloat, and the government has recently held off an Islamic fundamentalist movement that threatened another big money maker—tourism. The country has been a crossroad for international trade for millennia. But, dealing with foreign investors is quite another matter, one that's very much bound up with the nation's colonial past. While not sporting any high-growth economic figures, Egypt still attracts a great deal of both trade and investment interest.

COMMON STRATEGIES

- FOR TRADE: Aggressive, Secretive, Exploitative
- FOR INVESTMENT: Consensus, Jekyll and Hyde, Self-Righteous

NOTES FOR NEGOTIATORS

Haggling is a national pastime in Egypt. Foreign traders had better come prepared for some schooling in how to bargain. Nothing has a set price from day-to-day, and a sharp haggler is greatly respected. In fact, not attempting to bargain aggressively will be taken as an insult.

The legacy of Egypt's British colonial past is a bureaucracy not unlike India's. Lots of delays, official reviews, and rubberstamping of documents will be part of any medium to large project. Use Egyptian contacts to help smooth the way or circumvent officialdom, but in no way should the bureaucracy be confronted or criticized. Once it closes ranks against your project, Moses himself couldn't find an escape route.

While you may admire punctuality, your Egyptian counterpart will most likely have a more relaxed approach to time. Lateness and postponements aren't unusual and they fit in quite well with the local tradition that whatever happens was meant to be. Arrange appointments in advance of travel and confirm them regularly upon arrival in-country.

By North African and Middle Eastern standards, the Egyptians are quite familiar with modern business practices, although they don't always apply them to local enterprises. Their own system is somewhat formal and hierarchical. Rarely are first names used among business acquaintances, and titles abound.

Foreign firms are warned to have a solid agenda agreed upon before arriving at the negotiating table. All but the largest Egyptian firms will take their cues from what they perceive to be more successful foreign companies. Much of the Egyptian strategy is reactive, even when in a buying position.

Contracts, regardless of detail, are considered guidelines for business relationships rather than full delineations. The content of the document may be renegotiated, revised, and appended many times throughout the length of that relationship. Constant contact must be maintained with Egyptian partners and their commercial "temperature" constantly monitored. In addition, government interference or outright interdiction in the negotiation or contract process may occur for large projects or those involving internationally recognized brands.

Don't enter into business negotiations until a fairly long period of relationship building has taken place. Having the right connections and doing business with the right people can (in and of itself) prevent a great deal of delay and expense. Intermediaries may be used early in the process, but long-term and close contact must take place on a personal basis.

FRANCE

COMMERCIAL ENVIRONMENT

The French view their business culture as singular, much in the same way that they view themselves as a special European people. Business is a means to an end, not an end in itself. The French don't often define themselves in terms of what they do for a living. Business is rarely conducted with a sense of urgency, and personal relationships are important. The French are generally considered to be a highly educated and sophisticated people. Well-read and cosmopolitan counterparts are appreciated. The economy tends towards socialism, and many of the largest industries are partially state owned. Social issues are often a major concern when business is discussed.

COMMON STRATEGIES

- FOR TRADE: Indulgent, Intimidating
- FOR INVESTMENT: Intimidating, Hierarchical, Social

NOTES FOR NEGOTIATORS

Unless you speak fluent French, use an interpreter. Proper use of the language is a sensitive cultural issue. Even when selling, the French consider rushing to be vulgar. The more you rush, the more they'll slow the process down.

Don't try to out-French the French. Even if your counterpart lacks basic social graces, allow him his sense of superior sophistication. Exploit it if you choose.

Corruption is tolerated rather than promulgated. If graft is part of your program, be discreet.

Be well prepared for every negotiation session. "Getting back" to someone will not do.

The French will discuss every point at length and will have a position on every topic. Avoid direct confrontation unless you're in a strong buying position. The French love debate but not intense criticism. It will be taken as a personal attack.

All French men and women fancy themselves to be philosophers. Early meetings may have a large component of nonbusiness discussion. Your opinions will be solicited and evaluated. Not having an opinion in France is worse than having a badly formulated one. Even if you're in an extremely strong buying position, resist the urge to "cut to the chase."

The French are notorious for coming to the table with a single strategy and its accompanying tactics. If they've made a completely inappropriate choice, major postponements may result while they reformulate their position. Possibly exploitable, always annoying.

This is a very social culture, and negotiators may find themselves at two-hour lunches. Drinking wine will be part of the process. Keep your wits about you. You may be wearing a US$2,000 suit, but it will mean nothing if you pick up the wrong silverware or shy away from the oysters.

Contracts may be long and involved, even when you are buying. All contracts must be completely in French, and commonly used foreign words cannot be substituted (e.g., computer).

This is the land where bureaucracy was invented. Red tape can be a big part of negotiating, especially when dealing with government-connected companies. Business abounds with regulations. No matter how intense negotiations become, avoid raising your voice. Doing so is a sign of poor breeding.

GERMANY

COMMERCIAL ENVIRONMENT

Germany's very efficient business sector is devoted to *ordnung* (order). It has the most expensive labor force in the world but maintains a respectable productivity level. The workforce is highly unionized, and union members sit on the controlling boards of companies. As many of the country's firms have moved their manufacturing overseas to remain competitive, unemployment has skyrocketed. Consequently, the German government (as well as regional officials) have actively sought out foreign investment. The Germans are considered to be the powerhouse of Europe and the keystone of the European Union. While the absorption of East Germany has continued to be a drag on the overall economy, no one foresees the Germans relinquishing their leadership role anytime soon.

COMMON STRATEGIES

- FOR TRADE: Impassive, Intimidating
- FOR INVESTMENT: Technical, Pragmatic, Hierarchical

NOTES FOR NEGOTIATORS

Codes and regulations dominate the business environment, so be prepared to comply with a rule for virtually every aspect of your project.

Contracts in Germany are even more detailed than in the litigious United States. Contracts, once signed, are strictly adhered to by all parties.

When selling, make straightforward presentations. The Germans will be interested in the reasons for purchasing goods or services, rather than the image that surrounds the purchase.

Maintain formality and observe all hierarchies. While the Germans aren't averse to the occasional raucous social event, business-related events should be designed to maintain the dignity of all parties.

Be punctual. This goes for meetings, delivery dates, payments and social gatherings. If you're allotted thirty minutes for a presentation, don't exceed it. All meetings are planned with a start and a finish time. Germany is a land of precision; a lax attitude toward time is seen as an indication of general slovenliness.

German is a difficult and precise language. Translated materials must be perfect or the content will be disregarded. The Germans appreciate anyone who has taken the time and trouble to master their language, but they tend to denigrate those who've taken half measures.

You must be thoroughly prepared to answer any and all questions regarding your proposals. The Germans have little regard for people who "have to get back" to them.

The Germans tend toward a just-the-facts approach when conducting business. Introductions and preliminaries are brief, so be prepared to get right to the point. If your technique relies on charm and guile, this country will be difficult for you to tackle.

The Germans frown on workaholics (the average vacation is four weeks). Business is seen as a means to enjoy the finer things of life, not an all-consuming passion. Personal lives are kept separate from business. Avoid personal inquiries or the volunteering of information about your home life.

Don't criticize your competitors or those of your German counterparts. Each company is judged on its own merits, without comparison to others.

The Germans love to delve into the details of a proposal and shun "big picture" type presentations. They tend toward the hierarchical and view dissension in the ranks as an indication of poor preparation.

Statistics and charts are a mainstay of the German negotiator and are often used to hammer home their superior technical knowledge.

INDIA

COMMERCIAL ENVIRONMENT

India has made great strides since departing from socialist economics in the early 1980s. Its currency, the rupee, is convertible, and the heavily bureaucratic control of business by the "license-quota-subsidy raj" has been greatly diminished, though not eliminated. All industries (with the exception of rail transport) are open to varying levels of foreign investment. The stock market has a functioning oversight board and is generally more sophisticated than that of rival China. While it has had trouble with a somewhat xenophobic nationalist movement in recent years, India is generally considered to be one of the more welcoming of the Asia's emerging markets. Predicted to have the largest population of any nation on the planet in the next decade, India is "in need" in virtually every economic sector.

COMMON STRATEGIES

- FOR TRADE: Social, Deceptive, Compliant
- FOR INVESTMENT: Consensus, Departmental

NOTES FOR NEGOTIATORS

India is an ancient culture with splashes of modernity throughout its business sector. Some companies run on a strict consensus basis, while others maintain more horizontal styles. Research each company thoroughly (at the highest contact level available) and find out the nature of their management style.

India has numerous dialects, and contracts must be written in the vernacular. English is widely spoken and will most likely be the language of negotiation.

Regardless of the efficiency of counterparts, bureaucracy at local and central government levels remains lethargic. Expect delays and kick your patience into high gear.

Avoid the use of your left hand for passing items—especially food. The left hand is considered unclean as it's used by Indians for personal hygiene. Be aware that much traditional Indian food is eaten with one's fingers, rather than with utensils.

Although it has numerous female political leaders, women rarely take part in business, let alone important negotiations. Female team members may be taken to be secretaries by Indian counterparts, and every effort must be made during discussions to establish their credibility.

Internal religious feuds and India's colonial past are very sensitive subjects. Avoid discussing them unless they have a direct bearing on the outcome of the project.

Many large companies are family owned and operated, with upper management the purview of siblings. Don't assume that good relations with a single family member constitutes access to the source of commercial power. Internal rivalries can be bitter, personal, and long-standing. Make associations carefully and only after dutiful research. Choices, good and bad, can follow you throughout this large but closely knit country.

Indians are a warm and welcoming people who enjoy harmonious relationships. Confrontation isn't considered a respectable form of discussion. Like many Asian cultures, directly saying "no" is thought to be rude. Indians would sooner postpone meetings or send along subordinates until the message gets across.

India is very diverse and regionalized. Don't assume that strategies that were successful in one city will necessarily work in another.

INDONESIA

COMMERCIAL ENVIRONMENT

Indonesia is the largest Islamic nation in the world. Its more than 13,000 islands and its 200+ million people are ruled by a strong central authority. Much of the commercial class is of Chinese ancestry and subject to considerable resentment by the native population. The government is a "mandatory" player in any large project. Key industries are petroleum production, tourism, textiles, and mining. Indonesia is one of the rising stars of Asia and has considerable resources, both natural and human. Primarily agrarian until just 30 years ago, the country has made enormous strides toward industrialization—an accomplishment for which it's held up as an example to other developing Asian nations.

COMMON STRATEGIES

- FOR TRADE: Deceptive, Compliant, Brinkmanship
- FOR INVESTMENT: Consensus, Hierarchical, Departmental, Indulgent

NOTES FOR NEGOTIATORS

Indonesians negotiate virtually every aspect of their daily lives, from taxi rides to groceries, so you can expect considerable haggling over even the smallest point. Part of this is a cultural norm, but much of it is an attempt to wear down the opposition.

This is an Islamic culture but hardly fundamentalist. Only in rare circumstances will foreign businesses have to make religious-based concessions beyond basic dietary and prayer requirements.

The Indonesians are hospitable by nature but are not beyond putting a foreigner "in debt" for kindnesses rendered. If you attempt to reciprocate for every indulgence offered, you may find yourself giving away important concessions for very little.

Like many societies in Asia, this one is prone to hierarchy. Managers only bargain with their equals, so you may find that negotiations take place at levels that correspond directly to job titles. The greater the number of people in your party, the more complex the discussions will become. Keep it simple.

While contract signings may be treated with great hoopla, don't assume that the document will be strictly adhered to by an Indonesian partner. Contracts are simply guidelines for the "harmonious" relationship. Be prepared for the continual monitoring of the contract's requirements.

Keep relationships healthy and avoid making the Indonesian side feel subordinate. Confrontation can cause enormous "loss of face," even when counterparts are clearly in the wrong. Subtlety and finesse must rule the day. Keep in mind that Indonesian courts and arbitrators rarely produce findings in favor of foreign companies. It's either get along or go home.

Bureaucracy is deep in a government rife with patronage jobs. There's no getting around it, and large projects will necessitate local input as to how to navigate through the red tape.

Bribery is a standard form of getting things done, and the price goes up if the recipient has to ask. These bribes may extend to the lowest level of transaction (you often have to make payoffs just to get your car through an intersection), so be prepared to grease some wheels, both big and small. Failure to negotiate a reasonable payoff will mark your company for continuous shake-downs. If your home country has severe restrictions on bribery, you may find that a number of "consultation" fees will be attached to your project. Budget accordingly.

IRELAND

COMMERCIAL ENVIRONMENT

Ireland merged from the shadow of being one of Europe's "sick men" to achieve the highest rate of GDP growth in the European Union. Many of the world's high-tech companies have flocked here to take advantage of the island's educational excellence and investment incentives. Ireland has made the full transition from agriculture to services (now 67 percent of GDP), with many financial institutions using the workforce for back-office operations. Conflicts from British-held Northern Ireland have ceased and no longer affect the Republic. The infrastructure has been massively improved through the injection of European Union funding, and no recipient country has matched Ireland's successful implementation. Its low corporate taxes make it a favorite of international firms and the object of scorn by more highly taxed neighbors.

COMMON STRATEGIES

- FOR TRADE: Compliant, Secretive, Social
- FOR INVESTMENT: Platoon, Divide and Conquer, Horizontal

NOTES FOR NEGOTIATORS

The Irish are noted for their shrewdness and are renowned as the best horse-traders in Europe. They can drive a very hard bargain and always appear ready to walk away from the table.

Ireland has been absorbing invaders for centuries and treats commercial arrivals much the same. Smiling hosts will charm even the most hardened negotiator into making concessions thought unthinkable days before. If you're charmed easily, watch out.

This a land of highly educated people; masters degrees abound at the managerial level. Highly technical presentations will be readily understood and appreciated. Any attempt to treat Irish counterparts as second rate will be met with much resistance. The error in judgment will be made evident quickly and pointedly.

The Irish language, Gaelic, is alive and well, especially in western Ireland, but English is used for most business. Government documents will be presented in both languages. The Irish are accomplished linguists, and translators for most European languages are easily obtained.

These are a very social people, and there is no such thing as a short conversation in Ireland. Politics, religion, and many other topics are wide open for discussion. Bear in mind that the Irish are extremely well read and will know more about your country than you will. Confrontation isn't something the Irish fear, so don't enter into one lightly, whether business-related or not.

The Irish have always been a clever people but have only recently had access to the capital necessary to maximize their skills. Centuries of poverty have made them very pragmatic, though not adverse to risk. Always willing to bet on a sure thing, they'll give equal consideration to a "long shot" if the odds are right.

When making presentations, offer the upside first, but don't worry about presenting the downside. The Irish will have no compunction about calling your bluff if they think you're hiding something. They're masters of secrecy themselves and can spot it in counterparts immediately.

Business and pleasure are regularly mixed, and your tongue may be loosened at the pub as part of a divisive strategy. Both guest and host are expected to "buy a round." Though drinking is quite prevalent, getting inebriated at a social function isn't considered businesslike. Enjoy yourself but stay on your toes.

ISRAEL

COMMERCIAL ENVIRONMENT

Starting in the mid-1980s, Israel changed its economic model from socialist to market-driven. Given its tumultuous internal political environment and its seemingly ceaseless conflicts with its Arab neighbors, the country has managed to remain one of the most successful emerging markets in the Middle East. It's a leader in food production, food processing, and diamond cutting. Recently both government and industry have placed a great deal of emphasis on research and development, transforming Israel into a high-tech center. The government is very protective of domestic enterprises and issues many subsidies for start-ups. Foreign investors are rarely permitted to have controlling stakes, except in the largest of enterprises involving guarantees of technology transfers. Israel has few natural resources; imports tend to run 40% above exports.

COMMON STRATEGIES

- FOR TRADE: Aggressive, Exploitative
- FOR INVESTMENT: Brinkmanship, Intimidating, Horizontal, Jekyll and Hyde

NOTES FOR NEGOTIATORS:

Generally Israelis see themselves as a special people and are thus not bound by rules—any rules. Internally, this independence is accepted behavior, but it can cause conflicts in the global marketplace. Israeli negotiators will often disregard the requirements of counterparts, even when they are in a weak selling position. A clear reminder early in negotiations about who is calling the shots can prevent misunderstanding.

Israel exists in a constant state of controlled chaos, which Israelis refer to as *balagan*. Punctuality and deadlines are demanded of foreigners but not of themselves. Israelis often attribute this approach to the country's tenuous political and geographical position and the Jewish history of rootlessness. Be prepared for late arrivals and a lack of urgency to get things done.

During discussions, expect to be interrupted repeatedly. While in most cultures this is considered rude behavior, Israelis consider it a sign of interest.

Israelis are very proactive negotiators and like to anticipate their opponents' moves. Unveiling your plans slowly keeps them preoccupied with guesswork and less focused on their own maneuvers. Sudden changes in personal style also tend to spoil their plans.

There's very little socializing attached to business; lengthy introductions or small talk will fall on deaf ears. Israel is a great place to do business if you enjoy a brisk pace and quick yes-or-no discussions. If your strategy involves long, drawn-out negotiations with numerous postponements, Israel will be a tough nut to crack.

Israeli discussions usually take the form of straight talk called "talking *dugri*," which is a no-frills, in-your-face approach to repartee. They'll have little compunction about calling your proposal unworkable or poorly researched. Expect no sugar coating. However, don't make the mistake of responding in kind. Israelis are very thin-skinned when it comes to foreigners and their criticisms.

Don't underestimate the role of Jewishness in doing business here. If you or members of your team are Jewish, play it to the hilt. If neither case is true, avoid discussion of religion. Don't try to disregard the fact that preference will be given to Jewish-owned businesses and their representatives. Finding and fostering the right connections in Israel will result in long-term success.

Avoid discussions about Middle East politics or the founding of Israel. You may be sounded out on this topic by Israeli hosts, but it's best to avoid the bait. Keep the talk focused on business.

ITALY

COMMERCIAL ENVIRONMENT

Italy is often considered a problematic member of the European Union. Its volcanic domestic politics, frequent bouts with inflation, mounting public debt, high unemployment, and high government spending have combined to make it almost impossible for the country to meet its European Monetary Union (EMU) goals. Despite these problems, Italy has turned in some surprising domestic market successes. Its manufacturing, auto, and clothing industries have continued to make progress, while high-tech companies are burgeoning. Italy tends to run trade surpluses (10 to 12 percent), and non-EU investors will find that acquiring an Italian partner is the most efficient way to gain market access.

COMMON STRATEGIES

- FOR TRADE: Social, Compliant, Exploitative
- FOR INVESTMENT: Consensus, Divide and Conquer, Social

NOTES FOR NEGOTIATORS

Time is not of the essence in Italy, but punctuality is appreciated. Schedule meetings far in advance and confirm them upon arrival in-country. Only deadlines that are repeatedly insisted upon will be met.

Connections are very important, a process the Italians refer to as *clientelismo*. This amounts to someone, or some company, giving a good reference about you to your potential counterpart. These are very personal references, much deeper than the standard letter of introduction. These connections take some time to develop as personal integrity and loyalty are at stake.

Italy is highly regional (there's very serious talk of the country splitting into three politically separate areas); much research and relationship building must precede any investment move. Even with simple trading, on-the-ground research is recommended.

More so than most other EU countries, Italy will require a patient outlook when approaching business deals. The Italians like to do business with not just friends but respected friends. It may take a while to gain their confidence, but the effects will be long lasting.

The Italian manufacturing sector is known for a high level of quality and accompanying prices. While cost control is everyone's concern, any indication that you want to do something "on the cheap" will get a poor reception. It's all in the phrasing, and interpreters have to be well-schooled in your country's vernacular.

Italians are impressed with counterparts who share their cosmopolitan tastes. Expressing a genuine appreciation of art, music, food, and fashion will keep you in good stead with the locals. Avoid the just-here-on-business approach.

Count on participating in a good number of social events and lengthy meals as part of business protocol. When it's your turn to reciprocate, seek the aid of a local—hoteliers or restaurateurs are good sources.

Italians can be argumentative about virtually everything. The raising of voices and flailing hand motions are national pastimes. Don't be fooled. This is just passionate discourse, not signs of anger. It's rarely directed at counterparts, but witnessing such an interaction across the table may give the wrong impression about the cohesiveness of the other team's position.

JAPAN

COMMERCIAL ENVIRONMENT

The "bubble economy" of powerhouse Japan burst long ago. Today, Japan's economy is what may be described as "sputtering." However, the country is a long way from destitution and will hold its status as one of the top economies in the world for some time to come. Japan is slowly (some say almost imperceptibly) moving away from its more interventionist approach to more competitive market economics and is breaking down the protective walls used for decades to shield its now-powerful industries. Illicit behavior in both the government and private sectors is now regularly exposed in a culture that, just a few years ago, would have considered the process unthinkable. Most observers regard this change as a sign of a more mature, less insular Japan.

COMMON STRATEGIES

- FOR TRADE: Consensus, Impassive, Ambivalent
- FOR INVESTMENT: Consensus, Divide and Conquer, Deceptive

NOTES FOR NEGOTIATORS

Letters of Introduction from a *chukaishu* (well placed go-between) are essential for doing business here. As in much of Asia, having connections in Japan is the only way to get through the front door, unless you represent an internationally recognized brand name.

Individualism is not a characteristic of Japanese negotiators; they rarely come to the table in groups smaller than three. If you're a solo act, you'll still be confronted with a team even for simple trades. Be prepared for a number of informal trade barriers and restrictions on foreign investment—they'll make no apologies for their protective system. Meetings will be very formal and the company hierarchies will be observed. Keep in mind that the person doing the most talking for the Japanese side will most probably *not* be the person in charge of the negotiations. This permits all mistakes to be covered by "speaking out of turn" excuses and prevents the company from making commitments until they've seen the entire proposal. The Japanese will not discuss points that are not part of the prearranged agenda.

Small talk will be kept to a minimum and inquiries into personal lives will rarely be made or accepted. Meetings will be highly orchestrated; the Japanese don't like surprises. Have your presentation materials translated into Japanese and keep them detailed.

Japanese negotiators are famous for their ambiguous responses to proposals. They view vagueness as a form of protection from "loss of face" in case things go sour. Contracts are viewed as guidelines and any problems are arbitrated, rather than litigated. Contracts will almost always include a *jijo henko* clause that permits complete renegotiation if circumstances change. The system works well in Japan but many foreigners, especially Westerners, find it disconcerting.

Consensus is a life-style in Japan and the *ringi* system of moving information up and down the chain of command can be a true test of patience for foreign companies. The Japanese aren't noted for being able to "think on their feet" so don't expect quick answers to any question or problem.

Cost of capital is very low in Japan (often less than 1 percent), and they can afford to take a long-term approach to profit making. The Japanese have traditionally sought market share over quick returns and they expect foreigners (especially investors) to share their commitment to long relationships. Be forewarned: a "quick" return on investment in Japan is about ten years.

The Japanese maintain harmony at all costs and will smile the most when they're the least comfortable. At the negotiating table, a toothy grin is a sign of trouble, not acquiescence. If your proposal is unacceptable, you won't be told "no" in a direct manner. Postponements and requests for further research should be interpreted as a prelude to failure.

MALAYSIA

COMMERCIAL ENVIRONMENT

Three decades ago, Malaysia was little more than rice paddies and rubber plantations. Today, it's home to one of the world's tallest buildings and touting its "high-tech corridor." Essentially an Islamic (though secular) nation, it has combined the innate talent and energy of its native population with the mercantile strength of its Chinese minority to produce one of the most dynamic economies of Asia. While it still maintains strong agricultural, petroleum, and rubber manufacturing components, this nation has hitched its wagon to high-tech and is positioned, both physically and economically, to become the major technical player in ASEAN. Though it suffered a serious currency devaluation in the late 1990s, the economy remains strong and attractive to investors and traders alike.

COMMON STRATEGIES

- FOR TRADE: Aggressive, Impassive, Ambivalent
- FOR INVESTMENT: Consensus, Hierarchical, Jekyll and Hyde

NOTES FOR NEGOTIATORS

Malaysia has a very formal, almost ritualized, culture. In a country with a potential for numerous ethnic and religious conflicts, the preservation of "face" and the importance of mutual respect keep things running smoothly. The country's colonial past makes Malaysians highly suspicious of foreigners—at least initially. When in doubt, stick to the formal and err on the side of appearing overly respectful. If it's too much, your Malaysian counterpart will discreetly make it known.

As in much of Asia, the direct approach is considered rude and lacking in finesse. Pleased reactions will be downplayed and negative ones completely covered with distractions and forced smiles. This isn't lying, per se, but a way of avoiding embarrassment for both sides. Until something is in writing, assume "yes" means "we can continue discussions," and don't ever expect a direct refusal.

The Malaysians are a detail-oriented people; discussions may drag on as every point is exhaustively dissected. Foreigners can take such nit-picking as a sign of great interest. Short discussions mean it may be time to reschedule your flight for an earlier one.

Consensus decision making and hierarchical lines of communication will be an additional drag on negotiations. Even the most powerful head of a Malaysian company will submit to group thought. You can't rush it and you can't avoid it, so just allow time for it.

Most large companies are Chinese owned, but by government edict they must have a native Malaysian component. Most of the ethnic Chinese have taken Malaysian-style names to downplay any resentment. Foreigners should avoid any mention or exploitation of this rift, and it's a criminal offense to incite ethnic rivalry. As far as you're concerned, all counterparts are simply citizens of Malaysia.

Most business discussions will involve some form of socializing, usually over a meal. The Malaysians are rightfully proud of their cuisine and see it as a national treasure. Don't expect alcohol to be served unless the major players are non-Islamic. If your in-country stay is lengthy, you'll be expected to reciprocate with a banquet of your own. Seek local help in setting this up, as the protocol is fairly rigid.

Contracts are considered secondary to the quality of the personal relationship of the principals. You must keep the relationship strong and current if you expect to succeed here. Almost all contracts contain some form of escape clause to release both parties if things go sour.

MEXICO

COMMERCIAL ENVIRONMENT

Mexico has been economically and politically turbulent over the last two decades. Massive currency and debt problems have been exacerbated by political assassinations and corruption at the highest levels of government. None of this, however, has seriously damaged the country's attractiveness to foreign investors. From the success and conversion of *maquiladoras* established just inside its borders by its northern neighbor to the growth of Japanese auto plants, Mexico continues to make a serious contribution to both NAFTA and world trade. Low labor rates and liberal (by other emerging market standards, at least) foreign investment packages further Mexico's drive for success.

COMMON STRATEGIES

- FOR TRADE: Compliant, Self-Righteous
- FOR INVESTMENT: Hierarchical, Consensus, Social

NOTES FOR NEGOTIATORS

Formality marks Mexican business at all levels. The system is very hierarchical, and communication is directed downward. Only "equals" address each other on familiar terms and only after a lengthy relationship. Meetings consequently take on a very stilted air and much care will be given to seating arrangements and introductions.

Mexican society, both cultural and commercial, puts a great deal of emphasis on the showing of proper respect among its participants. Slights, whether real or imagined, are potential dealbreakers, and Mexicans are noted for their sensitivity to foreign opinions. The smile that looks like a smirk or the fatigue that's mistaken for boredom can bring the most lucrative deal to a screeching halt. Even investors and buyers must steer clear of these sensitivities.

Relationships are extremely important here and even short-term business will require them. The establishment of these *palancas* is part of the system of reciprocity that's at the economy's core. There's little doubt that some of this relationship building will result in graft; foreign visitors should be prepared for that contingency.

Mexico has a well-deserved reputation for bureaucratic lethargy—the result of the entrenchment of the PRI as the nation's ruling party. While the situation is improving, projects involving foreigners (especially U.S. citizens) receive extra scrutiny. Even barring government intervention, life is slow-paced and patience will be required for even small trades. Those in a hurry are advised to look elsewhere for business opportunities.

Attitudes toward punctuality and deadlines are nowhere near the extremes of the *mañana* stereotype, but Mexicans do view work and business as a means rather than an end. If punctuality or a deadline are important, that sense of urgency must be instilled early in the relationship. Mexican businessmen will readily agree to deadlines and payment schedules that (in their eyes, at least) will be regarded merely as guidelines.

Contracts are a matter of personal interaction in Mexico, and this attitude is reflected in the scant commercial law. Contracts are only honored among "friends"; lawyers hold little sway. Foreigners should be reminded that Mexican courts are heavily weighted toward domestic companies.

Mexico is the land of *machismo,* with male dominance and gender roles placing high on the list of sensitive issues. Female foreign executives may find the going very tough when attempting to maintain their business role, and they'll see no female counterparts across the table. Mexican men simply don't take direction from women and they have little respect for men who do. Bucking the system will unquestionably have a deleterious effect on the deal.

PHILIPPINES

COMMERCIAL ENVIRONMENT

This island nation has come a long way from its status as the "sick man" of Asia. It has learned a great deal from the mistakes made by the other emerging markets of ASEAN and has sought growth at a manageable pace. Foreign investment laws have been revamped to grant majority ownership even in the banking industry. The country has pursued build-operate-transfer-style infrastructure investments to solve its energy and communications needs while attempting to avoid environmental degradation. It remains an agrarian-based economy with pockets of industrialization, and it sees itself as having a productive future in shipping and tourism due to its prime location in the Pacific Rim. The successive governments have instituted a program to emphasize deregulation and modernization while creating numerous Export Processing Zones and Special Development Programs throughout its far flung archipelago.

COMMON STRATEGIES

- FOR TRADE: Compliant, Secretive, Social
- FOR INVESTMENT: Indulgent, Hierarchical, Deceptive

NOTES FOR NEGOTIATORS

Negotiations in the Philippines are conducted in a very formal manner. Company titles are very precise and are used to maintain the hierarchy. Locals will take on a very rigid manner when dealing with foreigners in an effort to preserve what they believe is a professional appearance.

The Filipinos are strong believers in forging relationships and maintaining *pakikisama* (smooth relations) at all costs. Confrontation is unthinkable and a sign of disrespect. Part of this process is the *utang na loob* (reciprocity) system whereby one business (or political) connection leads to other, more lucrative, deals. Acceptance of a favor or reference will call for a larger one in return. Beware the Filipino bearing gifts—a simple "thank you" will not suffice.

While the government has made a genuine effort to attract foreign investment, it still takes action to override contracts and nullify their terms. This is all part of the "Filipino First" policy that it has pursued in recent years to protect domestic industries from foreign "exploitation." The policy usually comes in to play when lucrative deals are given to the more competitively priced foreign firms. Having *pakikisama* with powerful people will limit your risk of being victimized by this policy.

Tsismis (gossip) is both a hobby and a business weapon. Competitors, both foreign and domestic, can be the subject of the most ridiculous rumors imaginable. This effort to set up intrigues, thereby derailing negotiations or even contracts, is a standard procedure. Keep an eye on your *pakikisama*.

Like many former colonies, the Philippines puts a great deal of emphasis on maintaining one's *amor propio* (self-respect) when dealing with foreigners. If you're buying, make sure you do nothing to demean your counterparts as the revenge will be in missed deadlines and quality problems. If you're selling, learn how to bend over backward.

Laws of all kinds are very flexible in the Philippines and are applied in direct proportion to the amount of money at stake. *Lagay* (bribery) is very much a part of any business, especially big business. The money will be paid in some form or another, and individual negotiators must be prepared to satisfy both their Filipino counterparts and their home country judiciary. Leave your moral baggage at home and pack extra savvy.

Higher education and advanced academic degrees are held in very high esteem. If you have some academic initials to include after your name, do so and expect favorable results. When introduced to counterparts with similar distinctions, inquiries into the particulars of their education will be met with enthusiastic responses.

POLAND

COMMERCIAL ENVIRONMENT

Poland has moved from the sluggishness of a centrally planned economy to become the strongest commercial entity in Eastern Europe. Its growth figures are on par with the emerging markets of Asia, and its government is making a sincere effort to dismantle unproductive state-owned companies. Poland has a strong iron and steel sector, as well as formidable machine manufacturing facilities. It still imports a great deal of fuel and foodstuffs, often in exchange for manufactured goods. The Poles have a dynamic culture, clear-cut ideas about their economic future, and little desire to permit a repeat of the colonization that plagued their past.

COMMON STRATEGIES

- FOR TRADE: Intimidating, Stubborn, Social
- FOR INVESTMENT: Consensus, Departmental, Social

NOTES FOR NEGOTIATORS

While its culture and language are quite old, Poland as a nation is relatively young, and it has only recently emerged from under the shadow of the Warsaw Pact. Foreign negotiators must recognize that this is a country with a mission to make up for lost time. Don't start negotiations unless you're serious. If you're here to do research, make that clear.

Poland achieved a fairly high state of industrialization under Soviet dominance and is now looking for technical development. Negotiators will be pressed for technological transfers, not just for investment funds and plant construction. It's best to hold this concession until all other points have been dealt with effectively.

For all of their desire to move ahead, the Polish decision-making process is woefully slow. Consensus rules the day and communication is rigidly hierarchical. Much of their internal debate may take place away from the table, but it's time consuming nonetheless. Any postponements will most likely be the result of internal problems and not necessarily the result of a proposal's shortcomings.

Foreign negotiators from longtime capitalist economies must keep in mind that properly prepared financial statements and property valuation are new concepts. Trying to get an accurate answer about what the counterpart's company is worth or its potential for growth will be just that—a trying experience. It may seem that you're being intentionally deceived, but for the most part it's lack of training. If such documentation will be required, get preliminaries prior to travel so that you'll know how much work is ahead of you.

Don't arrive in Poland with only a single plan for trade or investment. Develop a variety of positions that can be presented as the negotiating terrain changes.

Be punctual and be prepared. This highly educated population sees punctuality and follow through as indicators of respect. Remember, this is the former Second World, not the Third World.

Socializing, especially drinking, is a big part of business life. If you're not a big imbiber, keep a low profile; it's better to abstain than to make fool of yourself. Women are rarely found at the managerial level, although the Poles will not object to female counterparts. Still, after-hours socializing may not include these female executives.

RUSSIA

COMMERCIAL ENVIRONMENT

Russia is the geographically largest sovereign nation on earth, with a wealth of natural resources that alternately suffers from exploitation and neglect. The fall of the Soviet empire left Russia with massive debts and a devalued currency that was inconvertible as late as 2006. Even now, U.S. dollars and euros are the preferred scrip. The "new" Russia originally made enormous strides in its effort to throw off the burden of central planning but began to reassert state control once the inequities of privatization became clear. Solid predictions of long-term, high single-digit growth are attracting large but prudent investments. Russia has seen the steady rise of the *mafiya* in business and the renewed scrutiny of business by the state.

COMMON STRATEGIES

- FOR TRADE: Aggressive, Intimidating, Deceptive
- FOR INVESTMENT: Hierarchical, Social, Intimidating, Brinkmanship

NOTES FOR NEGOTIATORS

Russians may be new to international commercial negotiations but they're old hands at negotiating with foreign powers. They have clear agendas (although you may never see them) and no strategy or tactic is off-limits. Russia is no place for amateurs. Send your best.

Arrive at the table with clear objectives and a hard-line stance. Make few concessions early in the discussions, but know that your Russian counterparts will make numerous, inconsequential ones. If you play by their rules, you're doomed. Remember that Russia needs practically everything—including you.

The Russian people are extremely warm and gregarious. It's very difficult to dislike them on a personal level and this can be used against you. Parties, dinners, and introductions to friends and family, while socially standard, can lull the foreigner into a belief that they'll be treated as friends at the negotiating table. Enjoy yourself but separate business from pleasure.

Much of the difficult discussion at the table will be about how the buyer pays the seller. If the Russians are selling, they'll want to be paid in advance with a "hard currency," which to them is just about anything but the ruble. When they're buying, payment will be delayed and you can guess what the preferred currency will be. Foreign investors should never, under any circumstances, agree to single block transfers of cash. Keep the transfers small and dependent on preset benchmarks.

Although it has left central planning behind, the Russian decision-making apparatus is very bureaucratic. Even the simplest deals will take a great deal of time when compared to other industrialized powers. Numerous trips will be required for medium to large ventures.

Just as the geography lies between Europe and Asia, so does Russia's attitude toward contracts. It's best to get as many details written into the document as possible, in the hope that most will be complied with during the course of the agreement. Important points must be continually emphasized, as the Russians tend to look at the totality rather than the details of a contract.

The *mafiya* is a major player in Russian business. Foreign businesses are regularly "shaken down" and their personnel "roughed up" by its representatives. Don't expect that you'll be able to exact any kind of pressure against them at the negotiating table. They're a de facto subgovernment and must be courted accordingly. Bribery is as common as taxation. If you can't deal with this unsavory aspect of business, Russia isn't for you.

SAUDI ARABIA

COMMERCIAL ENVIRONMENT

Saudi Arabia is both the center for Islamic culture and a wealthy petro-state headed by a royal family with absolute power. Oil is its only industry, and its huge land mass contains only 28 million people (that includes almost 6 million foreigners). Due to its wealth, much of the labor force is expatriate, imported from the poorer nations of Asia. The nation is dependent on foreign firms for the majority of its infrastructure and its construction. The Saud family oversees all major commercial deals and has tried to move the economy into the steel and cement industries with limited success. Most private businesses are services directed at the petroleum and petro-chemicals industry.

COMMON STRATEGIES

- FOR TRADE: Impassive, Arrogant, Social
- FOR INVESTMENT: Hierarchical, Stern

NOTES FOR NEGOTIATORS

Most of the people you'll be negotiating with will be directly associated with the royal family. While your punctuality will be taken as a sign of respect, your counterpart's lateness is a sign of power. The Saudis rarely see themselves as "needing" foreigners and do little to ingratiate themselves.

The Saudis are very wealthy but unwilling to admit to their limited business skills when it comes to dealing with nonpetroleum issues. Impassivity and stern countenances often belie confusion. It's best to permit the Saudis their facade of shrewdness, as long as you understand its depth.

Your Saudi hosts will want to "size you up" before getting down to business. Social banter will precede business; it should be left to the host to decide when there has been enough chit-chat. This social aspect of business requires that a lengthy "courtship" predate the actual deal. All business, regardless of contracts, is conducted on a person-to-person basis.

The Saudis see themselves as a special people. They take a very arrogant, almost take-it-or-leave-it, attitude toward foreigners. Most of the country's wealth came after World War II, and its people are still trying to overcome a past in which they were subject to foreign rule. Negotiators must understand the cultural background in order to understand their counterpart's posturing.

This is an Islamic (though not fundamentalist) state and home to the most sacred site in the religion, Mecca. Usury (the charging of interest for loans) is forbidden under Islamic law. Therefore, negotiators need to come equipped with a variety of imaginative financial packages in order to comply. Islamic banks don't charge interest but become partners in the project, thereby fully risking their investment.

Bargaining usually starts at an artificially high level when the Saudis are selling and below ground level when they're buying. Don't be put off by these sometimes ridiculous offers. It's just a traditional starting point and is used to provide the maximum room for maneuvering.

Women have absolutely no role in Saudi business. Bringing female executives to the negotiating table to wrangle with Saudi counterparts may spell disaster. If your company wishes to force the issue, do so only after performing in-depth research into the local customs regarding the appearance of women in public. Even the U.S. military had to make concessions on this point during the Gulf War—and they were in the strongest of "buying" positions.

SINGAPORE

COMMERCIAL ENVIRONMENT

Singapore is often held up as an economic model for other Asian countries. Strict civil and criminal laws are matched by regular government intervention in commercial activity. Its meteoric rise as a commercial power in Asia was funded largely by outside groups. Singapore was considered a "developing" nation as late as 1989 but is now seen as a hi-tech and financial services hub. It's a shipping and transportation powerhouse, and its wealthier companies are very active in investment throughout Asia.

COMMON STRATEGIES

- FOR TRADE: Aggressive, Impassive
- FOR INVESTMENT: Secretive, Consensus, Exploitative

NOTES FOR NEGOTIATORS

Singapore is a former colony and its independence is relatively new. Singaporeans are very suspect of outsiders, especially Westerners, and fear being bested at the negotiating table—as much for the economic loss as the perceived loss of status. When you're winning, avoid any appearance of smugness.

Pay close attention to details. There's scant legal protection for foreign companies here, and all loopholes will be exploited massively. Don't be shy about getting everything in writing, as your counterparts will be relying on your lack of confrontation to get their way.

The Singaporeans are practitioners of realpolitik and don't put much emphasis on the value of the personal relationship. While socializing may be part of the negotiation process, it's something that will be used to lull the visitor into a false sense of trust. The smiling face that treated you to dinner last night is the grimace that meets your gaze across the negotiating table today.

Singapore is a mixture of Chinese and Malay cultures but its pace is more on par with that of Tokyo or New York. Deals often move along quickly, and the tempo may quicken if they fear they're losing control of negotiations. Set a comfortable pace and stick to it, and under no circumstances should your counterparts know when you're pressed for time.

If you're selling, start high and work down. Starting off with a "fair price" will get you nowhere. If you're buying, assume that the price the Singaporeans are asking for is far higher than the one they expect to get in the end.

Arrive at the table with many options, including the possibility that this round of negotiations may fail. Singaporeans like to drive hard bargains and they have no mercy for counterparts who have a do-or-die negotiating mission. If they sense that you have no alternatives, expect a good hammering.

English is the language of business here and its study is a mandatory part of education. Older businesspeople may not be as fluent as their younger subordinates. Singapore is very cosmopolitan, and interpreters for most languages are available locally. Keep in mind that "misinterpretations" are a standard way for Singaporeans to cover mistakes in their tactics.

Contracts are taken very seriously in Singapore and aren't meant to be broken or continuously renegotiated. The contract may also contain language about how to maintain harmonious relations with your new Singaporean partners.

Corruption is minimal, especially when compared with the rest of Southeast Asia. The country has a very high GDP per capita and bureaucrats are well paid. Foreign negotiators offering bribes are dealt with harshly. This country is law abiding to the nth degree. In fact, some expats have nicknamed Singapore "Disneyland with a death sentence."

SOUTH AFRICA

COMMERCIAL ENVIRONMENT

South Africa spent many years in a state of international embargo and "divestment" by foreign firms. The end of apartheid has seen the return of investment and the restructuring of the nation's industries, but results have been far from stellar. High crime rates coupled with the induction of inexperienced managers into top positions has made South Africa decidedly unattractive to all but the most altruistic. It's rich with mineral resources and even in its current state continues to be the most industrialized of African nations. South Africa is also touted as having a bright future in shipping, due to its locale. Many investors are waiting for the cultural and political dust to settle before making a final assessment of the nation's potential.

COMMON STRATEGIES

- FOR TRADE: Pragmatic, Stern, Social
- FOR INVESTMENT: Consensus, Hierarchical, Self-Righteous

NOTES FOR NEGOTIATORS

The business atmosphere is as racially charged as South Africa's politics. Many new managers and CEOs are black and view their role as establishing a new order. Some take a very self-righteous view toward foreign investors, whites in particular. Visitors may play to this perception for advantage or downplay it altogether. Confronting or disparaging it will have disastrous effects. White-run companies, for their part, refuse to be held responsible for the history of apartheid and view opinionated foreigners as meddlesome. It's best to keep opinions on racial topics to yourself.

South Africans of all colors are somewhat new to the international arena and many believe that the outside world needs them more than South Africa needs foreigners. Don't be surprised if you encounter take-it-or-leave-it attitudes across the table even when you're buying. All negotiations should start off with a clear picture of how both sides stand to benefit from the completion of the deal.

This is a nation used to self-sufficiency, and its businesspeople tend to bristle when they feel they're being pressured. Trying to apply artificial deadlines or ultimatums will only further delay the process. South Africans like straight talk and low-key sales approaches. When South Africans are in a strong buying position, they'll intentionally slow down the pace of talks in order to extract concessions. Socializing is a big part of South African business protocol. Attending sporting events, after-hours partying, back-country tours, and even hunts are used as a way to "size up" foreign counterparts. If they don't like you personally, you may find it difficult to make headway at the negotiating table.

This isn't a litigious society, and businesspeople here don't like to quibble over details. Bringing an army of lawyers to the table will not be of great benefit. Contracts are composed very much along European lines, and South Africans prefer to allow the quality of the relationship to fill in any vagaries.

English is the language of commerce; interpreters for many European languages are readily available. Afrikaans businesspeople, who speak a form of Dutch in addition to English, will often bring their own translators to meetings with foreign companies.

SOUTH KOREA

COMMERCIAL ENVIRONMENT

The Republic of Korea (ROK), as opposed to the Democratic People's Republic of Korea situated due north, has made enormous strides in the last few decades and is now one of Asia's powerhouses. It's striving to become more of a global player and less of an Asian one. Modeling themselves on the success of their rival, Japan, the South Koreans continue to use their central government as the overseer and occasional planner of the nation's major industries. But moving quickly from an industrial base to technology has caused the South Koreans to suffer growing pains. The country has a number of Special Economic Zones set up to entice foreign investment as well as hoped-for technology transfers. Despite its outward-looking commercial policies, the South Koreans still regard foreigners, of all types, with suspicion.

COMMON STRATEGIES

- FOR TRADE: Aggressive, Intimidating, Secretive
- FOR INVESTMENT: Consensus, Divide and Conquer, Deceptive

NOTES FOR NEGOTIATORS

South Korea still maintains an air of siege mentality in its approach to foreigners. These are a tough people who will go toe-to-toe with anyone regardless of size. South Koreans have zero compunction about signing agreements with which they have no intention of complying. Foreigners are meant to be fleeced and there's no shame in it. If you sign a contract in the ROK be prepared to supervise its compliance on a regular basis.

Wearing down an opponent through constant repetition and lengthy negotiation sessions is a time-honored practice. It's also a way of making sure that every detail has been covered. Mistakes by Korean managers are dealt with severely, especially if they cause the company to "lose face" at the hands of a foreigner.

Being direct isn't considered a Confucian virtue; thus, such behavior is incompatible with Korean business practices. Even if your counterpart is telling a bold-faced lie, diplomacy must be your response.

Koreans often make emotional pleas part of their negotiating style. They're also not beyond painting themselves as poor, humble peasants, even though they have one of the higher GDPs per capita in Asia. If you demonstrate any compassion, it will be tapped again and again with no hope of reciprocation. In reality, the Koreans only respect hard-line, strong opponents.

Koreans always negotiate in teams, and they'll always attempt to be numerically superior. Exploiting dissent or contradictions in foreign counterparts is a common ploy. Unless your team is composed of highly skilled Cowboys, don't let anyone get separated from the group. The weakest members will be culled first, so keep a special eye on novices.

Much of the ROK's success is the result of sacrifice by the general population. Koreans work hard and play hard. Negotiations will be exhausting and after-hours socializing will be more a test of fortitude than a chance for relaxation. If you're not willing to *gun pei* (raise the cup) until the wee hours with counterparts, it's best to decline altogether.

Women play a very subservient role in Korean business and will only appear at negotiations as secretaries or interpreters. Visiting female executives will have to make a special effort to make their status known. Female negotiators, regardless of rank, will not be invited along for the after-hours carousing.

SWEDEN

COMMERCIAL ENVIRONMENT

Sweden is the most socialized country in the world, with over half of its GDP being in the public sector. Consequently, it also has one of the highest income tax rates in the world at 60 percent. Sweden's once highly touted social welfare system, *folkhemmet,* has taken its toll on the economy as domestic firms move operations abroad. Its major industries are steel, automotive, precision machinery, and wood products. This densely populated country is very dependent on foreign oil and imported foodstuffs. Foreign investors, though continually attracted to the highly skilled and educated workforce, are often deterred by what are viewed (at least by outsiders) as confiscatory taxes.

COMMON STRATEGIES

- FOR TRADE: Pragmatic, Social
- FOR INVESTMENT: Impassive, Horizontal, Technical

NOTES FOR NEGOTIATORS

Make appointments well in advance and be punctual. Rest assured that Swedish counterparts will do the same. These are a precise and disciplined people, and they expect the same from those wishing to work on their turf.

The high level of education makes technical acumen quite common, and the Swedes are reknown for their engineering skills. Presentations should be detailed with additional data at the ready. Keep proposals realistic and play up the pragmatic aspects. Exaggeration or melodramatic presentations will be met with classic Scandinavian indifference.

The Swedes are tough bargainers but they rarely haggle. Their approach is to remain staunch in the own position while constantly demanding concessions from counterparts. They will comb through the details of your proposal looking for loopholes. Be prepared.

This is a very formal, law-abiding society, and bribery is completely out of the picture for negotiations. If your strategy relies on conducting business under the table, you'll find yourself alone under there, or worse, incarcerated.

Upper-level Swedish managers often delegate a good deal of decision-making authority to middle-level management. Don't assume all power is at the top and do your research to make sure that you have decision makers sitting across the table from you. Many Swedish companies use the executive suite as a preretirement holding area. A company president may be so in name only.

Contracts are very detailed; expect them to be followed to the letter. The Swedes will expect the same from counterparts. While this seems quite efficient, be reminded that only that which is in the contract will be attended to and little more.

Swedish counterparts will most likely request to see your entire proposal before coming to the negotiating table. This is not just to limit surprises but an efficient use of time. It also serves to avoid potential conflicts or confrontations—both highly undesirable here.

The Swedes like to combine business with pleasure but not of the raucous type. Business meals will be fairly formal and toasting will be moderate. Avoid all signs of inebriation. Women make up 48 percent of the workforce and hold high positions in government and business. Contrary to the image of sexual abandon, Swedish men actually maintain a rather traditional attitude toward women in society as a whole. Foreign female negotiators can expect to be subjected to a good deal of Old World manners and "ladies first" deference.

TAIWAN

COMMERCIAL ENVIRONMENT

Taiwan, along with Korea and Japan, was one of the early Asian miracles of the 1960s and 1970s. Its commercial sector is still a leader in the global market and its GDP per capita is five times higher than that of its larger cousin across the straits. Taiwan is both an industrial and a technical power that has seen a sharp decline in foreign investment in the last few years, due to higher labor rates and uncertainty about its relationship with mainland China. To hedge its bets, Taiwan has poured investments into China and its neighbors. The island's businesspeople are highly schooled in international business, and thousands of them are sent throughout the world, on a regular basis, searching for opportunities.

COMMON STRATEGIES

- FOR TRADE: Aggressive, Compliant, Secretive, Social
- FOR INVESTMENT: Consensus, Hierarchical, Indulgent

NOTES FOR NEGOTIATORS

The Taiwanese are more expert at international negotiations than any other Asian group. The insular nature of their economy and their tenuous political position have kept them on the global scene for decades. They'll know more about your society, culture, business, and company than you will. Similar research on your part is absolutely vital. Learn everything you can about your counterparts, but be discreet when tapping for information in Taiwanese business circles—they're quite clannish. Expatriates with on-the-ground experience are the best source.

The Taiwanese are Chinese by heritage but "special Chinese" by circumstance. Attempting to treat them like naive mainlanders or cosmopolitan Hong Kongers will meet with disappointment. These Chinese are believers in realpolitik and have no delusions about their position in world economics. If they're buying, expect a tough stance; if they're selling, be prepared for a healthy dose of indulgence, but keep your hands on your wallet.

Come to the table prepared. The Taiwanese are highly educated, more so than Hong Kongers, and they take business very seriously. Poorly prepared counterparts will be quickly shown the door, though very politely.

Under no circumstances should you go on a "fishing expedition" under the guise of true negotiations. While the Taiwanese aren't beyond doing this themselves when overseas, they frown on turnabout. Foreigners who are caught doing it will find it difficult to get appointments anywhere on the island when they wish to negotiate in earnest. News travels fast.

The Taiwanese tend to front-load their concession process with numerous, inconsequential ones early on. Bigger concessions are saved for the end and given with great reluctance. The Taiwanese often practice the envelopment of opponents. You'll be wined and dined, hotels (perhaps offered airfare) and drivers will be provided, and you may even be taken to a remote resort for the negotiations. All of this puts you "in debt" to your hosts. It also makes you psychologically dependent on them for even the simplest things. Enjoy the ride, but stay on your toes.

Visiting foreigners are often amazed by the amount of after-hours partying that accompanies business here. Your host will most likely pull out the stops during negotiations in an attempt to wear you down. Remember, they can always find new team members for the following day's discussion and none of their team will be suffering from jet lag. Take it easy and when in doubt, call it an early night.

THAILAND

COMMERCIAL ENVIRONMENT

Thailand has been one of the "mini dragons" successes of Asia. It has long been a target for foreign investment, especially hotels and resorts, and tourism is the major source of foreign currency. The economy also supports sizable textile, agricultural, and aquiculture industries. Thailand's numerous banking industry scandals have caused the country to seek international bank funding. This has brought with it a great deal of external scrutiny and the rethinking of many projects involving foreign private funding. The downturn in the high-growth rate of Thailand (less than 5 percent) and continued political chaos have had a chilling effect on FDI here and in the regional emerging markets as well.

COMMON STRATEGIES

- FOR TRADE: Aggressive, Social, Exploitative
- FOR INVESTMENT: Consensus, Divide and Conquer, Indulgent

NOTES FOR NEGOTIATORS

Personal relationships are a very important part of doing business in Thailand. Having the right connections and knowing when to use them will greatly facilitate long-term success. Start working on these relationships well in advance of attempting to schedule negotiations.

Patience is highly regarded in Thailand, and Buddhist countries in general. Thais believe in keeping a "cool heart" during negotiations and meetings. Showing open frustration or making demands to speed up the proceedings will not be seen as a show of strength but rather as personal weakness. Any concerns in this area should be discussed via back-channels—never in public.

It's very important to maintain a united front when dealing with Thais. Although they'll be just as willing to exploit discrepancies as the next negotiator, disunity also carries the burden of disharmony, which will cause Thai counterparts to doubt the project's potential.

Punctuality is very much appreciated, although its appeal declines in proportion to the distance one is from Bangkok. Agendas should be discussed and agreed upon prior to arrival in-country, but don't be surprised if your Thai counterpart suddenly attempts to add or detract from the original. Spontaneity is a big part of Thai business culture.

Bargaining should be done in such a manner as to be obviously concerned about all sides of the deal. Any appearance of haggling just as a show of superiority will have detrimental effects. Proceed as if the relationship was more important than the profits.

Thai is a difficult language to master and your attempts at it will be appreciated. While English and Chinese are widely spoken, translate all materials, including business cards, into Thai for presentation. Since Thai speakers aren't all that common outside of the country, this procedure may have to be done upon arrival in Thailand.

Thailand is a functioning monarchy and the people are devoted to the royal family. Criticizing or insulting the king or his family can result in criminal charges.

Very few, if any, Thais will take kindly to a foreigner making even the smallest critique of the monarchy.

Graft and corruption are part and parcel of the commercial sector. Requests for "tea money" and the inclusion in projects of inflated consulting fees for government officials are all part of the price of doing business in Thailand. Prepare your counterstrategy for these requests before getting to the negotiating table.

TURKEY

COMMERCIAL ENVIRONMENT

Free-market policies adopted in the 1980s have moved Turkey from being a fringe economy to one of the most thriving of the emerging markets. Recently rebuffed by the European Union, the country still remains a major supplier to the global marketplace. Turkey is now a service economy (63 percent of GDP), but the economy continues to support substantial manufacturing and textile industries. There are still a substantial number of large state-owned companies (KITs) that put a drag on growth as they operate in subsidized, protected industries. Istanbul is a major transportation link for trade throughout Europe, the Middle East, and the Asian subcontinent. Investors continue to be attracted to the educated workforce and strategic locale Turkey offers.

COMMON STRATEGIES

- FOR TRADE: Aggressive, Exploitative, Indulgent
- FOR INVESTMENT: Hierarchical, Jekyll and Hyde, Social

NOTES FOR NEGOTIATORS

The Turks are known for their hospitality. Foreigners are often taken aback by the extent of their hosts' generosity. Experienced negotiators may see this outpouring of goodwill as a manipulative technique, and, to a degree, it is. However, it can be taken at face value as part of a long-standing Turkish custom.

Punctuality is considered standard operating procedure, and its absence is considered a sign of disrespect. Make appointments well in advance of travel and confirm upon arrival in-country. This common courtesy can make or break early negotiation sessions.

Like much of the commerce in this part of the world, haggling is commonplace and nothing has a set price. If you're selling, start high, almost absurdly so, and work back down. When buying, start at the bottom and begrudge every move upward. Always give the impression that you can walk away at anytime. If the Turkish counterpart sees that your needs exceed your wants, this weakness will be immediately exploited.

Much general conversation precedes business discussion, and there's a Turkish dislike of "cutting to the chase" just for the sake of expediency. Business moves at a slow pace; the Turks don't like to be rushed, especially by foreigners. Even when you've come to buy with cash in hand, expect a lot of chit-chat before a deal is cut.

Due to its location, Turkey is chock full of polyglots. English, French, and German are widely spoken, and translators for most European and Asian languages can be easily located. Contracts will be signed in the local dialects, and all business materials should be translated for presentation.

Contracts are usually stated in general terms with the specifics being hammered out over the extent of the relationship. Any insistence that quality control be made part of the contract will be met with considerable resistance. Counterparts will consider it insulting that a foreigner believes a Turk would deliver anything but the highest standard. Don't belabor the point.

Western business dress is favored among executives, and it's always best to remain conservative in appearance. Overly casual or exotic dressers will not be taken seriously regardless of wealth or title. Temperatures run the gamut in Turkey; visitors should do some meteorological research prior to negotiations.

Home and family are sacred in Turkey and to be invited to a counterpart's home is a great honor. Never refuse this invitation unless it's absolutely impossible to comply; it's not offered lightly, and a casual refusal is a grave insult. While there's a good deal of socializing, don't expect wild after-work partying. Alcohol isn't always offered, as this is an Islamic, albeit secular, country.

UNITED KINGDOM

COMMERCIAL ENVIRONMENT

The United Kingdom is a leading economy of the European Union. However, high growth and low unemployment (by European standards, at least) seem to vindicate the U.K.'s standoffish approach to the European Union's single-currency policy. The United Kingdom has been a top player in international trade for centuries—it was certainly its first global practitioner ("The sun never sets on the British Empire"). It also attracts an enormous amount of foreign investment to its own shores for high-tech, automotive, and food processing. The country supports considerable financial services, insurance, and transportation industries. Few international companies would consider their reach total without some form of U.K. presence.

COMMON STRATEGIES

- FOR TRADE: Financial, Stern, Arrogant
- FOR INVESTMENT: Hierarchical, Platoon, Legalistic

NOTES FOR NEGOTIATORS

The British are old hands at international business; their history of negotiation in that area goes back centuries. The depth of their knowledge is without comparison. Arrive in the U.K. thoroughly prepared and equipped with numerous options. Don't attempt to learn how things work "at the table" or your British counterpart will "hand you your head."

British business moves at a more deliberate pace than American business. Presentations should be detailed, with a minimum of hyperbole. The British have seen everything "under the sun" and there's nothing new there, so get to your point.

The class system is still very much alive and proper connections will make a difference for long-term projects. Government agencies and industrial associations are good starting points for small- and medium-size deals. Larger projects may require social introductions. Britain is an orderly society and punctuality is mandatory. Arrange appointments in advance and present an agenda as early in the process as possible. The British side will insist on having one, so it's best to get your version in first.

Start your bargaining at a point only slightly distant from your projected goal. You can leave yourself some negotiating room but don't be excessive. Your British counterpart will have already researched the true value range of the deal.

Finance is a major sector of the British economy; you should have no problem exploring options. British manufactured goods are generally of high quality and there's little need to build provisos on that matter into the contract. Transportation and delivery requirements should be stated clearly.

The British tend toward detailed contracts littered with legal lingo. They may also insist upon having the contract bound under British law, although most international disputes on large matters will be settled in Brussels. If you're not from a society bound up with commercial contract law, be careful what you sign. Contracts in the U.K. are very binding and penalties can be severe.

Even in the post-Thatcherite U.K., unions are still very strong. Joint-ventures should be heavily researched to uncover the possible effects of respective union involvement. Political intervention in this area isn't unusual; keep in mind that the most recently elected government is the Labor Party.

The business lunch has been institutionalized in Britain; much negotiating will be done with knife and fork in hand. The British can be exceedingly charming and their manners put the world to shame. Enjoy the surroundings but resist the charm. It's all just so much posturing—usually perfect.

UNITED STATES

COMMERCIAL ENVIRONMENT

The United States is the largest economy in the world with its nearest competitors, Japan and China, being less than half its size. Low inflation, low interest rates and low unemployment have stymied economists and thrilled foreign investors. The United States dollar is still the most widely used currency in the world and, like it or not, every country measures themselves against an "American" yardstick—another blow to the metric system. Its companies have some of the most commonly recognized international brand names, and its entertainment industry dominates world culture. The ability of the American economy to quickly recover from even the most substantial blows, makes it a top choice for FDI even during the worst periods. The United States has hollowed out its manufacturing sector in recent decades and moved solidly into services and high-tech.

COMMON STRATEGIES

- FOR TRADE: Aggressive, Legalistic, Arrogant, Technical
- FOR INVESTMENT: Cowboy, Platoon, Intimidating

NOTES FOR NEGOTIATORS

The Americans (as they're called, to the chagrin of the other occupants of North and South America) have only recently gained a grudging respect for other economies in the international marketplace. Formerly labeled naive, Americans now use this stereotype to their favor as unsuspecting counterparts approach the negotiating table. Their business schools are the best in the world and their society combines aspects of every other one on the planet. You may not like their style but don't underestimate their acumen. They aren't number one by accident.

True to history, Americans believe in winning wars by accepting a few lost battles. U.S. negotiators are extremely nimble and can change strategy and tactics during a ten-minute break. You had better be able to respond in kind.

They're the practitioners of the original Cowboy mentality, and an American company will usually send its negotiators into the field with an unusual amount of authority. They often assume that counterparts have similar authority and are very disappointed with "errand boys" masquerading as executives. Individualistic by nature, they can also be good team players, but only when they get to select the team.

Americans have a blindspot in that they believe everyone else in the world wants to be like them. They also believe that all markets should be as open as theirs purports to be. Even when you're on your own turf, the Americans want to play by their own rules. If you're on their turf, their lawyers will take great care in laying out the rules for you.

The American style is very direct, and they try to demand the same from counterparts. To not do so is to be labeled deceitful. Americans want you to look them straight in the eye and "lay it on the line." They love confrontation and are not subtle in their intimidation techniques. The Americans play for big money and they play for keeps. As they're fond of saying, "if you can't take the heat, stay out of the kitchen."

U.S. negotiators generally start off from a strong position (at least in their minds) and are quite miserly with concessions. They've learned patience over the years, mostly from dealing with the Japanese, and can wait until the end of negotiations to concede major points if necessary. Americans do, however, prefer speedy negotiations and chafe under too much extraneous socializing or postponement. They used to cut deals early (and to their disadvantage) just to save time. Nowadays, they can afford to just leave.

VIETNAM

COMMERCIAL ENVIRONMENT

The Socialist Republic of Vietnam is one of the few remaining economies that's controlled by a communist leadership. Its *doi moi* policy, established in the mid-1980s, was designed to remedy the shortcomings of the centrally planned, profitless commercial sector. Foreign investment, both private and government subsidized, flooded in during the early 1990s but has slowed to a trickle as the less than stellar results have been tallied. The country has a formidable bureaucracy, and corruption is rampant in both the government and private sectors. Vietnam's workforce is still predominantly agricultural, and it is one of the world's top rice exporters. The government has licensed numerous automotive companies to operate assembly plants, and some inroads have been made in developing light industry and technology. Tourism and agriculture still remain the country's top sources of foreign currency. The local currency, the dong, is inconvertible on the open market.

COMMON STRATEGIES

- FOR TRADE: Aggressive, Secretive, Self-Righteous
- FOR INVESTMENT: Consensus, Hierarchical, Deceptive

NOTES FOR NEGOTIATORS

The Vietnamese are accustomed to exercising enormous patience, something they perceive others, especially Westerners, as being unable to do. "Time is money" isn't a Vietnamese concept; they're patient because the current pace of their culture makes patience feasible. Make sure that you're not locked into too tight a schedule. It will only work against you.

The Vietnamese will often change agreed upon terms overnight, and seemingly arbitrarily, as a way of shifting the balance in their favor. Since there is little commercial law to enforce contracts, make sure that only the minimum amount of capital necessary for a project is turned over to the Vietnamese at any one time. It's not advisable to extend unsecured credit to a Vietnamese partner.

Until recently, the Vietnamese were able to play one anxious suitor off against another. But an investment downswing has tipped the scales in favor of foreign capital. Let it be known that your company is willing to do business, but only in areas that show promise of investment returns within a reasonable period of time. This may be the most effective negotiation tool available to you.

Many terms will be left unspecified by the Vietnamese, especially if they feel it's not to their advantage to clarify them. Your attempts to obtain a specific response will be met with vague nods or rapid changes of subject. Don't sign anything until the contract terms are "transparent." It's hard enough to enforce a contract in Vietnam without adding vagueness to the procedure.

Bureaucratic red tape is often used as an excuse for delays. The easiest way to deal with this is to play off of the competitive spirit of the Vietnamese. Make it known early on in your discussions that your company will be pursuing many other projects within the country, that your appointments are numerous, and your agenda organized. Any business that can't be completed in the time allotted will be postponed indefinitely. Most delays will evaporate when the specter of competition enters the negotiation—but make sure that you can back up your claims.

The Vietnamese will generally hire their own interpreter. In many cases, this is a necessity, as the primary decision maker will not be fluent in your language. If the negotiations aren't proceeding in their favor, however, the Vietnamese will often claim that most of the problems are the result of linguistic or cultural misunderstanding. Bringing your own interpreter can counter this tactic.

CHAPTER 20

Glossary

THE TERMS LISTED below are general terms used in negotiating around the world as well as a number of generally American (U.S.) business slang terms that have entered common usage. The use of slang, of course, is very problematic in international negotiations as it is culturally based and often does not translate.

ABOVE BOARD Dealing honestly and in plain view. Implying fair play. In gambling it refers to keeping hands, and one's cards, on the table, or above board.

ACE IN THE HOLE (ace up one's sleeve) An undisclosed advantage, usually one that will ensure success when revealed.

AGENDA The list of topics to be covered during a negotiation session. An agenda may be arranged in either an ascending or descending order of importance. The side that exerts the greatest control of the agenda will be the most effective in attaining their goals. Negotiation session strategy will be based on the agreed upon agenda.

AGENT A third-party representative who acts on behalf of a client during negotiations or as part of the distribution chain once a deal has been signed. Agents can be from either the public or private sector and are often used during negotiations to handle difficult or sensitive issues.

AT THE TABLE The location where negotiations take place. It may be a real table around which negotiators sit, a cocktail party, an airport lounge, or a golf course. Experienced negotiators are always prepared to negotiate in any setting.

BACK CHANNEL Discussions that effect negotiations that take place between high-ranking subordinate team members away from the negotiating table. Back channel discussions can be productive in situations where direct and public discussion of sensitive issues might cause disharmony (loss of face) or cause unwanted media attention. Such discussions are also called "side meetings."

BACKTRACK 1) To change one's position on an issue, 2) To retrace the steps one has taken in a process.

BAIL OUT To abandon a failing project or product before losing more money, time, or labor.

BARGAINING CHIP Something of value that can readily be given as a concession in negotiating a contract.

BIG PICTURE The overall scope of a project or business transaction. In negotiations, senior executives and chief negotiators typically deal with the big picture of a project, while members of the negotiating team handle the detail oriented issues.

BLOODYING The means by which negotiators gain expertise by making mistakes while "doing battle." Experienced negotiators will develop enough "calluses" from past "battles" that they do not bleed so easily in the future.

BLUE SKY Something with little or no value. Ideas that are not realistic. In negotiating, one side may offer a "blue sky" provision.

BOILER PLATE Standard contract provisions, often printed in small type and referred to as "fine print."

BONA FIDES Latin for "good faith." Refers to documents, materials or promises issued by negotiators to show their commitment to a proposed outcome.

BOTTOM LINE 1) The net profit of a business. 2) The final result of a contract negotiation or deal.

BRIBERY Payments or concessions given to an individual holding a position of trust to influence the outcome of a negotiation. While the term implies illegality, each society has its own rules about what constitutes the acceptability of such payments. Moral considerations aside, bribery is an entrenched part of international business.

BUILD-OPERATE-TRANSFER (BOT) The construction and then operation of a manufacturing or service facility in a foreign country for a set period of time after which it is handed over to a local government authority for a nominal fee. BOT is usually used as a means of financing large or complicated infrastructure projects in developing economies unable to finance the project themselves.

BULLETPROOF (also: ironclad) A contract that has no loopholes. (A contract that can withstand the impact of bullets.) Rarely is a contract "bulletproof," as so much depends upon the willingness of the principals to follow through on its provisions and the ability of local governing law to protect the rights of the parties to the transaction.

BURNING BRIDGES To close off all avenues of retreat or future contact. Often used when one makes permanent enemies of someone who might be helpful in the future. In international negotiating it is unwise to burn bridges.

BUSINESS COOPERATION CONTRACT (BCC) An agreement by two companies to work together for mutual benefit, but without a long-term binding contract. Either side may cease the BCC at will.

CHERRY PICK The selection of the best terms and conditions of a proposal while disregarding troublesome or unprofitable items. Cherry picking is utilized by very strong or highly inexperienced negotiators.

CHIEF NEGOTIATOR (CN) The head of a negotiating team (or a solo negotiator) responsible for developing and implementing the overall strategy and tactics of a negotiation. Full responsibility for success and authority to contract lie with the CN.

CLOSING SPECIALIST The member of a negotiating team responsible for 1) tracking the progress of the negotiations, 2) recognizing when it is time to stop talking and start signing, and 3) bring the negotiations to a successful conclusion. The closing specialist is usually on the selling side but can also be a savvy buyer.

CONCESSION 1) Individual terms and conditions of a proposal that are granted to the opposition, usually in exchange for concessions of equal value or importance. Proposals often have terms and conditions built in for the express purpose of concession during the negotiating process. 2) A right granted to a counterpart in return for another right or as a means to influence the overall outcome of negotiations. The importance of a concession is relative to each company's strategy.

CONFIDENTIALITY The giving or keeping of secret or proprietary information. Getting both sides in an international negotiation to maintain confidentiality is difficult, especially when the stakes are high.

CONSULTANT NEGOTIATOR A professional negotiator employed by companies on a project-by-project basis. Companies that do not have the required expertise in-house often hire consultant negotiators. They can act either as chief negotiators or advising team members. Consultant negotiators typically deal with larger bargaining issues and should not be confused with technical specialists.

CONTROLLING INTEREST Ownership or control of enough of the stock of a corporation to control decision making. Controlling interest is usually assumed to be at least 51 percent of the voting stock of a corporation, but it may be less depending upon the ownership characteristics of other blocks of stock. In international joint ventures it may be possible to control an enterprise with less than a 51 percent stake in the company.

DEADLINE The time or date by which something must be done.

DEAL BREAKER A term or condition in a proposed transaction upon which negotiators for both sides cannot gain agreement and that can cause the transaction to fail. Deal breakers may relate to price, payment terms, quality issues, politics, or requests for illegal payments.

DEVIL'S ADVOCATE An individual who is given the role of the opposition in discussions preparing for negotiations. Devil's advocacy derives from taking the side of evil during a theological debate.

DOWNSIDE The potentially unprofitable or troublesome part of a proposal or contract. The negative, less desirable alternative.

DOWNTIME Unproductive time during foreign business travel when no business is being transacted or formulated. Not to be confused with leisure time, which is time spent resting.

DUE DILIGENCE Investigative research to independently establish the background of a potential partner. Matters investigated typically include financial statements, legal status and any key matters that affect the viability of the partner to follow through on a particular transaction. Openness and access to records are not standardized globally, and as a result the ability to conduct such research may be greatly restricted by the legal structure of individual economies and company policy. See also: TRANSPARENCY.

ENVELOPMENT The subtle but constant control of a counterpart's every moment, whether social or business. It can run the gamut from the heavy-handed methods of a Chinese tour of a cultural site, replete with "special guides," to the London financier who miraculously secures tickets to a sold-out show. It can also take the form of choosing a remote meeting site with limited communications and transport.

ETHICS Moral principals and values in personal and business relationships. The word derives from the Greek for "character" and is generally taken to describe an attitude having to do with moral duties and obligations. Obviously, ethics vary widely around the globe and it would be incorrect to automatically assume that your counterparts share the same moral base as you. Cultural values often affect ethical standards and it is best to research both before conducting negotiations in a particular region or country.

EXPAT Short for expatriate. Individuals who work for extended periods of time in foreign countries without becoming citizens. Expats are an excellent source of cultural and commercial information on a country.

FACE Respect given to an individual's dignity and prestige by others due to performance in business and actions taken in personal life. Though this is primarily an Asian expression, the concept is universal. In many societies, an action resulting in the loss of face can result in the immediate cessation of business negotiations.

FACILITATION PAYMENT A payment or consideration given to a government official or worker in order to get them to do what they should have done anyway. Unlike a bribe, the facilitation payment seeks no special consideration and is usually legal.

FISHING EXPEDITION False negotiations conducted for the purpose of 1) gaining experience for future talks with a competitor or 2) to test the market value of a product, service, or company. See also: PRACTICE NEGOTIATIONS.

FOREIGN CORRUPT PRACTICES ACT An act passed by the U.S. Congress that makes it unlawful for U.S. citizens or their agents to bribe foreign officials to gain commercial advantage. Violators can be charged with a felony in U.S. Federal court. The FCPA has been criticized by some Americans as an impediment to U.S. businesses whose competition does not face similar restrictions in the global marketplace.

GET-OUT-OF-DODGE A hasty retreat. An American "Wild West" term to describe a quick and usually clandestine exodus from a country (Dodge is a small city) where talks have soured and the threat of violence or incarceration is very real. Some negotiators hold dual or duplicate passports to facilitate such exits from politically, socially, and economically unstable countries.

GLAD HANDING The effusive greeting of counterparts with overblown handshakes and flowery language. Glad handing is often a front for those with little to offer at the negotiating table. It can denotes a level of insincerity that politicians generally exhibit when accompanying overseas commercial junkets.

GO-BETWEEN An intermediary employed by foreign firms for the purpose of gaining contacts, language ability, or knowledge of local business practices. A go-between can be effectively used by either side in a negotiation to help smooth over a variety of social, political, and business issues.

HARMONY The good personal relations between two sides of a business transaction. (Commonly used term in Asia.)

HEADS UP A warning or advice given to negotiators to be on the look out for a counterpart's action or potential reaction. Researchers and cultural consultants should issue these before and during negotiations.

HIDDEN AGENDA Undisclosed intentions or issues.

HOME TURF ADVANTAGE The advantage that comes from being in one's own cultural, economic, or geographic landscape, usually as the host. It does not always indicate that the host is working in his or her native country. Visiting the facilities of a counterpart's overseas subsidiary located in your country may still actually cause you to perform as if you were in someone else's "home turf."

HONCHO From the Japanese "han cho," it means group leader and generally refers to a strong leader with a high level of command capability. Many negotiating teams disguise the identity of their honcho, the ultimate decision maker.

INSIDER An employee or other individual who is privy to special financial or technical information not made available to the public.

INTERMEDIARY An individual or firm that acts as a go-between for two companies seeking to do business. An intermediary often arranges for the preliminary meetings that lead to serious negotiations. Companies must be careful of whom they select for intermediaries as many do not have the connections or expertise they say they have. See also: GO-BETWEEN.

JOINT VENTURE (JV) An agreement by two companies, typically one foreign and one domestic to work together for mutual benefit with specific ownership percentages specified in a long-term contract. The terms of some joint venture deals are regulated heavily by governments as to limits of foreign ownership and the minimum amounts of money or assets invested.

KICKBACK A secret commission paid to an individual (usually illegally) to secure a contract.

LAY-IT-ON-THE-TABLE To speak directly about circumstances, to tell the facts about a situation.

LETTER OF INTRODUCTION (LOI) A statement, often by a third party, in letter form, that briefly profiles a company with an eye toward doing business together. When written by a third party it will take on the form of a recommendation. Some societies will not consider doing business with foreign firms without the submittal of an LOI.

LEVEL PLAYING FIELD An environment where everyone plays (sports or business) by the same rules and where the winner wins on merit.

LIP SERVICE To support something in words but not in actions. Simply implies that someone supports a cause using their lips (by talking).

LOOP, IN THE To be informed about and involved in an activity or enterprise. Those in the know (in the loop) vs. those on the outside (out of the loop).

LOOPHOLE A means of escape from a difficult situation by taking advantage of a technicality or ambiguity in a law, regulation, or contract.

LOOSE CANNON An unpredictable person who has trouble maintaining self-control. It is inadvisable to have a loose cannon on a negotiating team.

LOWBALL An extremely low quoted price, cost estimate, or purchase offer used in a deceptive manner to mislead either a buyer or a seller.

MEMORANDUM OF UNDERSTANDING (MOU) A formal statement by two or more firms stating their desire and intent to do business together. In some countries a MOU is considered to be a contract. Do not sign an MOU until all signatories are aware of its ramifications.

NEEDS Items included on an agenda that a company must gain concessions on if the overall negotiations are to be considered successful. See also: WANTS.

NEGOTIATIONS The activities (including discussions, transfer of information, compromise, etc.) leading to a settlement or agreement concerning a business transaction. Each party to the negotiation must gain enough from the process to make it worthwhile to themselves and concede a sufficient amount to keep counterparts interested. Everyone negotiates, but some gain more than they concede.

ON HOLD The indefinite suspension of plans. Some deals are put "on hold" until better conditions present themselves.

ON-THE-GROUND Research conducted in the very area (culture, country, city) which it describes. It is the best, most expensive, and highest level of first-hand information.

PAYBACK A concession given in return for another or the retribution that comes about when one has run afoul of a counterpart. All strategy and tactics should be viewed with an eye toward eventual payback.

PEEL THE ONION To unveil the contents of a proposal slowly, as in the layers of an onion. It is used to either frustrate the speedy tactics of counterparts or to measure how much they will really require from a project without exposing the full content.

POKER FACE A countenance that does not reveal either pleasure or pain. Such impassivity is used to keep counterparts from determining whether they are winning or losing. It is derived from a poker player's desire to conceal the contents of his playing hand.

PRACTICE NEGOTIATIONS 1) Negotiations conducted by a company in-house with its own staff playing the roles of both parties so that team members can gain experience and insight into upcoming negotiations. 2) False negotiations conducted by a company in an unscrupulous manner, pretending to bargain in good faith with another but participating only to garner experience or technical information to be used in the future.

RECONNAISSANCE (a.k.a. recon, recce) On the ground research and investigation of a company, product, or market. This special form of research requires actual travel to the country and culture that will be the target of negotiations. First-hand, on-the-ground experience costs more than second-hand information but it pays much higher dividends.

REPRESENTATIVE OFFICE An office opened in a foreign market as a first step for establishing a relationship with buyers or sellers. A "rep" office in a foreign market allows a company to show its commitment to the new arena while permitting more intense on-the-ground commercial research. Many developing economies have tight restrictions on the opening and operation of representative offices. Central government approval may be required and significant restrictions may apply.

REQUEST FOR PROPOSAL (RFP) (a.k.a. request for quote) A document issued by a purchaser seeking purveyors for very specific goods or services. The RFP will give basic technical requirements and possibly price restrictions. Purveyors will respond with either a request for more data or a bid for providing the goods or services.

RIGHT FIT An association between two companies where each brings specific, important, and complimentary capabilities to the association.

SHOOT THE WORKS The presentation of a firm's entire negotiating position all at once. It can be used to either intimidate counterparts or expedite proceedings. The opposite of peeling the onion, whereby a company presents its position one piece at a time.

SIDE MEETING Scheduled ad hoc meetings, usually between subordinate negotiators, used to settle technical details or pass along communications that would cause embarrassment or delays if broached at general sessions. They can also be used to acquire information useful for determining the presence of dissension in a counterpart's team.

SIZE UP THE OPPOSITION To assess the strengths and weaknesses of counterparts in a negotiation.

SMOKE SCREEN A diversionary tactic designed to confuse and mislead.

STONEWALL To be inflexible in a negotiation or to refuse to acknowledge a point or issue.

STRATEGY The science of creating a careful plan using all the social, economic, political, legal, and other forces available to achieve a goal.

STRAWMAN A false leader propped up by the opposition in an attempt to disguise real power or motive.

SUGAR COAT To present something in the best possible manner.

TABLE (U.S.) To place an issue aside for consideration in the future.
(U.K.) To bring up an issue for immediate discussion.

TACTIC An individual movement or action taken in a negotiation designed to achieve a particular end.

TECHNOLOGICAL ECONOMY Societies economically focused on high technology, information, and financial services. Manufacturing and agriculture play subordinate roles, with manufacturing being mostly contracted out overseas.

TELECONFERENCE Simultaneous negotiation by telephone by two or more parties. In some instances verbal agreements can be concluded by telephone but are typically followed up by written agreements.

TRANSPARENCY The clear understanding by all parties of a uniform set of rules, standards, and laws governing a transaction. Since some form of deception is part of every negotiator's style, full transparency is never achieved, only various levels of visibility.

UPPER HAND, TO GAIN THE Control and advantage in a negotiation.

UPSIDE The potentially profitable or positive part of a proposal or contract. The positive, more desirable alternative.

WANTS Items included in a proposal or agenda that a company would like to gain at the negotiating table but are not vital to a successful outcome. See also: NEEDS.

WIN-WIN A negotiating strategy where both parties gain roughly equal advantage. Contrasted to a win-lose strategy or a zero-sum strategy.
See also: ZERO-SUM GAME.

WINDOW OF OPPORTUNITY A limited period of time during which an opportunity exists.

WRIGGLE-ROOM Purposely vague conditions or terms that are included in a negotiation or contract to allow for future renegotiation.

ZERO-SUM GAME The concept that one side's gains are directly offset by another side's losses. When all the gains and losses from each side are totalled, the sum is zero. See also: WIN-WIN.

CHAPTER 21

Resources

Acuff, Frank L. *How to Negotiate Anything with Anyone, Anywhere Around the World*
American Management Association, New York, New York. 1993.

Axtell, Roger. *Do's and Taboos of Hosting International Visitors*
John Wiley & Sons, New York, New York. 1990.

Beckman, N. *Negotiations.*
Lexington Books. Lexington, Massachusetts. 1977.

Cavusgil, S.T., and P.N. Ghauri. *Doing Business in Developing Countries*
Routledge, Lincolnwood, Illinois. 1990.

Country Business Guide Series
World Trade Press, San Rafael, California. 1994-1999.
12 country-specific comprehensive texts on doing business in major and emerging markets.

Fuller, George. *The Negotiator's Handbook*
Prentice Hall, Englewood Cliffs, New Jersey. 1991.

Hall, Edward. *Beyond Culture*
Anchor Press, Garden City, New York. 1976.

Hinkelman, Edward G. *Dictionary of International Trade*
World Trade Press, San Rafael, California. 1997.

Jeannet, Jean-Pierre and Hubert Hennessey. *Global Marketing Strategies*
Houghton Mifflin, Boston, Massachusetts. 1992.

Mitchell, Charles. *A Short Course in International Business Culture*
World Trade Press, San Rafael, California. 1999.

Moran, Robert, et al. *International Business Case Studies*
Gulf Publishing, London. 1994.

Passport to the World Series
World Trade Press, San Rafael, California. 1996-1999.
25 country-specific books on the business culture of countries.

Reilly, Leo. *How to Outnegotiate Anyone*
Adams Media Corporation, Holbrook, Massachusetts. 1994.

Terpstra, V. and K. David. *The Cultural Environment of International Business*
South Western Press, Cincinnati, Ohio. 1985.

BIOGRAPHY

Jeffrey Edmund Curry, MBA, Ph.D., is an international businessman and educator. He is a visiting professor at numerous universities in Europe and Asia as well as a member of the International Affiliate Faculty at the Audencia Ecole de Management in Nantes, France. He is the author of books about business practices in Vietnam and Taiwan (*Passport Vietnam* and *Passport Taiwan*) as well as books on marketing and economics (*A Short Course in International Marketing* and *A Short Course in International Economics*). He resides with his wife and son in San Francisco.